CAMPO BAEZA

SELECTED WORKS

MO
WIT
NESS

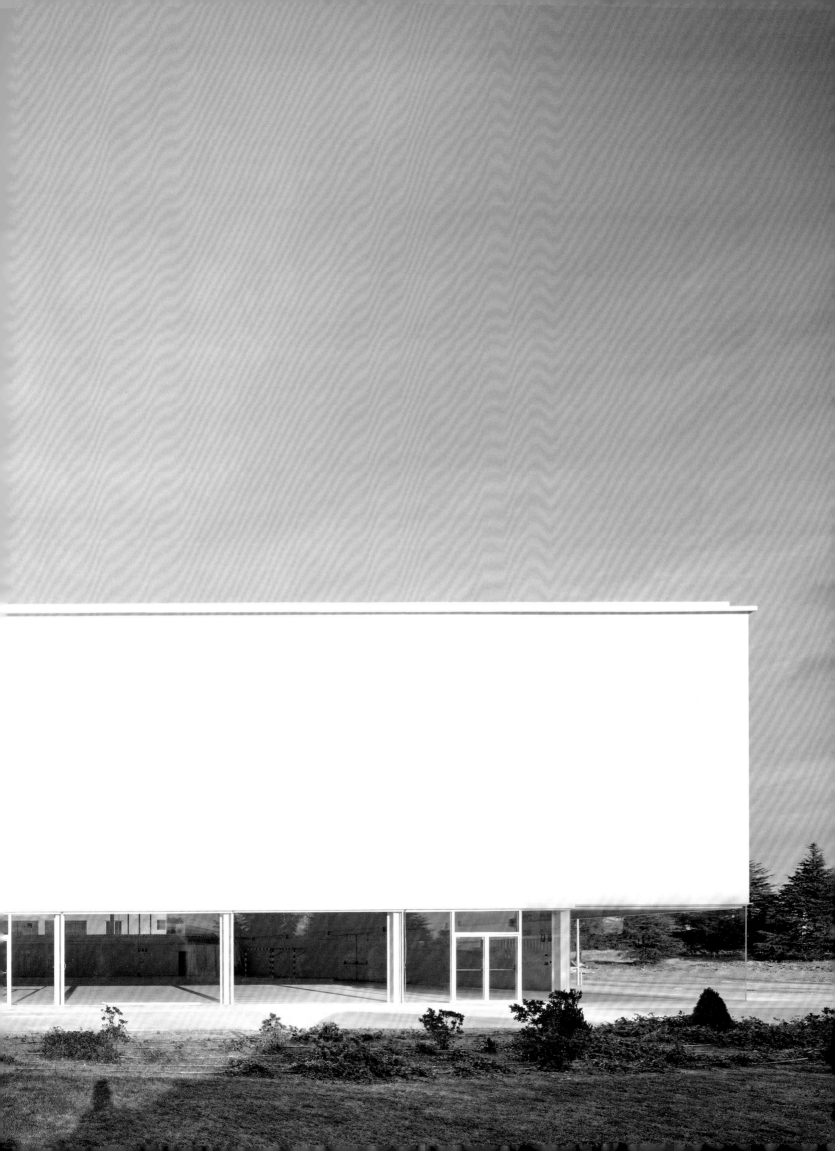

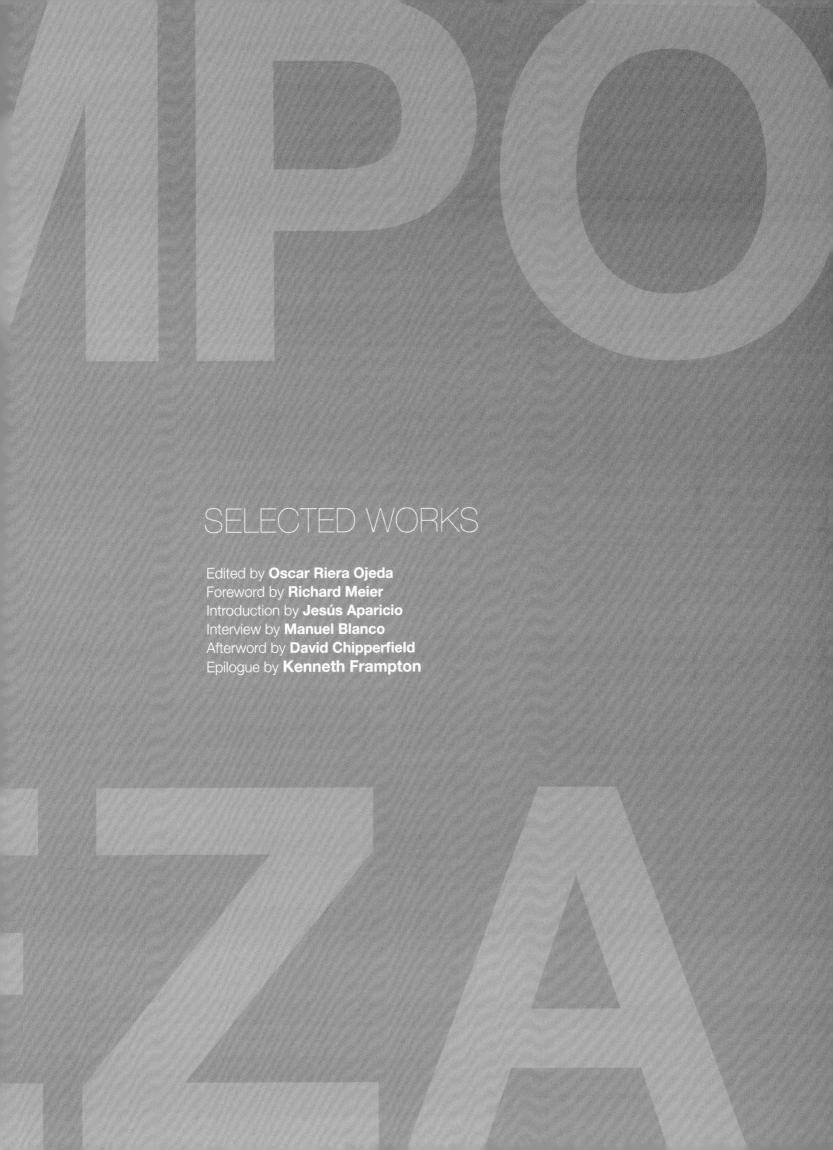

SELECTED WORKS

Edited by **Oscar Riera Ojeda**
Foreword by **Richard Meier**
Introduction by **Jesús Aparicio**
Interview by **Manuel Blanco**
Afterword by **David Chipperfield**
Epilogue by **Kenneth Frampton**

Table of Contents

Dedicated to my father who while over a hundred
years old is still thinking about others.
From him, I have inherited the spirit of ANALYSIS.
To my mother, to whom I owe my firm decision to
be an ARCHITECT.
To them both, for their extraordinary generosity,
I owe everything.

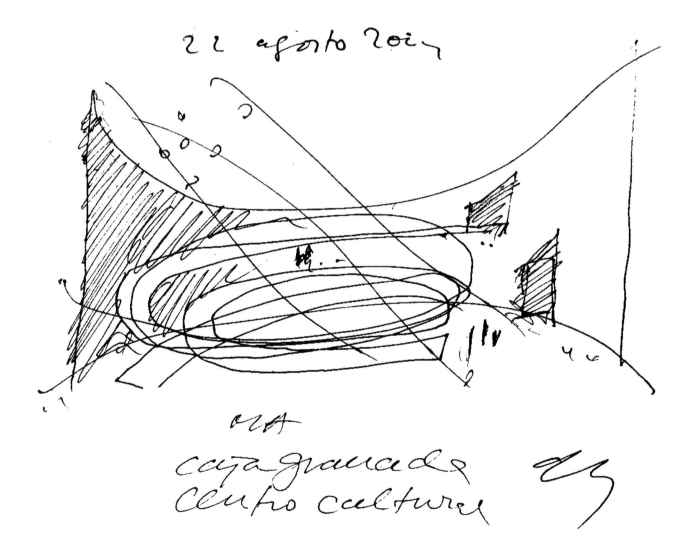

Acknowledgments
by Alberto Campo Baeza

THANKS, THANKS, THANKS

The gratitude I owe to so many people is so great that there wouldn't be enough pages in this book for me to express it adequately.

So many people have been extremely generous with me over the years that I don't have enough words to express my gratitude.

To my father, to whom I owe everything, who at the age of 101 can boast enviable mental and physical health, I dedicate this book. He was a wonderful surgeon and professor, with a gift of analytical acumen that I hope to have inherited. And with a very good sense of humor. And to my mother, who, as the good daughter of an architect, made a point of inculcating in me a love of architecture.

I also owe nearly everything to my masters, the Spanish architects who as teachers showed me so much: Alejandro de la Sota and Asís Cabrero and Rafael Aburto, and Julio Cano Lasso who later called on me to collaborate with him. And Javier Carvajal who led me into a teaching career at ETSAM, the Madrid School of Architecture. And also to Oiza and to Fisac. I will never forget any of them.

To Kenneth Frampton who wrote the prologue to my *Young Spanish Architecture* in 1986, and from that time on has written the prologues to nearly all my books. To Richard Meier and to David Chipperfield, whose words in this book are beautifully expressive. They honor me with their friendship.

To Tadao Ando, who generated and encouraged my exhibition at the MA Gallery of Tokyo in 2009. With him were Kazuyo Sejima and Toyo Ito and Kengo Kuma. And to Toshio Nakamura who made me a "correspondent" in Madrid for his important journal *A+ U.*

To Jørn Utzon whose generosity is reflected in the letters he wrote praising my undeserving works. I never knew how to thank him for that.

In the field of teaching, it is only fair to mention here Ignacio Vicens, Jesús Aparicio, and Juan Carlos Sancho. These three men today are tenured professors at ETSAM. I am, I feel, a bit guilty for their academic success. They have always helped me a lot. And they are, all of them, extraordinary architects.

To my clients who gave me the most important thing, freedom. I can attest that they are happy with their houses. From Roberto Turégano, Gaspar and Pepe Guerrero, Nancy Olnick and Giorgio Spanu, or Paco de Blas and Javier Asencio, to Rufino Delgado and Luis Moliner. Or Julio Rodríguez, to whom I owe the Caja Granada Savings Bank or to Antonio Claret, to whom I owe the MA in Granada. Also to Tom Ford, who commissioned me to design his house in Santa Fe, New Mexico, which local laws prevented from being constructed.

To Manuel Blanco, architect and tenured professor at ETSAM, who is the curator and spirit behind all of my exhibitions. From the exhibition at CROWN HALL in Chicago in 2003 and that of the URBAN CENTER in New York in 2002, those at the BASILICA PALLADIANA in Vicenza in 2004, at the BASILICA of SAINT IRENE in Istanbul in 2005, to the exhibition at the MA GALLERY in Tokyo in 2009. And in 2010, he prepared the exhibition at the NATIONAL GLYPTOTHEQUE in Athens. And at the Tempietto SAN PIETRO IN MONTORIO and that of the MAXXI in Rome in 2011. All sites that I do not deserve.

To the collaborators in my little studio who have been many and very good, the best, in these recent years. And I will name those who are with me now: Ignacio Aguirre, Alejandro Cervilla, and Miguel Ciria, along with Gaja Bieniasz. Not many, but they are worth a lot. Much better than I.

And to Oscar Riera Ojeda, who back in distant 1997 published one of the first monographs about me and now, this book.

Thank you, thank you, thank you.
GRACIAS, GRACIAS, GRACIAS.

Foreword
by Richard Meier

I first met Alberto Campo Baeza on a trip to Madrid in 1979. He was at the beginning of his career, and I can't help but still think of him as a young architect. Today he has the same vitality and enthusiasm that he had then, though the work has matured in a way that has been a delight to behold. He has become an architect of international stature and distinction, a master practitioner and teacher. Campo Baeza's many built projects in Spain, Italy, and now the United States continue to amaze by their purity, their strength, and their deeply felt dedication to modernist principles of architecture.

On a second visit in 1988 with my young son in tow, Campo Baeza and I spent some time together looking at architecture in Madrid. In the mix of all the historic work we were seeing he showed me the newly completed Turégano House, a beautiful white cube and a sublime exercise in minimalism. Looking back on those early residences, one can see that Campo Baeza has always been, to borrow a phrase from American sports parlance, a "big game player," no matter the scale. He had the prescience to recognize opportunity, select his clients carefully, and work in contexts within which it was possible to forge unforgettable relationships between the built and the natural environment—all extremely difficult feats for any young architect. From the outset of his career there has been an understanding and command of the history of architecture that brings a startling lucidity and substance to the work. The clarity of architectural ideas expressed in Campo Baeza's buildings have ranged in scale from small but beautiful residential structures like the De Blas House to cultural facilities such as Andalucía's Museum of Memory in Granada, an addition to his earlier large-scale achievement, the Caja Granada Savings Bank.

Campo Baeza's is an architecture of understanding and investigation, of intellect without mannerism. Critical to the impact of his work are a clear distinction between what is natural and what is man-made and a pitch-perfect articulation of elemental tension between solid and void, indoor and outdoor space, light and volume. The strength of form and composition, set against the backdrop of two cathedrals of Cádiz, an industrial neighborhood of Majorca, or an escarpment on New York's Hudson River Valley establishes a connection that is at once powerful and calm.

Gravity, space, light, and time are all intertwined as forces in Campo Baeza's work. There is no more powerful way to mark time than to speak in the language of light, which is ever-changing. The light in Campo Baeza's work is by turns bathing, piercing, dappling, and always brilliant. His investigation of light and mass is vital not only to the success of his career but also to the identity of what modern architecture continues to achieve. Architecture for our time evokes a feeling of what is important to us today, but good works of architecture also capture an enduring quality. It is a simple idea, but that pride of place and profound sustainability is the key difference between creating spaces with a life beyond our own and creating structures that ultimately become part of the past. Campo Baeza is interested in that enduring quality. Exacting attention to detail, from geometry to proportions to materials, has been consistently evident in his work from his days as a student to his current work in progress. While his style seems to be immune to trend or fashion, this is not to say his work is not bold; his excellent proposals for the Mercedes-Benz Museum and the Copenhagen Philharmonic are the forceful and daring work of an artist at the height of his powers. I have noticed that while the single family homes have led to cultural, public, and commercial projects of international significance, Campo Baeza has continued to create spaces for preschools and day care centers, most recently the much-lauded Benetton Day Care Center in Treviso, Italy. This is a wholly appropriate expression of his ideas on architecture: a simplicity and discipline that connects with young minds, which have no threshold for false notes or contrivance. Here both space and occupant are joined with the past and the future.

Richard Meier

RICHARD MEIER RECEIVED HIS ARCHITECTURAL TRAINING AT CORNELL UNIVERSITY AND ESTABLISHED HIS OWN OFFICE IN NEW YORK CITY IN 1963. HE HAS RECEIVED THE HIGHEST HONORS IN THE FIELD INCLUDING THE PRITZKER PRIZE FOR ARCHITECTURE, THE GOLD MEDAL FROM THE AMERICAN INSTITUTE OF ARCHITECTS, THE AMERICAN ACADEMY OF ARTS AND LETTERS, AND THE ROYAL INSTITUTE OF BRITISH ARCHITECTS AS WELL AS THE PRAEMIUM IMPERIALE FROM THE JAPAN ART ASSOCIATION. AMONG HIS BEST-KNOWN PROJECTS ARE THE ACCLAIMED GETTY CENTER IN LOS ANGELES; THE HIGH MUSEUM IN ATLANTA; THE BARCELONA MUSEUM OF CONTEMPORARY ART; THE FRANKFURT MUSEUM FOR DECORATIVE ARTS; THE CANAL+ TELEVISION HEADQUARTERS IN PARIS; THE CITY HALL AND CENTRAL LIBRARY IN THE HAGUE; THE JUBILEE CHURCH IN ROME ITALY. CURRENT PROJECTS INCLUDE THE ITALCEMENTI ITC LAB IN BERGAMO, ITALY, THE ST. DENIS OFFICE COMPLEX IN PARIS, THE ROTHSCHILD TOWER IN TEL AVIV, AND THE SOMA NEWARK MASTER PLAN.

The Alchemist of Space
by Jesús Aparicio

Closeness to someone or something may simplify the perceived reality or make it more difficult, since it is easy to distinguish the details but often hard to apprehend the whole unblurred.

I wouldn't want this text to obscure in any way the integrity and magnitude of the work of such a figure of architecture as Alberto Campo Baeza. To try to ensure this doesn't happen, it seemed appropriate to me to subject his buildings to a systematic architectural analysis that starts from the gaze the architect projects onto reality and concludes with an architectural interpretation of the work Campo Baeza has been building as a unified and complete legacy, even with its variations and transformations.

So, this essay begins with that gaze that is indispensable to the work of every architect and that in Campo Baeza's work is centered on aspects such as function and place: a gaze belonging to a sensitive, rigorous, and essential person.

A. The Gaze the Architect Casts on Function and Place

Alberto Campo Baeza casts a double gaze that can be distinguished in each one of his works: that on function and that on place. In both cases, his is a gaze in which intellectual abstraction is wisely combined with sensory experience. This dual vision is incorporated in the perception of the spaces he builds, spaces whose center is always man, the human being in whom are combined, as in Leonardo's Vitruvian Man, universality, geometry, proportion, and particularity.

For that reason, Campo Baeza's architecture simultaneously represents and interprets both the function it contains and the place in which it is situated. His constructed work encompasses the most diverse functions: domestic buildings (homes), institutional buildings (educational institutions, offices, day care and nursery schools, and museums) and urban interventions (squares and plazas). Among these functions, the house naturally stands out as a place that is simultaneously and indivisibly temple and school.

But all of the aforementioned *utilitas* is transformed and interpreted to provide a universal and specific answer to a man and to a place. Thus, one can see how the houses are introverted or exposed, composed of horizontal, vertical, or diagonal spaces, depending on their location. In each case, they are the precise response to the man that inhabits and to the place that receives them. Topography, geology, biology, latitude, views, sunlight, and other aspects are all included in this architect's gaze upon the place, and like an alchemist of space who distills its essences in his beaker of knowledge, he finally achieves that wonderful perfume of architecture.

But this variation of spaces according to place not only occurs in the houses. The same is also true of the public buildings, which are sometimes hidden behind courtyards, while others rise like towers and still others lie within the landscape. That they should do one thing or another is the consequence, in most cases, of the reflections the architect has made about the place, whether it is open countryside, the suburb or the city, and all its respective possibilities. This, I believe I can say, I have learned from this master: the architect has to look upon the place as a unique, unrepeatable possibility. And this is applicable to each one of the places in which he may project a construction. There are no bad places for the architect, only bad readings—insensitive readings—of places. Alberto Campo Baeza knows this well and his work demonstrates it. Some of his most canonical works are the result of an apt and intense reading of places that are not exactly idyllic. It just happens that he knows well that the architect works with reality, with the reality of the place and of the construction.

The work of good architects organizes functions and constructs harmony in the place if it did not exist there previously, and in the case of privileged places, it underlines their beauty. We find numerous examples in Campo Baeza's work of how to perform this far from simple task, as he knows very well, whether it is a case of David confronting Goliath, when what he builds must conquer the place, imposing itself upon it, or whether the intervention is more like the Trojan horse, and beauty remains hidden in the innards of the architecture, since what is built can hardly achieve the complete transformation of its surroundings.

The Fene City Hall project constructs a new reference between the place and the main buildings with two courtyards surrounded by arcades, which also serve as a transition between the public building and the adjacent park on its north side. Thus, in regard to the relationship with the place, the rationality of the constructed space is wisely blended into continuity with the park.

The San Fermín School in Madrid does not establish any continuity with its degraded surroundings; instead, the building is closed on one edge, opening itself to the opposite side as though it were a wall protecting it from what it voluntarily wishes to exclude from the place.

The Turégano House in Madrid is resolved wisely, as it is implanted on the topographical slope of the lot, so that the topography comes to form part of the space of this tripartite house. This operation is different from that of the Gaspar House, in Cádiz, in which a beautiful setting without tension voluntarily merges in its horizontal perception into a house of two-dimensional tensions so as to be revealed in a vertical foreshortening behind the courtyards as even more beautiful, as the evergreen pines rise over the white walls that construct its perimeter. In this canonical house,[1] the function is organized with a space that is doubly tripartite, a space that accentuates a horizontal continuity delimited by the border of the enclosure. From the outside, it is revealed as a white object, a poetic reaction, that holds the secret of its space within.

And so we may continue to follow Campo Baeza in his guise of the architect who organizes functions and places. The Drago Public School in Cádiz, set in an urban context, magnificently combines a function that requires concentration with the inalienable condition of its situation facing the sea. Or the Center for Technological Innovation in Majorca that, situated in an industrial area, constructs behind its marés stone walls an area that forms a continuous space of offices and garden.

Campo Baeza uses very few elements to abstract, underline, or transform a place: a box, a plane, or an enclosure. These austere and economically constructed architectural elements achieve their objectives effectively and are the "more with less" that the architect so often refers to.

The Telefónica Tower in Madrid is a good example of decision when establishing a function in a place. In a lot that was initially earmarked for a "low intensity" and "low height" building like those around it, Campo Baeza boldly and aptly chooses the typology of maximum density: the skyscraper. He achieves many things with this sought-after intensity: firstly, an effective resolution of the function, in which corridors are minimized; secondly, he transforms those landscaped areas that appear in all horizontal urban developments—which tend to be non-places pertaining to neither nature nor culture—into a park with a dimension clearly belonging to nature, so that from it, the tower is the only cultural reference; thirdly, he provides the company the best emblematic image possible from a distance, the tower itself; and fourthly, the tower allows its users to bring the park, the city, and the horizon together within the office. We thus find another of the constants of Alberto Campo Baeza's architecture in this tower design: the precise combination of compactness of function wherever possible and free expansion wherever it most suits man and the place.

Continuing to reflect on this triple aspect of man, function, and place in Campo Baeza's architecture in other designs and projects, one discovers how in the De Blas House in Madrid the function of living spaces—in a glass box on a plane facing the horizon—is distinguished from those of sleeping, eating, and washing—within a concrete box: the plane and the box, the cabin and the cave, the air and the earth. In this project, something appears clearly that could already be seen in the Center for Technological Innovation

---

[1] About this house I heard professor Salvatore Bisogni of the Naples School of Architecture say that it was the best courtyard house constructed since Mies van der Rohe, which is the same as saying that it is the best courtyard house built in the twentieth century.

and in the Telefónica Tower, the dual consideration of space as cave—stereotomic—and as cabin—tectonic. And this dual appreciation is the consequence of a reflection on the place, a place in which there is always a dialogue between earth and air, between solid and vapor, between the closeness of opacity and the infinity of transparence. And there are functions that have more to do with one state or another of the material. Campo Baeza first intuited it and in De Blas House, he already knows it.

From this moment, this double reading of place, earth-air, and of function, public-private, becomes clearer all the time, and while the architect continues to trust geometric lines as a horizontal mode

pavilion for meetings. This superposition coincides with the use of different materials: cement, steel, and glass. In this way, the building responds to a triple consideration of the scale of the place, whether it is understood as terrain/parcel, as the border of a highway, or as an observatory of the horizon of the city and the mountains of Madrid. This in turn is adapted to the three functional aspects of the building: storeroom, offices, and meeting rooms.

Two public buildings set in their location by horizontal designs can be found among the architect's projects: the Montenmedio Museum, which, constructing an almost infinite wall in an oak

Campo Baeza uses very few elements to abstract, underline, or transform a place: a box, a plane, or an enclosure. These austere and economically constructed architectural elements achieve their objectives effectively and are the "more with less" that this architect so often refers to.

of colonizing the site, from the beginning of the millennium, he has established his work with a greater and clearer vertical superposition. In this way, in this period, one can continue to appreciate the horizontal geometric designs—expressed clearly in the floor plans—that take over the place, principally when it is urban, as occurs most sharply in the plaza of the Cathedral of Almería (a competition won in 1978 and constructed more than twenty years later), in the square of the Caja General de Granada (headquarters of the Caja Granada Savings Bank) and in the Asencio House, the Montenmedio Museum, the Entrecatedrales [Between Cathedrals] space in Cádiz and in Andalucía's Museum of Memory in Granada. These designs are references to the place which in many cases coincide with a property limit that the architect makes coincide with the border establishing the grounds of the space.

Nonetheless, the vertical references to the place and to the function—which, basically, are narrated through sections— are more frequent all the time. A piling up that consists of the superposition of the earth, cave, cabin, and air in a certain arrangement so that the function is adapted to the place. We can find examples of these circumstances in the Caja Granada Savings Bank, in which the condition of cave emerges beyond the gradient of the terrain, constructing a central space open to the sun in its ceiling. The offices of the Andalucía Regional Government construct a lookout post, a stone wall of vertical proportions containing offices, on which a glass cabin is situated, used as a meeting room that serves as an observatory over the city. Or the building for Mercedes-Benz in Stuttgart (Germany) in which a cement podium is constructed, emphasizing its horizontal character and quietude, so that some helicoid ramps can be erected on top of it that belong to the world of mobility. Thus, quietude—stability and mobility—balance are juxtaposed.

One finds a triple piling in the central headquarters of the SM publishing company: the basement, the box of offices, and the

grove, divides the world in two halves, with the simultaneously artificial, white, and horizontal reference of this landscape, and the Benetton Day Care Center in Treviso (Italy) in which he erects a cylindrical enclosure that contains four prismatic pieces, constructing a hermetic area on the site that distinguishes outside from inside and within the interior combining the centrality of the circular and of the cross.

The Moliner House in Zaragoza, the Rufo House in Toledo, and the Olnick Spanu House in New York once again organize the place and architecture by means of piling up uses, materials, and different spaces that are almost always counterposed through juxtaposition and contraposition. And the same happens with the plane that constitutes the space Between Cathedrals, under which the ruin is left as a theoretical foundation and over which a very light small building closed with gauzes faces the horizon of the sea.

This section could not be complete without mentioning two projects with designs different from those already considered: the Center for Nature Interpretation in the salt flats of Janubio, Lanzarote, and Andalucía's Museum of Memory. They are two different, nearly opposed projects. While the first wishes to disappear into the landscape, constructing a black horizontal plane over the salt flats, the second is pure raised presence, with a vertical plane confronting the highway and the valley, which in turn provides a backdrop for the already mentioned building of the Caja General.

B. The Order of Matter: Structure, Geometry, and Light

There is a triple order in the architecture of Campo Baeza: that of the structure, that of geometry, and that of light. While the first belongs to the resistant quality of the material, the second is made according to an intellectual abstraction of geometry itself, and the third is framed within the experiential condition of the material and of astronomical science. Nonetheless, they all construct a common order: the order of architectural space.

Gravity establishes the order of the physical structure, the brain constructs that of geometry or the rational structure, and the mobility of the universe and man's sensitivity produce the order of light. Alberto Campo Baeza knows all of this, and he makes it clear, both in his texts and in the framing of his projects and designs. An idea of order imposes itself upon the gaze Campo Baeza casts over the place and the required function, an order that is first the abstract translation of a thought to later become the material construction.

Sometimes, due to its simplicity—which is by no means simple—the order appears obvious. However, that is not the case. That the order might appear obvious, due to its simplicity once revealed by the architect, does not mean that it is. One must remember that most great discoveries—and architecture in some ways is one—do not entail resolving complicated questions but rather simple ones. We may recall how the drawing of figures such as the square, the circle, the cube, or the sphere is defined by only one parameter. The Pythagorean Theorem and the Law of Gravity define three variables. The same occurs with Campo Baeza's architecture, which, though it is defined with few parameters, ends up possessing great spatial intensity thanks to its very simplicity.

While function and place are usually variables given to the architect, gravity and light are realities that exist, and structure and geometry are questions that he decides. The table of architecture is a tripod: resting on what the client requests, what the world gives, and what the architect proposes. Campo Baeza's response to any given function in any place, always bearing in mind the laws of light and gravity, is a rational response in which all of the above is ordered with geometry and structure.

After analyzing the circumstantial—function and space—and the universal—light and gravity—in their variables and constants, Campo Baeza decides upon the designs of an architecture conceived from and for man in response to the above: an architecture of geometry and a structure of pure forms.

Thus, parallelepipeds and cylinders end up defining the lines of these designs. A formal purity in which the identity of the place and the delimitation of the space in reference to man, inside and outside, is superimposed on the architecture. Apart from these geometric figures, Campo Baeza has only used one triangle, one helicoid, and one ellipse in all his work.

This geometric purity mirrors a Platonic and rational mental clarity. This rationality is translated into a geometry of parallels and orthogonalities, with which nearly all of his work can be defined. When they do rarely appear, the other geometries (triangle, curves, etc.) usually correspond to the imposed conditions of urbanistic alignments.

The geometry that defines the lines of the structure in Campo Baeza's architecture is an encompassing geometry, one that gets the most dimension out of the place, the function, and the budget. To obtain this maximum dimensional possibility, an economy of means is necessary that translates into constructive sobriety. For that reason, it is not odd that his walls are made with rough brick, pointed, coated, and painted white and that the floors are made of inexpensive stone from Cabra, in a light sand color. However, this extreme material sobriety—since what we could call restraint or "spatial sobriety" always exists in his work—becomes even more evident in his residential and educational architecture.

While structure and geometry are abstract organizations and therefore susceptible to using symmetry in their construction, the same is not true of light, which with its asymmetrical variation constructs together with the person that inhabits the architecture, the most vital aspect of the space: that which escaping mathematical perfection overcomes it as it penetrates deep within the territory of the transcendent and the poetic.

Reviewing the work of Alberto Campo Baeza, the aforementioned extremes can be observed, together with the factor that entails constructing with pieces of architecture that become greater as they take on every possible aspect of the place. Thus it happens that from the exterior, they are a reference to their urban or territorial surroundings, while their interior space expands, multiplying its capacity to be perceived, by means of the spatial mechanism of doubling the experience of seeing and stepping through the space.

A spatial operation of this kind is carried out in the project of the Fene City Hall, so that in its two main facades, the main building falls over two arcaded areas that establish a new limit between the building and the park or the city. One of these arcades continues until joining it. In the case of the San Fermín School, the classroom wing serves as a habitable wall that is closed on one of its sides, with its classes opening on the opposite side (the south). In the center of the wing, a cylindrical space of glass blocks is built that simultaneously illuminates the communications core and provides the pavilion with a lobby.

The canonical house, Turégano House, is structured according to geometry and light, as it adapts to the slope of the terrain. It could be said that the house is sheltered in a cubic volume measuring 9 m around the perimeter, which is broken up according to the solicitations of light and topography. The result of these luminous and topographical solicitations, added to the function and to the primitive cubic figure, produces the structural order of the house.

With regard to the order of the material, two different attitudes on the architect's part can be distinguished, depending on whether the work is situated in an urban lot—in which case, it tends to adhere to the site—or whether it is constructed in a medium without level or alignment definitions—in which case, geometry is used to define an exterior enclosure that assumes the space or opens up to the existing surroundings. Nonetheless, in any of the aforementioned cases, the architecture is defined in its interior by a pure geometry that sometimes has its origin in the exterior border of the building and other times is counterposed to it.

Thus, Campo Baeza's architecture may be classified within the following parameters:

1. According to its location
      a. In an urban medium
      b. In nature

2. According to its exterior geometry
      a. Adhering to natural levels or alignments or preexisting urban parameters
      b. Work defined by a geometry of pure forms

3. According to its interior geometry
      a. As an echo of the exterior enclosure
      b. Pure form different from the exterior border

4. According to its relation to the topography
      a. Imposing itself in it
      b. Superimposing itself upon it

5. According to the relationship of the space to the view
      a. To illuminate
      b. To see

From the above five points some interesting observations regarding Alberto Campo Baeza's architecture and its evolution can be made.

In regard to location, while usually belonging to an urban surrounding, some of his architecture has been raised in natural or undefined landscapes due to an absence of legal parameters that have determined its situation in one way or another. Such is the case of the Gaspar House and Guerrero House in Madrid and the Olnick Spanu House in New York, or the Montenmedio Museum and the Center for Nature Interpretation in Lanzarote.

With regard to geometry, it can be said that Campo Baeza's architecture is mostly established in its exterior volumes with a geometry of pure forms, except in the few cases in which the existence of different slopes, alignments, or exterior borders require otherwise, as in the case of the Drago Public School and Asencio House in Cádiz, the Cathedral plaza in Almería, and the Center for Technological Innovation in Majorca.

With regard to the interior geometry of his buildings, there is a dual decision in the structural order. First, when it is the reflection of the exterior definition of the building; that is the case in most of his work. Second, when the order of the interior structure is counterposed to that established by the exterior, as occurs in all his architecture when it adheres to slopes, alignments, or an exterior border, and in some buildings in which this opposition is voluntarily sound and is the determining factor of the space of the design (as occurs in the Benetton Day Care Center or in Andalucía's Museum of Memory).

With regard to topography, two attitudes exist: imposition in the topography or superposition upon it, though one is found more often. In this aspect, one can say that Campo Baeza's architecture usually imposes itself on the landscape, without hiding, with that classical attitude of the Greeks with their temples in which a respect for the place is revealed in the knowledge of its material, its scale, etc. On rare occasions one finds Campo Baeza's work adhering to the place, and when this occurs, it is due mainly to two reasons: a building with an excessive dimension, which would end up becoming a problem of scale if it didn't fragment (as is the case of the Montenmedio Museum) or a natural or cultural preexistence that must not be touched (as occurs with the archaeological ruins in the space Between Cathedrals in Cádiz or with some versions of the Center for Nature Interpretation in the salt flats of Janubio, Lanzarote).

Finally, the relation of the interior of the spaces to the exterior is established by the following aspects: the relationship with natural light, the relationship with the view, or with a double relationship of light and view.

Light alone is in itself a determining factor of the interior spaces in the San Fermín School, the Turégano House, the Caja Granada Savings Bank, and the Asencio House. The gaze is fundamental in the Fene City Hall, the Gaspar House, the Center for Technological Innovation, the Telefónica Tower, the De Blas House, the Cathedral plaza, the offices of the Regional Government of Andalucía, the Mercedes-Benz headquarters, the SM building, the Guerrero House, the Olnick Spanu House, the Center for the Interpretation of the Landscape, the Rufo House, the Between Cathedrals space, and Andalucía's Museum of Memory. Within these examples, one can distinguish whether the gaze of the space is introspective (Gaspar House) or whether it is made toward the exterior (De Blas House), and also whether the gaze is frontal (Gaspar House) or foreshortened (Andalucía's Museum of Memory) and whether it is horizontal or vertical.

Finally there are a few examples in which light and the gaze coexist with comparable intensity, as occurs in the lobby of the Drago Public School, the Montenmedio Museum, and the Benetton Day Care Center.

C. Boxes, Planes, and Enclosures

Another way to approach Campo Baeza's spaces is to classify them according to the archetypes of the box, the plane or podium (horizontal wall), and the enclosure or vertical wall. Throughout his career, the kind or kinds of space he works with have become more obvious each time, thanks to his clarity: boxes of light and planes of air.

The space of the box is characterized as a pure volume, some-times cubic, which grants the space a change of scale that is constructed with the vertical dimension. This vertical dimension is revealed by means of the light that runs through it. Thus, one can see the connection between the space of the box, the change of scale due to the increase of the vertical dimension, and the light. Logically, given the previous parameters, it is not difficult to imagine how these spaces tend to coincide with the public or served areas of the same. Sometimes these boxes are exposed to the exterior as a unique space the project has erected, other times they remain hidden in the edificatory de-signs intersecting with them.

A few examples of this kind of space can be found in the San Fermín School, where a luminous cylinder of glass blocks in-tersects the general design of the building and constructs the common space and vertical circulation. In the Turégano House, the box manifests itself as a single volume from the exterior, while from the interior, it is comprehended as the foreshortened concatenation of the home's public spaces that, providing mul-tiple oblique views, make it almost infinite as solid light crosses through them. The canonical example of the box in Campo Baeza's work is the Caja Granada Savings Bank, in which the building is like a geode that hides a space of another scale, vertical and shared, within its interior: a courtyard of operations bathed in light. The four colossal columns that traverse it, while born of a structural necessity, are also the representation of the same thing, additionally revealing the parameters of scale and light.

We can find box spaces inserted into the structural lines of the vestibule of the Drago Public School or in the living room of Gaspar House, in which the box, unlike what usually happens in Campo Baeza's work, constructs a shadow space in its verti-cal dimension, just as occurs in the Guerrero House. A different case is the box that he builds in the center of the Benetton Day Care Center, surrounded by rooms and enclosed by a circular wall; or the box of Moliner House, situated on top of a plane like a vertical space of diffuse light.

Thus, work with light can be made with solid light (the Caja Granada Savings Bank), with shade (Gaspar House), with dif-fuse light (Moliner House), or with light combined with views (Drago Public School).

Another characteristic space of Campo Baeza's work is the podium or horizontal plane of the borderless floor where man can fix his gaze on the infinite horizon. If the box is the space of vertical extension and light, the plane is the space of horizontal extension and the gaze: the space of man. These continuous and horizontal spaces sometimes extend toward the infinite horizon, as is the case of the Telefónica Tower, the De Blas House, the SM building, the Olnick Spanu House, the Center for Nature Interpretation, the Rufo House, and the space Between Cathedrals.

WORK	According to its location	According to its geom. exterior	According to its geom. interior	According to its topographical relation	According to its relation to the sense of the view
Fene City Hall	A	A	A	A	B
San Fermín School	A	B	A	A	A
Turégano House	A	B	A	B	A
Drago Public School	A	A	B	A	A+B
Gaspar House	B	B	A	A	B
Center for Techn. Innovation	A	A	A	A	B
Telefónica Tower	A	B	A	A	B
De Blas House	A	B	A	A	B
Cathedral Square	A	A	B	B	B
Caja Granada	A	B	A	A	A
Asencio House	A	A	B	A	A
Delegation of Public Health	A	B	A	A	B
Mercedes-Benz Museum	A	B	A	A	B
SM Public Offices	A	B	A	A	B
Guerrero House	B	B	A	A	B
Montenmedio Museum	B	B	A	B	A+B
Benetton Day Care Center	A	B	B	A	A+B
Olnick Spanu House	B	B	A	A	B
Moliner House	A	A	B	A	A+B
Center for Nature Interpretation	B	A	A	B	B
Rufo House	A	B	A	A	B
Between Cathedrals	A	B	A	A	B
Museum of Memory	A	B	B	A	B

It is interesting to note the different positions in which glass is placed in the boxes and in the spaces between the planes in Campo Baeza's architecture. While in the boxes, glass is placed in the exterior beams reconstructing the solidity of the box to appear virtually completed in the reflection in the glass (Turégano House), the second leaves the glass built-in, hidden in the shadow in order to disappear and thus accentuating its transparency (De Blas House, the Center for Technological Innovation, and the Olnick Spanu House).

Other times, the plane open to the infinite is not possible or convenient, so the architecture adheres to an area within which the absolute control of the continuous space is possible. Such is the case of the Gaspar House, in which the perimeter walls protect a continuous interior space with the courtyard of lemon trees and light, the room in the shadow (the box constructing the roof of shade to which we referred before), and again another courtyard with lemon trees, light, and water. Something similar occurs in the Center for Technological Innovation, in the Cathedral plaza, and in some way occurs—even combining this space with that of the box—in the Asencio House and the Guerrero House. The Benetton Day Care Center is a space in which centrality, continuity, and frontality[2] are combined. Centrality is constructed in the spatial relation that exists between the box of the central vestibule and the circular wall-enclosure. Continuity is the consequence of the two possible directions between the classrooms that unite the center with the enclosure. Frontality is constructed in the spatial

---

[2] It would be a good idea to clarify what is understood by the concepts here. Centrality is constructed by a space equivalent to 360° of the plane, so that from inside (the center) toward the outside (the perimeter), what can be called a centrifugal centrality exists, outside (the perimeter) toward the inside (center), what is called a centripetal centrality. It is a flat space of infinite directions and radial orientations. Continuity is constructed when the space succeeds in one direction and equivalently toward either end. Frontality is constructed when the space succeeds according to one direction, but in a different way in each one of its orientations.

relation between the classrooms and the surrounding grounds. The Moliner House establishes its continuity over the plane of the floor that is enclosed between the walls.

One can say that the plane open to the infinite and the enclosure are two modes of constructing continuity in Campo Baeza's work, in the same way that the box is the consequence of a desire for discontinuity with the place in an architecture that turns in on itself. Therefore, the box separates the interior space from the exterior, the plane unites them, and the enclosure constructs an exterior space of controlled nature that belongs to architecture itself.

Notwithstanding the above, and even as Campo Baeza's architecture is of an astonishing clarity—his proposals that have won competitions so often are, like the story of Columbus's egg, of an unquestionable simplicity—several of the ideas outlined earlier coexist in his work. In the Gaspar House, a box of shady roof nuances the enclosed continuity in a few white walls; in the De Blas, Olnick Spanu, and Rufo houses the box and the continuous

dimensions, with another scale, providing the entire whole with meaning. The existence of these spaces can be seen throughout his work. These are the spaces that best summarize his architecture and for which it is recognized.

They are the generous and measured served spaces that often correspond to the lobbies of his public architecture (the Fene City Hall, the San Fermín School, the Drago Public School, the Caja Granada Savings Bank, the SM building, the Benetton Day Care Center). Other times they correspond to courtyards (the Center for Technological Innovation or Andalucía's Museum of Memory) or to the spaces between two planes that offer a view into the distance (the upper floor of the Telefónica Tower, the rooms in the top floors of the office building of the Regional Government of Andalucía and of the SM building or in the canopy of Between Cathedrals). With regard to the houses, the spaces become splendid in their quality and dimensions as living areas, as can be found in the concatenation of the living room-dining room in Turégano House or in the shaded space between two luminous courtyards in Gaspar

With regard to geometry, it can be said that Campo Baeza's architecture is mostly established in its exterior volumes with a geometry of pure forms...

space pile up; in the Asencio House a box is built within some walls and in the Guerrero House the enclosure that surrounds the continuity acquires a vertical dimension so as to begin to construct a box. The building for the headquarters of Mercedes-Benz is the counterposition between the static nature of the box and the mobile infinitude of the exhibition ramp. Andalucía's Museum of Memory constructs an area that goes beyond being a perimeter space to become the central articulating courtyard. A courtyard that, as it is elliptical, adds to its initially central condition the direction in which its spotlights are aligned, a direction that is not ambivalent in its two directions but rather that has the nature of a frontal foreshortening as it confronts the vertical body that rises perpendicular to it on one of its sides.

D. Compactness and Expansion

These analytical observations of Campo Baeza's work would not be complete without speaking of another element that is fundamental and constant to it. It happens that, once he has been given a place, a function to resolve, and a budget, Alberto Campo Baeza decides on the administration of the spaces following the guidelines of what could be called a splendid sobriety, something like: "let's be austere in the required *utilitas* in order to be magnanimous in the chosen *venustas*."

This translates into a clear division in all of his projects between the served space and the service space—*utilitas*—characterized by its compact and austere design, without concessions, to benefit the first. However, in his buildings the served space, without being in the least bit capricious, always appears generous in its

House or Guerrero House, or in the glass boxes in De Blas House or Rufo House, or in the living space above the golf course in Asencio House, or that overlooking the Hudson River in Olnick Spanu. In one instance, Moliner House, that expanded and generous space corresponds to a work area, to write with a diffuse and constant light.

CONCLUSIONS

Having sought to analyze Campo Baeza's work through the words above and through the occasional drawing, it is worth thinking about what is substantive in this body of constructed work over some thirty years. The essential thing is what spins in the architect's head again and again and that results in a body of work that transcends the expression of an age and a place because it belongs to the universal and the eternal.

Thus, the universal and eternal constants that construct his work are gravity, light, and man. Constants that build a universal space and a suspended or eternal time. In this architect's thought, Aristotelian and Platonic ideas, the poetry of San Juan de la Cruz and Santa Teresa of Ávila, and the sound of the music of Bach are teachers that join his architectural masters, the always universal Iktinos and Kallikrates, Anthemius of Tralles and Isidore of Miletus, Bernini, Le Corbusier, Mies van der Rohe, Barragán, and Utzon.

Campo Baeza's work is timeless; while belonging to a place, it transcends it in the search for eternal parameters—gravity, light, and man—in constructing the beauty of its spaces. It is a beauty constructed by means of the architect's rigorous gaze that orders and organizes the space in the place, with an unquestionable order of priorities, selecting and situating the substantive and the circumstantial reality to correspond to his poetic gaze.

Campo Baeza organizes his spaces following a hierarchical server-served chain of order that starts from and constitutes a complete, encompassing, and eternal idea. For example, in his houses, the bedrooms structure the closet and bathroom areas; everything is done in accordance with the living area and that, in the end, constructs a relation of light or of views between the constructed idea and the place. Something similar happens in the Caja Granada Savings Bank, where the washrooms and communications are contained in the cement walls, that, like the best Kahn of the Exeter Library, define the work space. At the same time, this space constructs the great empty central space that moves according to the diagonal of its floor plan and section to best trap light in the space; that substantive space of the project, built with concrete and sun.

Alberto Campo Baeza is a poet of space. It is unthinkable to decipher the intensity of his work without recognizing this. Just as a poet carefully selects his concepts and juxtaposes, opposes, or lines them in sequence, creating the music of ideas through the chosen word, Alberto Campo Baeza selects his proportions, his measures, his lines, and his light to make that eternal music of ideas resound—sometimes in the transgression of the established disciplinary rigor—through the space of his almost white architecture, a whiteness that does not want to veil abstraction and light.

Given the work and the thought of this enormous architect, one always feels fortunate to be his disciple, because Alberto Campo Baeza is that master who with apparent facility resolves simply and indisputably problems that seem unsolvable. Like a good master, he uses the Socratic method; a commentary of his, reformulating the question, often leads the student to obtain the response he was hoping for. It is a method that makes the disciple learn to think, to formulate the appropriate questions in order to reach a lucid answer.

Another characteristic of Campo Baeza's architecture is that it is pedagogical, since one can learn a lot from it—needless to say, I have been doing so for the past thirty years—and one can teach a lot with it, which I have also had the opportunity to do for the past twenty-five years.

The master taught me first with the rigor of his work, then with his poetic sensibility, and later with his deep thought. Finally, having given me his friendship, I have had the fortune of knowing that beyond his masterly architecture, his sober and sensitive gaze upon the world and the bottomless significance of his knowledge, what is truly extraordinary in him is the person, himself. Thank you, maestro.

Jesús Mª Aparicio Guisado
Professor of Architectural Design, ETSAM

JESÚS Mª APARICIO GUISADO IS AN ARCHITECT. HE GRADUATED FROM THE ESCUELA TÉCNICA SUPERIOR DE ARQUITECTURA DE MADRID (ETSAM), WITH HONORS IN BOTH BUILDING DESIGN AND URBAN DESIGN IN 1984, AND HE LATER TAUGHT ELEMENTS OF COMPOSITION AT THE SAME INSTITUTION. HE HAS WON THE ROME PRIZE IN ARCHITECTURE AWARDED BY THE ACADEMIA DE BELLAS ARTES DE ESPAÑA IN ROME, AND A FULBRIGHT/M.E.C FELLOWSHIP. HE WAS VISITING SCHOLAR AT COLUMBIA UNIVERSITY, NEW YORK, WHERE HE OBTAINED A MASTERS IN ARCHITECTURE AND BUILDING DESIGN. HE HAS A PH.D. IN ARCHITECTURE AND, SINCE 2009, HAS BEEN A PROFESSOR OF BUILDING DESIGN AT ETSAM. HE HAS BEEN A VISITING PROFESSOR AND LECTURER AT NUMEROUS SCHOOLS OF ARCHITECTURE IN EUROPE, THE UNITED STATES, AND SOUTH AMERICA. HE AND HIS WORK HAVE WON SEVERAL INTERNATIONAL AWARDS.

WORK	YEAR	ORDER STRUCTURE GEOMETRY	MATERIAL	PLACE NATURE & CULTURE	FACES OR PLANES	COMPACTNESS & EXPANSION
Fene City Hall	1980		Mortar.	Park border.		Compact boxes. Balcony plane.
School in San Fermín	1985		Brick. Glass brick.	Suburban Zone.		
Turégano House	1988		Mortar.	Development (suburban).		
Drago Public School	1992		Mortar and stone baseboard (flat). Classic.	Urban lot.	Adhering borders and emptied boxes. Plane over the sea. Planes to look from.	
Gaspar House	1992		Mortar and flat stone floor.	Outdoor courtyard nature.		
Center for Technological Innovation	1998		Stone. Glass. Concrete.	Industrial compound lot.		Transparency doubles the space.
Telefónica Tower	1999		Concrete. Steel. Glass. Stone. Supporting + severy.	Outskirts. Ordering of the place.		
De Blas House	2000		Concrete + Steel. Supporting + severy.	Development. Transformed Nature.		
Plaza of the Cathedral of Almería	2000 (1978)		Marble paving slabs. (form and deform).	Urban plaza.		
Caja Granada Savings Bank	2001		Concrete. Stone. Alabaster - glass. Adding to continuity and light.	Lot.		

Project	Year		Material	Site	Concept	
Asencio House	2001		Mortar Stone.	Development.		
Delegation of Public Health Offices	2002		Stone. Base + cabin.	Urban site.	Box with back and front.	
Mercedes-Benz Museum	2002		Reinforced concrete.	Industrial area.		
SM Group Headquarters	2003		Steel in the facade. Leveled glass. Wood skirting board.	Facing the highway (scale).		
Guerrero House	2005		Mortar. Reticule Reinforced Concrete. Reinterpretation of Gaspar (one more step).	Nature and courtyard abstraction.		
School in Montecarmelo	2006		Mortar.	Nature.		
Benetton Day Care Center	2007		Mortar. Stone.	Industrial zone.		
Olnick Spanu House	2008		Concrete. Stone. Steel.	Nature. Same references that began with the archetype of the De Blas House.		
Moliner House	2008		Mortar. Glass.	Development.		
Center for Nature Interpretation	2009		Steel and concrete.	Nature.		Expansive flat structure constructs the space.
Rufo House	2009		Concrete.	Development.	Subtracted box.	
Between Cathedrals	2009		Stone.	City.		
Andalucía's Museum of Memory	2009		Concrete + mortar.	Site.		

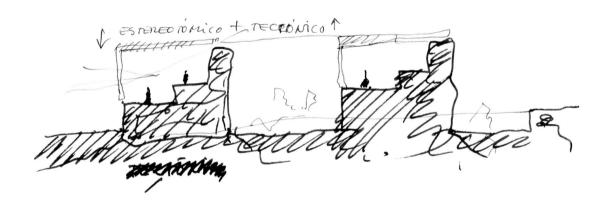

FEAR

WEAR

Rotonda House

Rotonda House

Madrid, 2021

A HOUSE FOR ANA

Situated at the very summit of a hill north of Madrid, with the sierra as a backdrop in the distance, a house for Ana.

Once again, we are trying to build the loveliest house in the world. And to capture that 360° panoramic landscape, we proposed a belvedere at the top of the house where one feels in seventh heaven.

Supporting this belvedere, we built a two-story podium made of local Colmenar limestone, in which we carved out the required openings for windows, providing light and ventilation to the rooms.

Geometrically the structure is based on a 12 x 12 m square, divided into nine 4 x 4 m squares. Like an exercise from Durand's *Précis des leçons d'Architecture*. With a certain Palladian flavor.

On the south-facing ground floor, a spacious living room, protected by a light veranda where vines and jasmine can grow. The floor plan extends to a pool at the edge. On the north facade is the main entrance to the house. Alongside it, the large kitchen and the dining room. In the center of that floor, a 4 x 4 m square general hallway through which the staircase and the elevator can be accessed.

On the upper floor, the bedrooms at all four corners. Three identical bedrooms with en suite bathrooms, and a larger primary bedroom with a dressing room.

And supporting this construction in the steep topography of the hill is a concrete podium, in a color matching the stone, which houses the garage, storage, and service areas.

Previous spread. Exterior view from the north.
Right. Aerial view from the northwest with the surrounding landscape.

Above. Exterior view from the southwest.
Right top. Partial view from the northeast.
Right bottom. West elevation.

Above right. Entrance door detail.
Right. Exterior view from the northwest.

Above. Second floor. Rooftop canopy.
Right. Second floor. Glass box. Transparency.
Following spread. Second floor. Rooftop canopy.

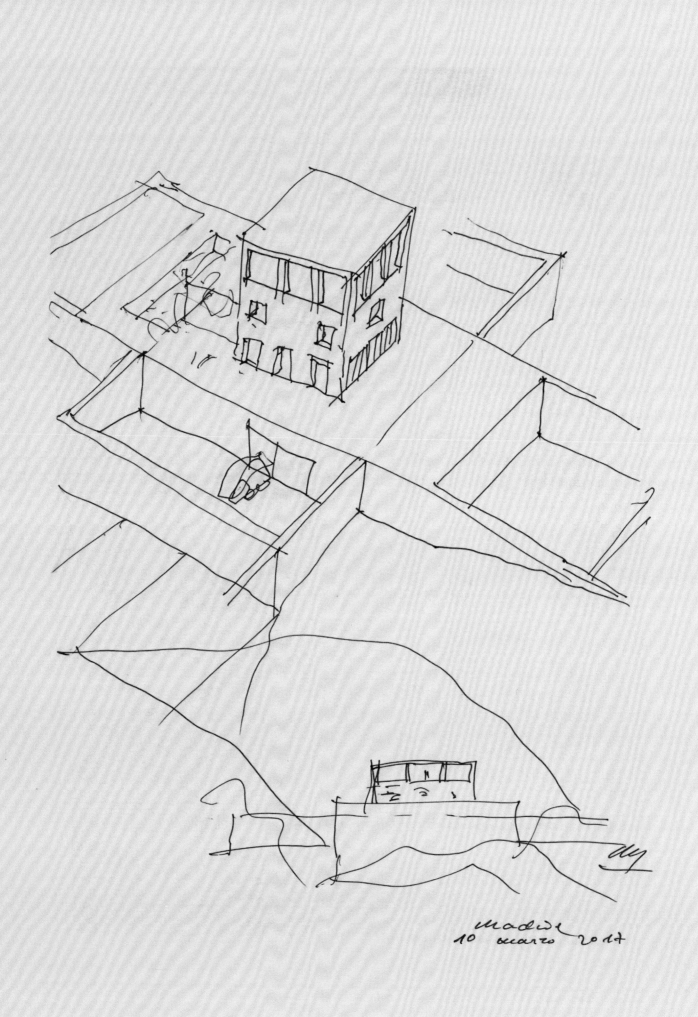

madrid
10 marzo 2017

CASA ROTONDA

casa para Ana
31 marzo 2017

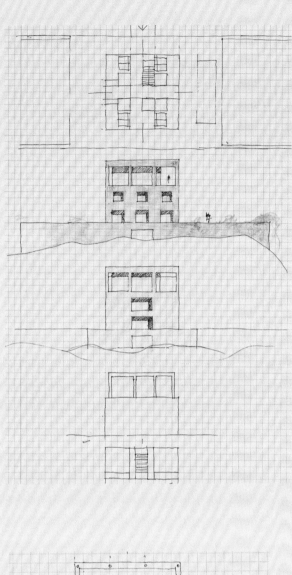

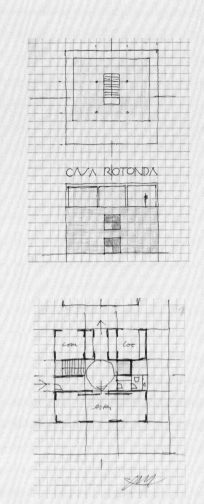

CASA ROTONDA

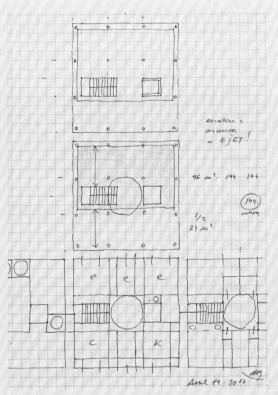

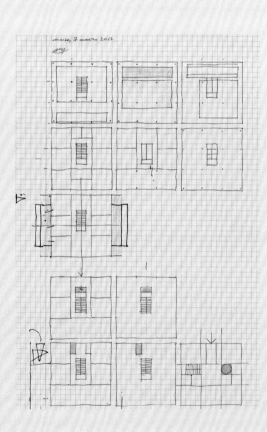

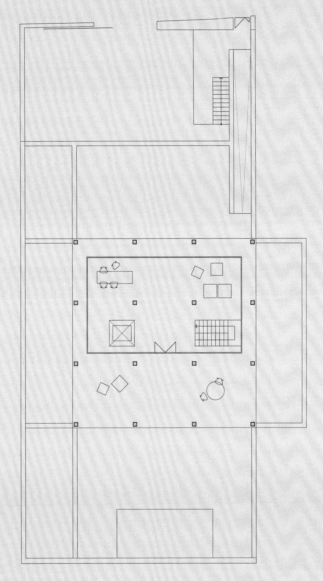

second floor plan

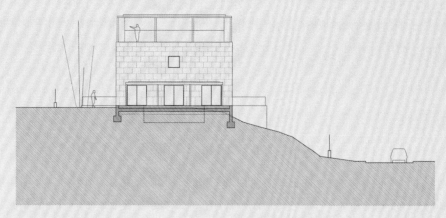

south elevation

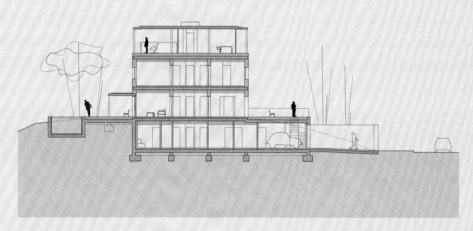

longitudinal section

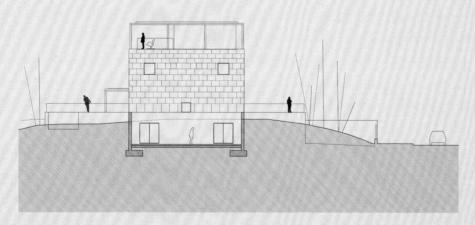

east elevation

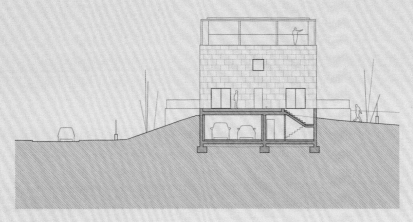

north elevation

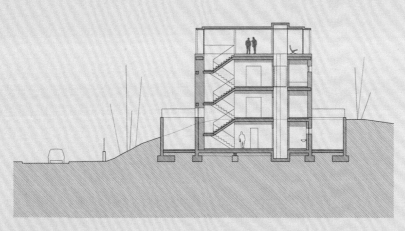

cross section

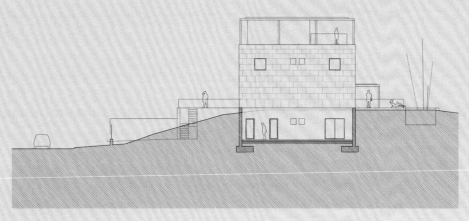

west elevation

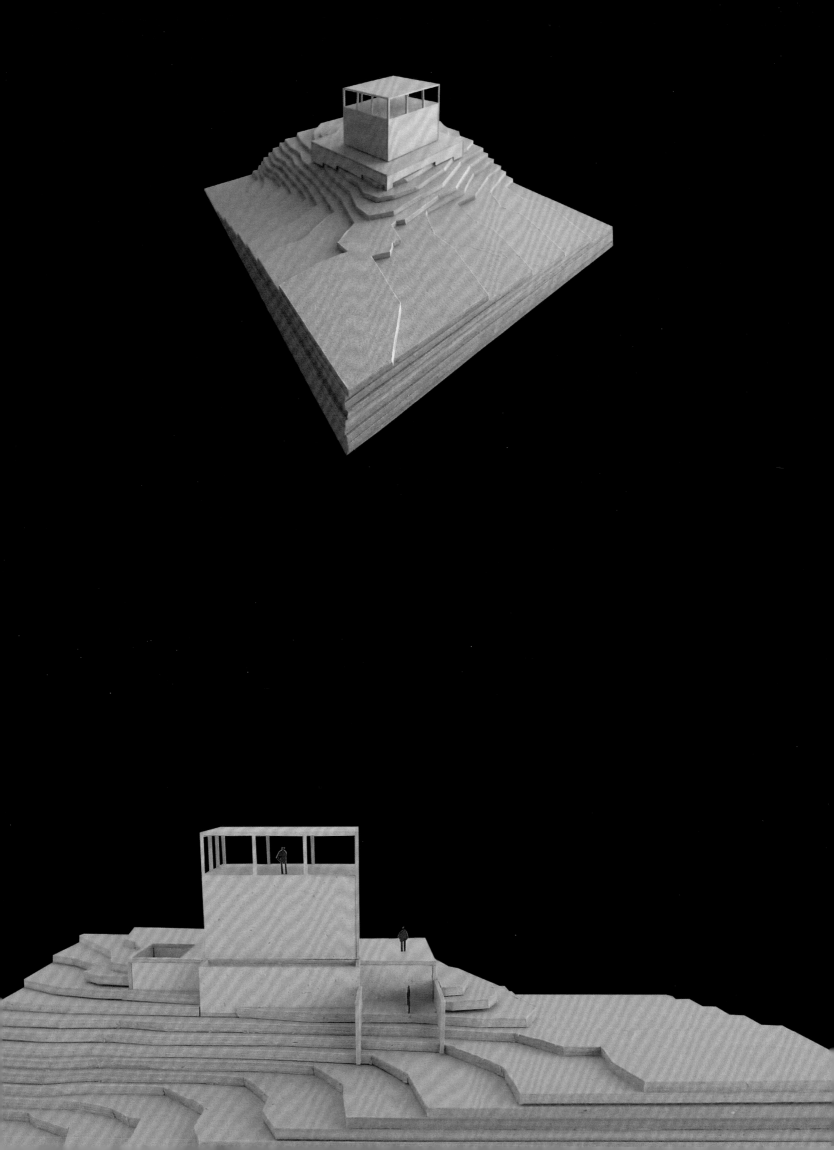

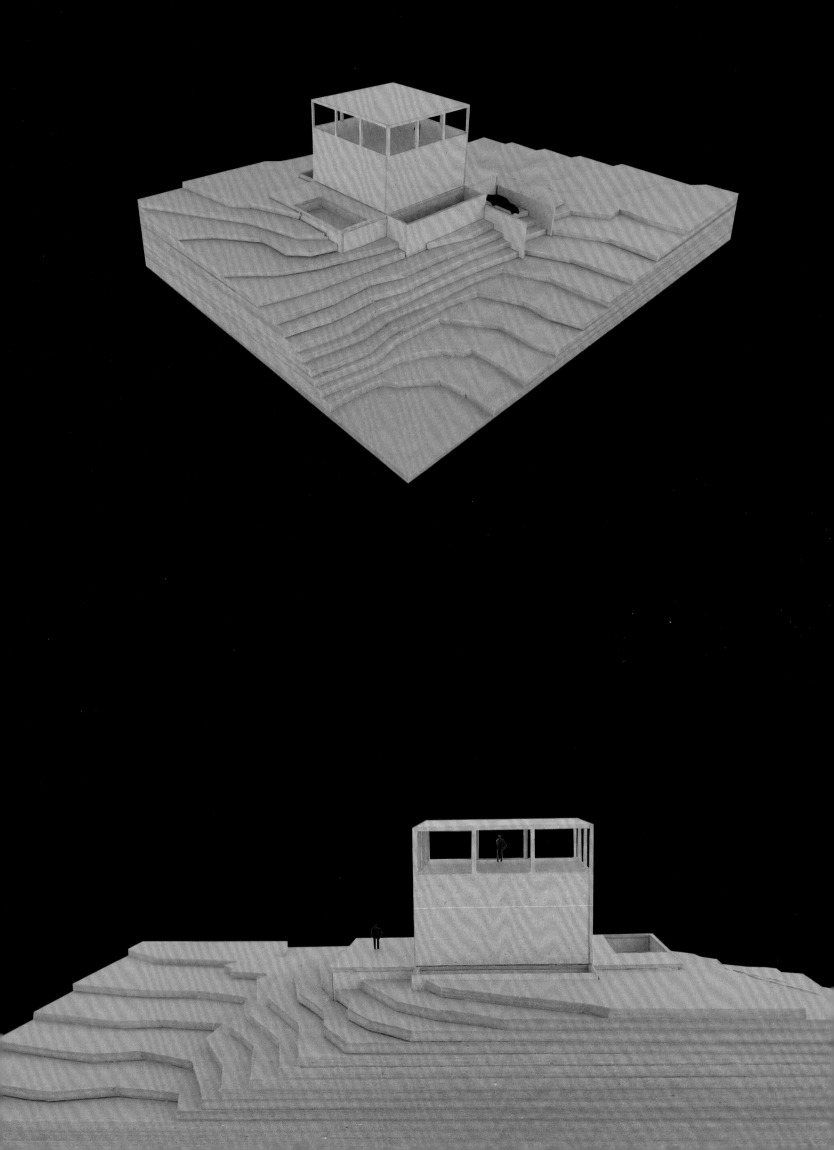

Work:
Rotonda House

Location:
Madrid, Spain

Client:
Private

Project:
2017

Built:
2021

Building Area:
500 m²

Collaborators:
Ignacio Aguirre, Alejandro Cervilla, María Pérez
de Camino, Elena Jiménez, Joan Suñé, Alfonso
Guajardo-Fajardo, Tommaso Campiotti, Sara
Fernández de Trucios, Francesc Abajo

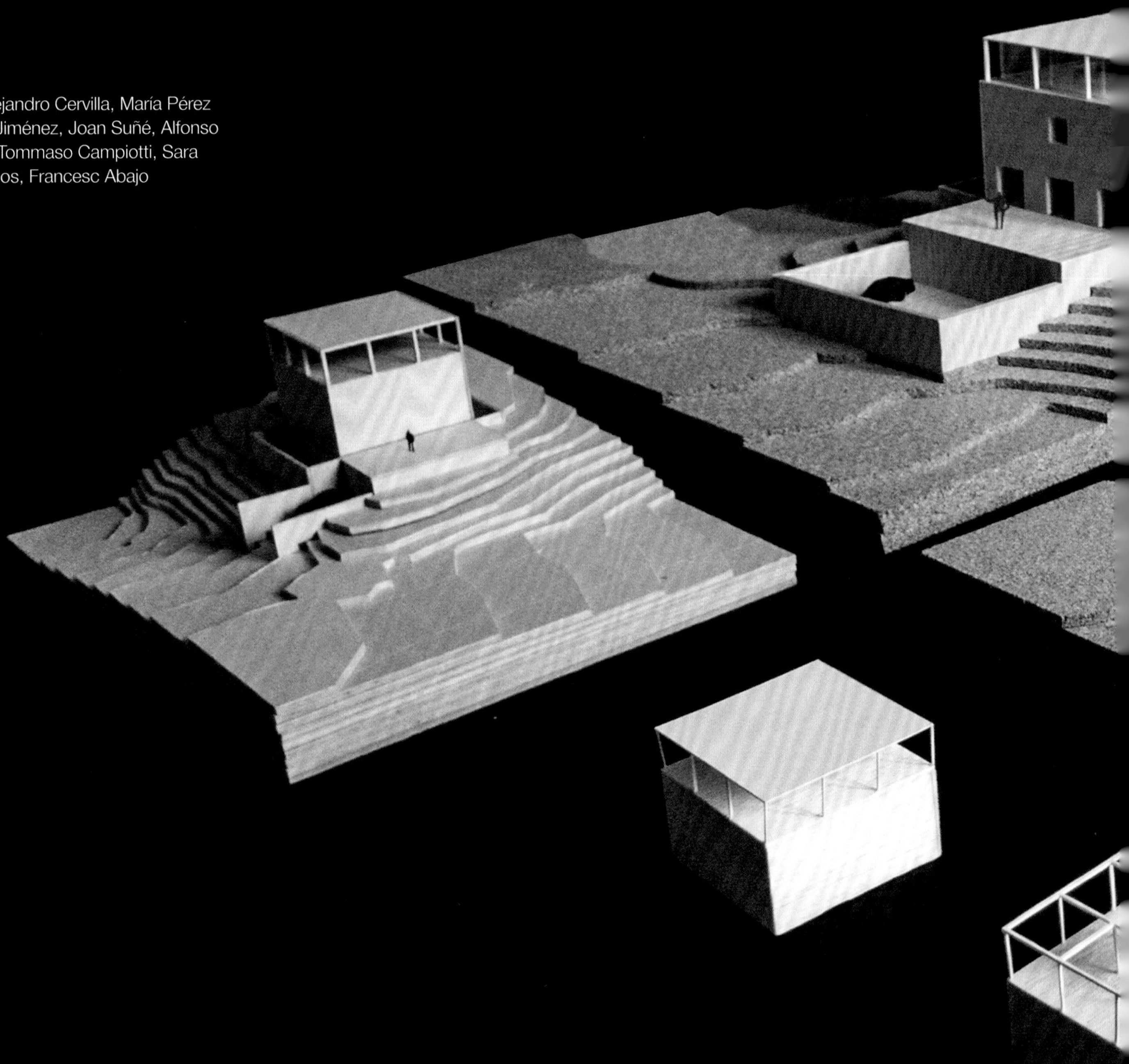

Triaedrus

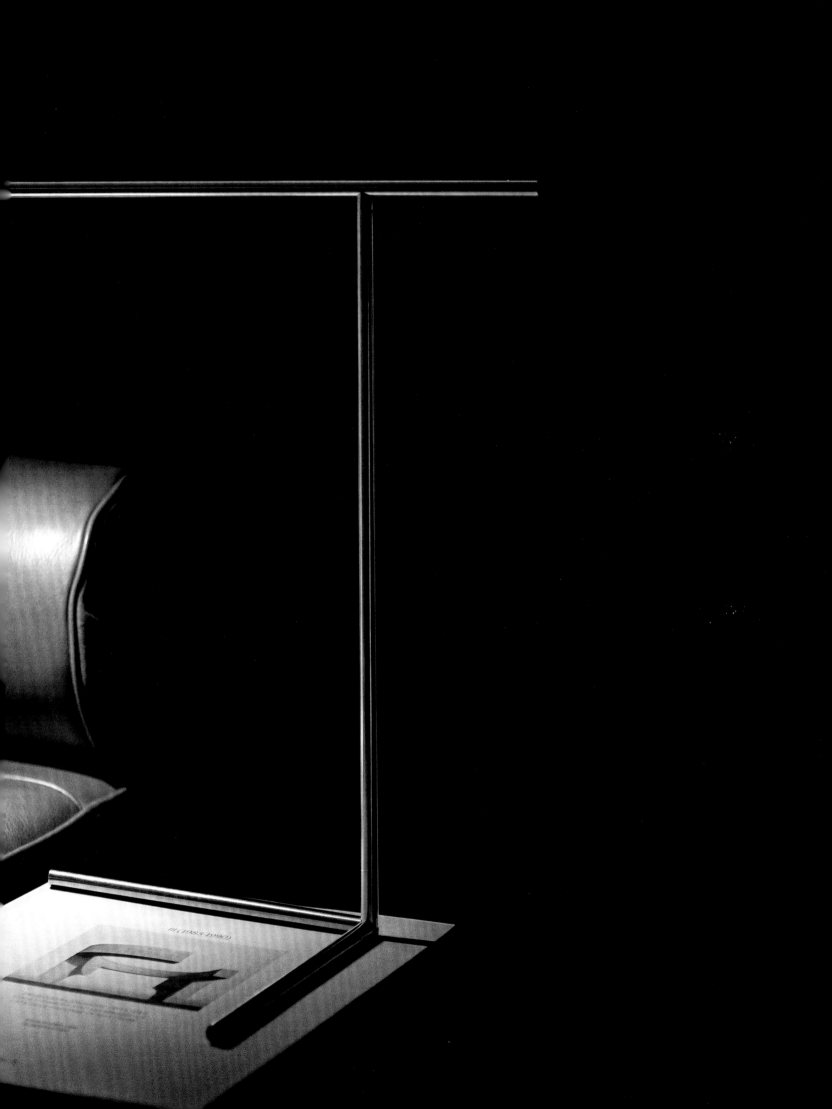

Triaedrus: A Lamp Like Me
Triaedrus Lamp, 2020

Some time ago, the prestigious Spanish lighting manufacturer FERRAM commissioned me to design a desk lamp as part of its project ARCHITECTS on DESIGN.

They had also commissioned lamps from Álvaro SIZA, Eduardo SOUTO, David CHIPPERFIELD, and Kazuyo SEJIMA. All of them masters of architecture, all of whom I admire so much. It is an honor for me to be included alongside them in this adventure.

FERRAM is a renowned lighting company. FERRAM illuminates ZARA, EL CORTE INGLÉS, and MANGO, among others.

I must admit that I have put my heart and soul into this lamp, and FERRAM and its technical team also have. And I can only extend my infinite thanks to everyone, and especially to FERRAM, for this entire adventure. To use the expression Curzio Malaparte famously coined when he commissioned his house by the architect Adalberto Libera, I would have to say that this is "a lamp like me."

Previous spread. Triaedrus Lamp and Day Bed by Mies van der Rohe.
Right. Triaedrus Lamp and Plywood Chair by Charles and Ray Eames.

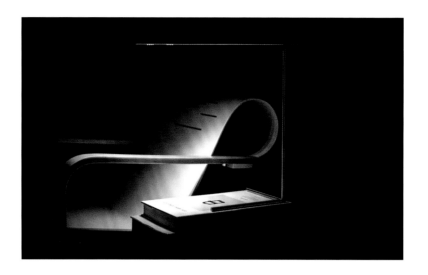

Left. Triaedrus Floor Lamp stainless steel prototype (in progress)
and Wire Chair by Charles and Ray Eames.
Above. Triaedrus Lamp and Paimio Armchair by Alvar Aalto.
Below. Triaedrus Lamp, view from above.
Bottom. Triaedrus Lamp in a working environment.

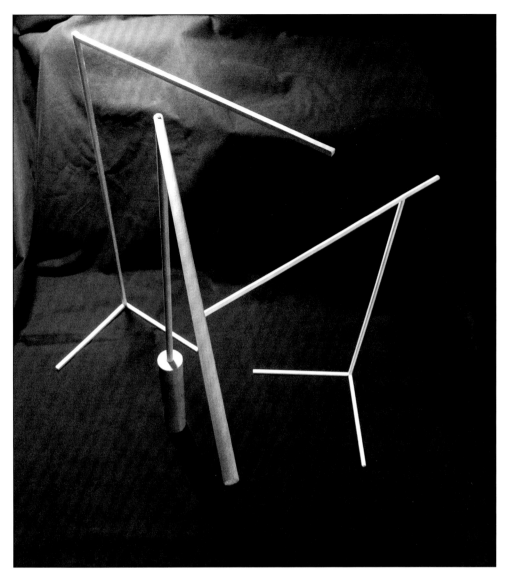

Top. Models.
Below. Triaedrus Lamp, site view.
Right. Triaedrus Floor Lamp prototype painted white. In progress.

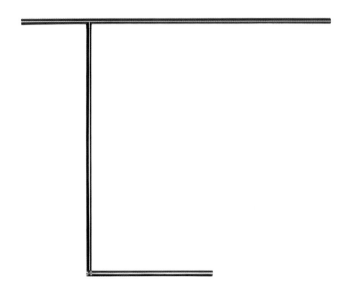

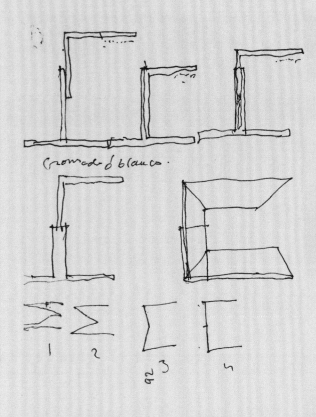

Cromado blanco.

1   2   3   4

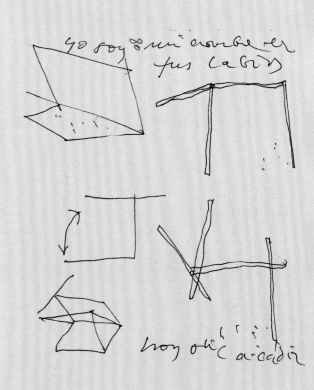

yo soy un hombre en tus labios

hoy solo caridad

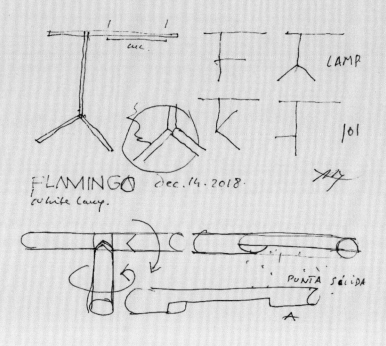

FLAMINGO   dec. 14. 2018.
white lamp.

LAMP

101

PUNTA SÓLIDA
A

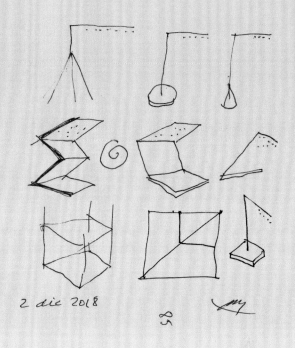

2 dic 2018

85

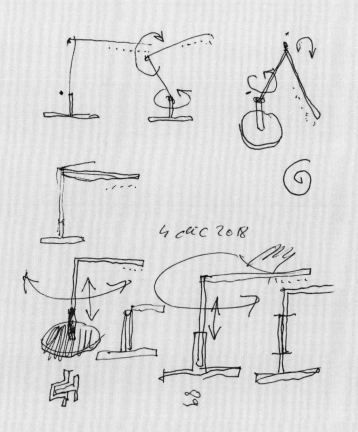

4 dic 2018

69

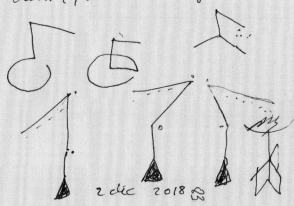

si pienso en pantalla, te llama
led orgánico que pienso en
una lámina plegada capaz de
poner un plano luminoso en la
posición deseada

si pienso en punto, pienso en una
varilla, una varita mágica.

2 dic 2018   83

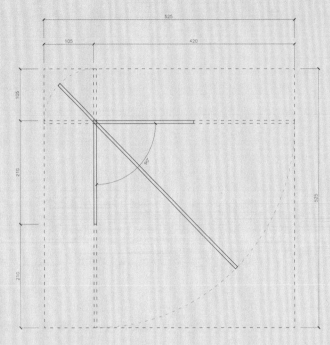

tubular: 10 mm

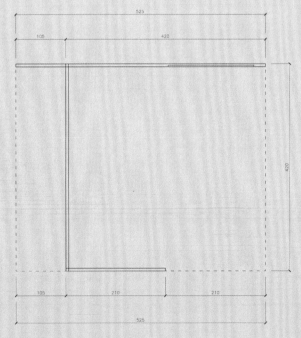

tubular: 10 mm

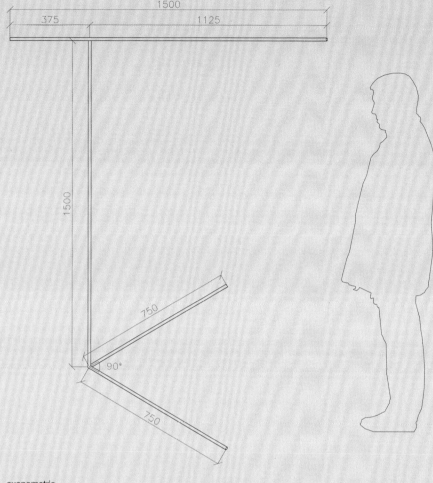

axonometric

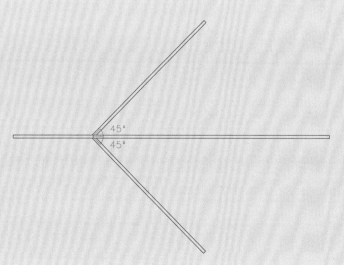

plan

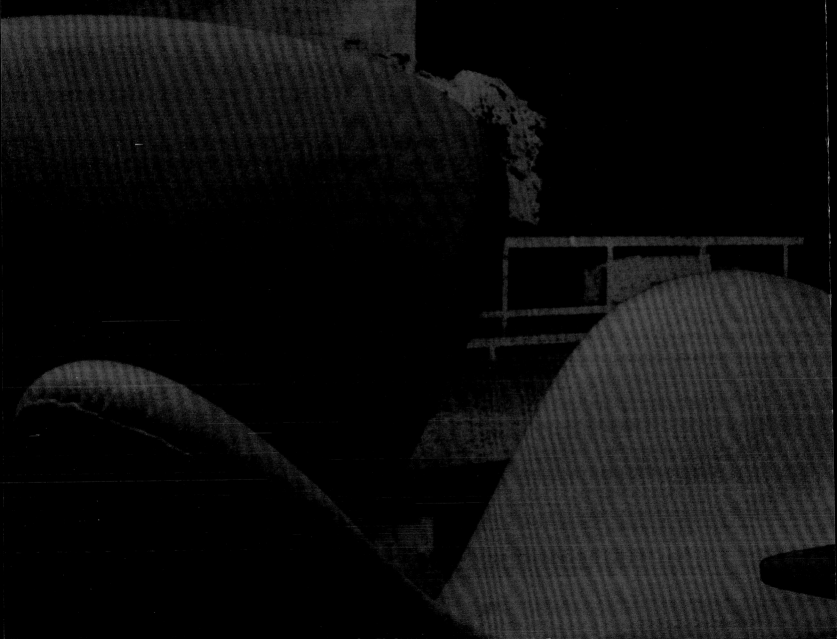

Il Cielo in Terra

Il Cielo in Terra
Venice, 2019

TOMB IN VENICE

We would like to make the most beautiful house in the world, but also the simplest. On a small plot within the Capoluogo Cemetery in San Doná di Piave in Venice. A piece of heaven on earth.

It will be a shaded box, pierced by light, a reinforced concrete cube of 3 x 3 x 3 m. To bring the light inside, we will drill the corners of the six square planes that make up the cube, producing a square 60 x 60 cm opening on each plane, so that two holes never coincide in the same trihedron.

We will begin by drilling the top with its opening oriented in such a way to allow the sun, breaking the shadows, to penetrate the interior diagonally.

On the main facade, the one closest to the access road, we will open a door in the concrete, so that when closed, the planimetric layout is reestablished. And the 60 x 60 cm hole corresponding to the isotropic operation on that facade will be altered so that it is at eye level and from it one can see inside.

And in the geometric center of the shady cubic space crossed by the moving sunlight we will hang a bright white marble 60 x 60 x 60 cm cubic urn, which will float in that space supported by four fine steel cables.

The opening corresponding to the ground plane will be excavated to reveal the thickness of the concrete and a mirror will be placed at the bottom.

During the course of the day as the rays of sunlight cross the openings on the concrete cube, they will fall on the white marble of the floating urn and a kind of luminous transfiguration will take place capable of producing the suspension of time.

Previous spread. **Main facade view.**
Right. **Detail facade view. White marble urn.**

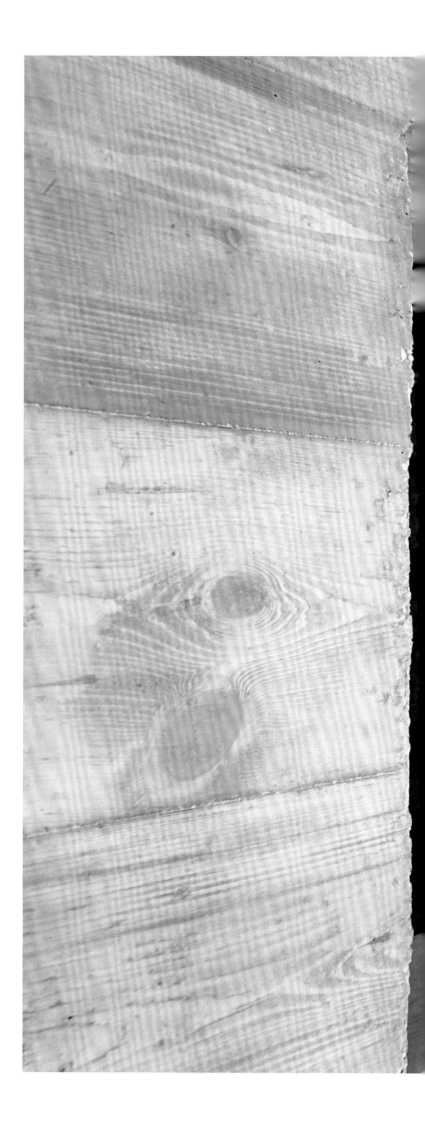

The cinerary urn, that gleaming white Thassos marble cube, will be in a single piece. A cavity will be hollowed out inside to contain the ashes. It will have an upper lid, which, when closed, will not show anything. The four very fine steel cables will go, two by two, from the sides of the urn to the inner edges of the cube.

The reinforced concrete cube will be built with care and attention but never to excess. Without any kind of enclosure, the openings will let in light and air, as well as wind, rain, and snow, the stars and even birds. With the holes set at the corners, two of its sides will be in continuity with the adjoining walls. The other two sides will show the strong thickness of the concrete.

The cube will be supported on a podium in the same concrete that will be flush with the podiums of the adjacent constructions. Thus, the inside floor of the cube and that of the outside will not be on the same plane. Given its 30 cm height, a possible step is contemplated.

Left, above, and below. Interior view with the hanging marble urn.

MESTRE
10 Ottobre 2016

MESTRE

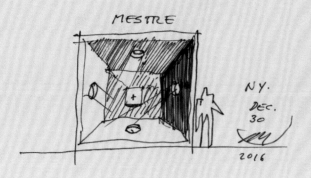

N.Y.
DEC.
30
2016

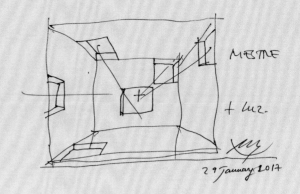

MESTRE

+ luz.

29 January 2017

MESTRE Dec 21 2016
un pezzo di cielo stellato!

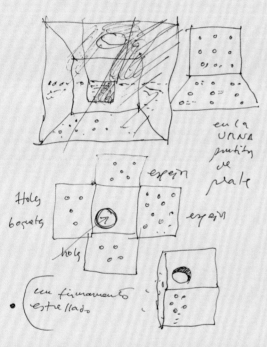

en la
URNA
justita
de plate

Holg
boquets

espejn

espejn

Holg

• un firmamento
estrellado

TOMBA
MESTRE

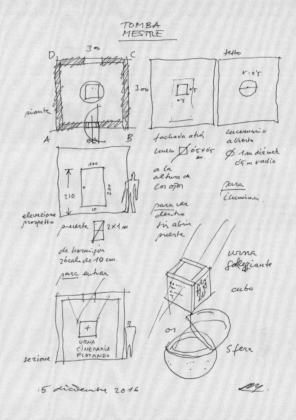

tetto

planta

fachada atrá
hueco ☐ 0'5×0'5
m.
a la altura de
los ojos

para ver
dentro
sin abrir
puerta

lucernario
abierto
Ø 1m diámetro
0'5 m radio

para
iluminar

elevazione
prospetto

puerta ☐ 2×1 m

de hormigón
zócalo de 10 cm.
para entrar

urna
galleggiante

cubo

sezione

URNA
CINERARIA
FLOTANDO

sfera

15 diciembre 2016

S MESTRE·S LUCE

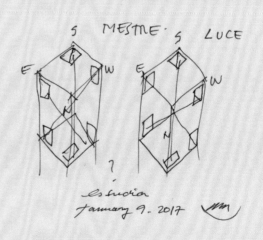

estudio
January 9. 2017

site plan

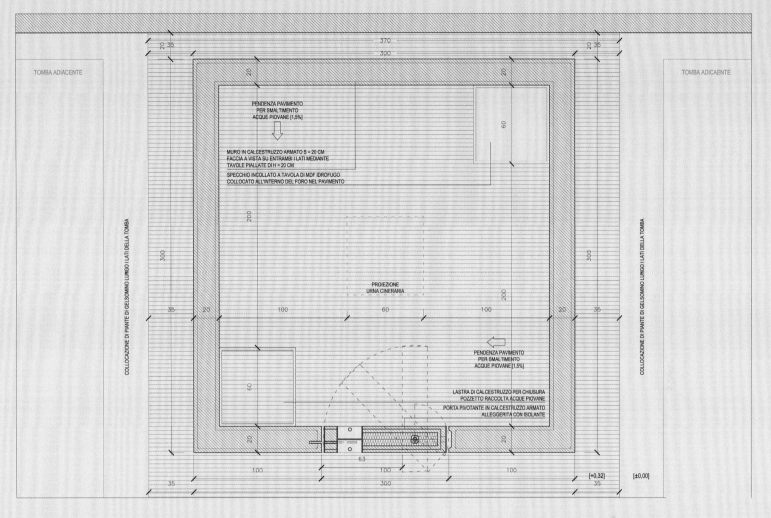

TOMBA ADIACENTE

370

300

20

PENDENZA PAVIMENTO
PER SMALTIMENTO
ACQUE PIOVANE (1,5%)

MURO IN CALCESTRUZZO ARMATO S = 20 CM
FACCIA A VISTA SU ENTRAMBI I LATI MEDIANTE
TAVOLE PIALLATE DI H = 20 CM
SPECCHIO INCOLLATO A TAVOLA DI MDF IDROFUGO
COLLOCATO ALL'INTERNO DEL FORO NEL PAVIMENTO

60

200

300

PROIEZIONE
URNA CINERARIA

200

100   60   100

PENDENZA PAVIMENTO
PER SMALTIMENTO
ACQUE PIOVANE (1,5%)

LASTRA DI CALCESTRUZZO PER CHIUSURA
POZZETTO RACCOLTA ACQUE PIOVANE
PORTA PIVOTANTE IN CALCESTRUZZO ARMATO
ALLEGGERITA CON ISOLANTE

60

63

100   100   100

[+0,32]   [±0,00]

35   300   35

COLLOCAZIONE DI PIANTE DI GELSOMINO LUNGO I LATI DELLA TOMBA

TOMBA ADICAENTE

COLLOCAZIONE DI PIANTE DI GELSOMINO LUNGO I LATI DELLA TOMBA

plan

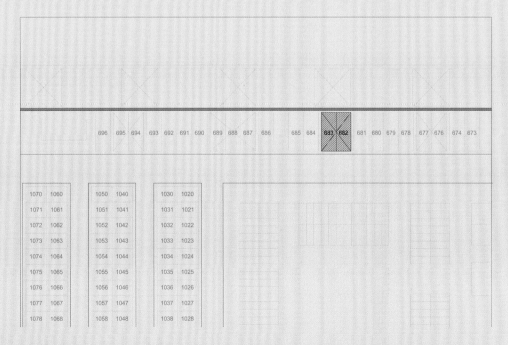

| 696 | 695 | 694 | 693 | 692 | 691 | 690 | 689 | 688 | 687 | 686 | | 685 | 684 | 683 | 682 | 681 | 680 | 679 | 678 | 677 | 676 | 674 | 673 |

1070	1060		1050	1040		1030	1020
1071	1061		1051	1041		1031	1021
1072	1062		1052	1042		1032	1022
1073	1063		1053	1043		1033	1023
1074	1064		1054	1044		1034	1024
1075	1065		1055	1045		1035	1025
1076	1066		1056	1046		1036	1026
1077	1067		1057	1047		1037	1027
1078	1068		1058	1048		1038	1028

location

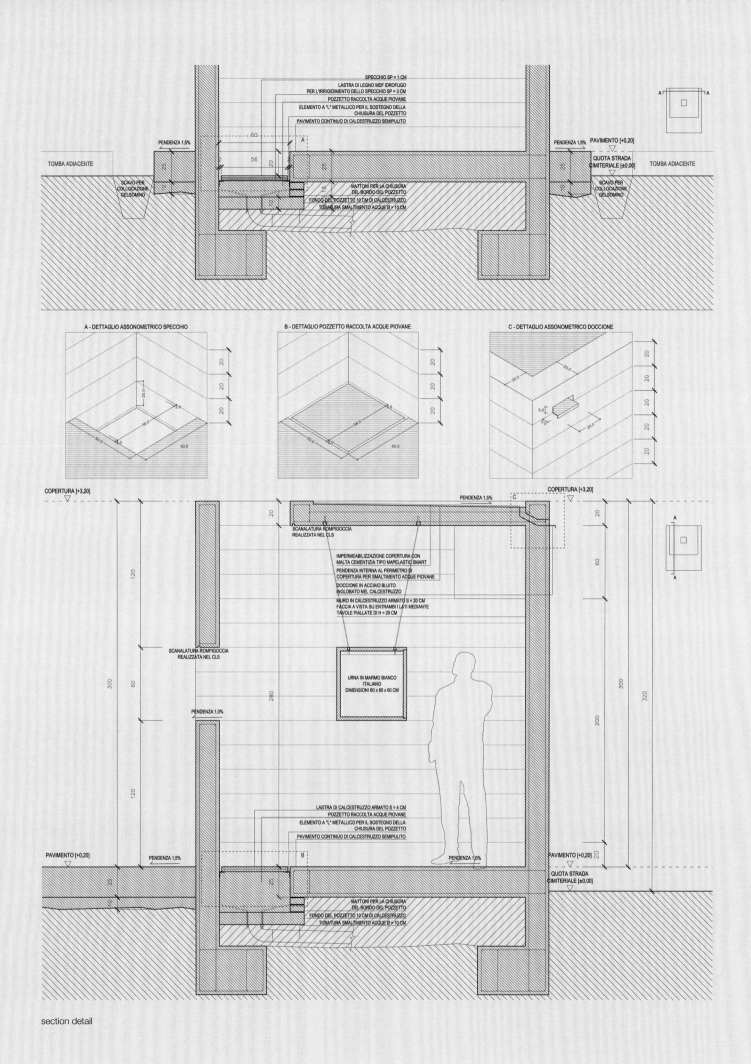

SPECCHIO SP = 1 CM
LASTRA DI LEGNO MDF IDROFUGO
PER L'IRRIGIDIMENTO DELLO SPECCHIO SP = 3 CM
POZZETTO RACCOLTA ACQUE PIOVANE
ELEMENTO A "L" METALLICO PER IL SOSTEGNO DELLA
CHIUSURA DEL POZZETTO
PAVIMENTO CONTINUO DI CALCESTRUZZO SEMIPULITO

PENDENZA 1,5%
PENDENZA 1,5% PAVIMENTO [+0,20]

TOMBA ADIACENTE
QUOTA STRADA
CIMITERIALE [±0,00]   TOMBA ADIACENTE

SCAVO PER
COLLOCAZIONE
GELSOMINO

SCAVO PER
COLLOCAZIONE
GELSOMINO

MATTONI PER LA CHIUSURA
DEL BORDO DEL POZZETTO
FONDO DEL POZZETTO 10 CM DI CALCESTRUZZO
TUBATURA SMALTIMENTO ACQUE Ø = 10 CM

A - DETTAGLIO ASSONOMETRICO SPECCHIO

B - DETTAGLIO POZZETTO RACCOLTA ACQUE PIOVANE

C - DETTAGLIO ASSONOMETRICO DOCCIONE

COPERTURA [+3,20]

PENDENZA 1,5%

COPERTURA [+3,20]

SCANALATURA ROMPIGOCCIA
REALIZZATA NEL CLS

IMPERMEABILIZZAZIONE COPERTURA CON
MALTA CEMENTIZIA TIPO MAPELASTIC SMART
PENDENZA INTERNA AL PERIMETRO DI
COPERTURA PER SMALTIMENTO ACQUE PIOVANE
DOCCIONE IN ACCIAIO BLUITO
INGLOBATO NEL CALCESTRUZZO
MURO IN CALCESTRUZZO ARMATO S = 20 CM
FACCIA A VISTA SU ENTRAMBI I LATI MEDIANTE
TAVOLE PIALLATE DI H = 20 CM

SCANALATURA ROMPIGOCCIA
REALIZZATA NEL CLS

URNA IN MARMO BIANCO
ITALIANO
DIMENSIONI 60 x 60 x 60 CM

PENDENZA 1,0%

LASTRA DI CALCESTRUZZO ARMATO S = 4 CM
POZZETTO RACCOLTA ACQUE PIOVANE
ELEMENTO A "L" METALLICO PER IL SOSTEGNO DELLA
CHIUSURA DEL POZZETTO
PAVIMENTO CONTINUO DI CALCESTRUZZO SEMIPULITO

PAVIMENTO [+0,20]
PENDENZA 1,5%
PENDENZA 1,5%
PAVIMENTO [+0,20]

QUOTA STRADA
CIMITERIALE [±0,00]

MATTONI PER LA CHIUSURA
DEL BORDO DEL POZZETTO
FONDO DEL POZZETTO 10 CM DI CALCESTRUZZO
TUBATURA SMALTIMENTO ACQUE Ø = 10 CM

section detail

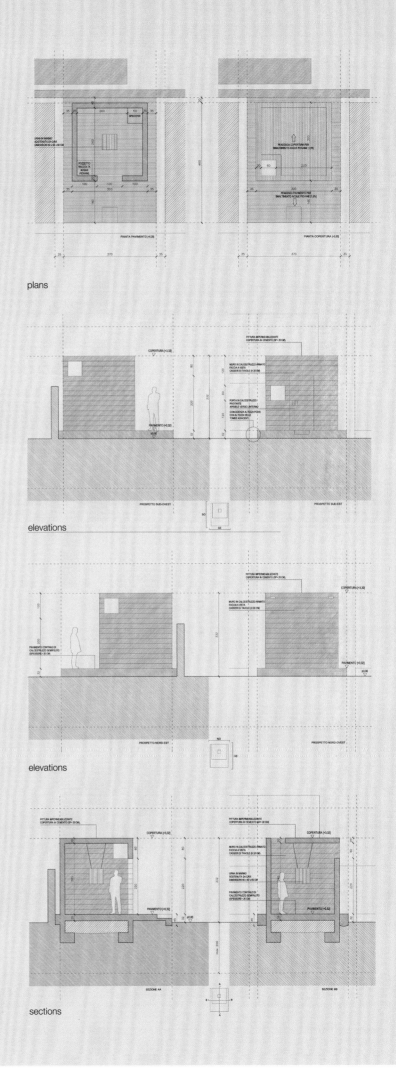

plans

elevations

elevations

sections

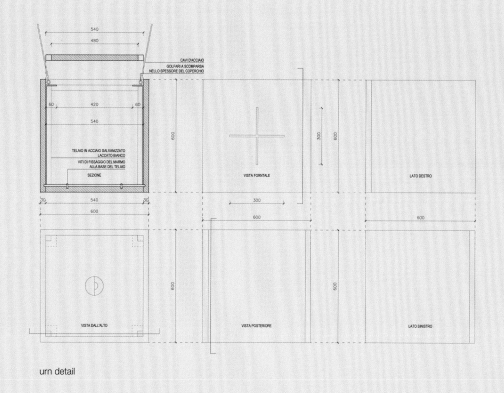

urn detail

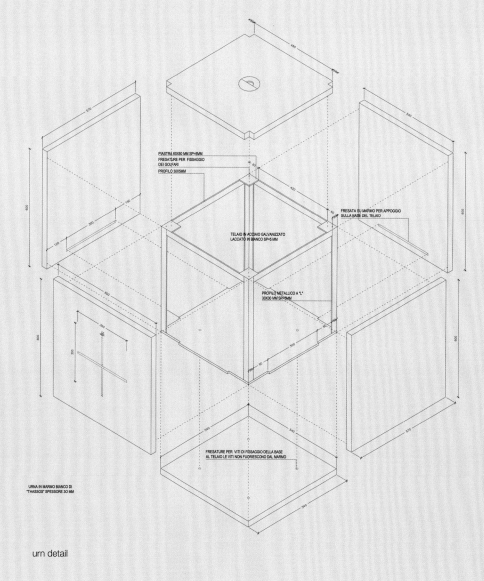

urn detail

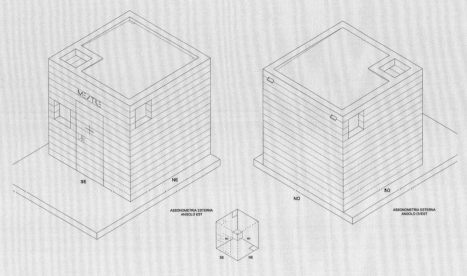

exterior axonometric

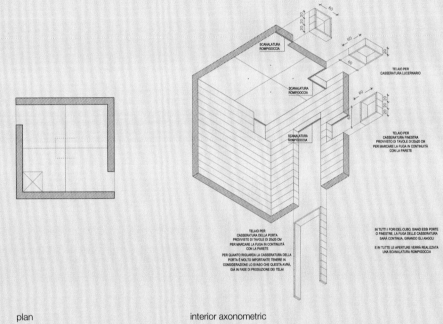

plan

interior axonometric

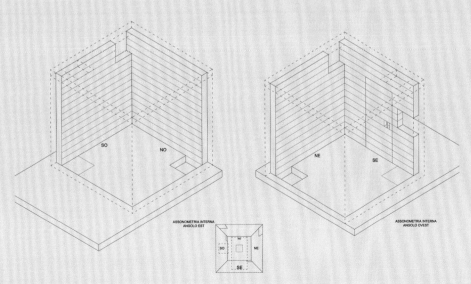

interior axonometrics

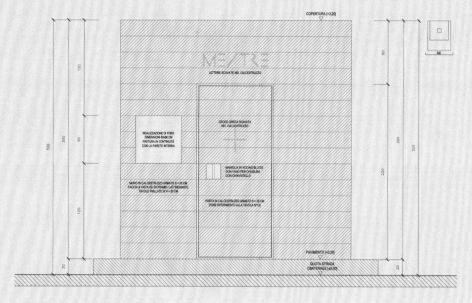

elevation

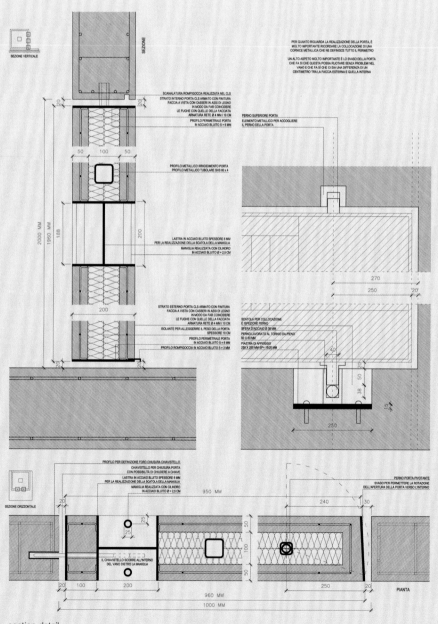

section detail

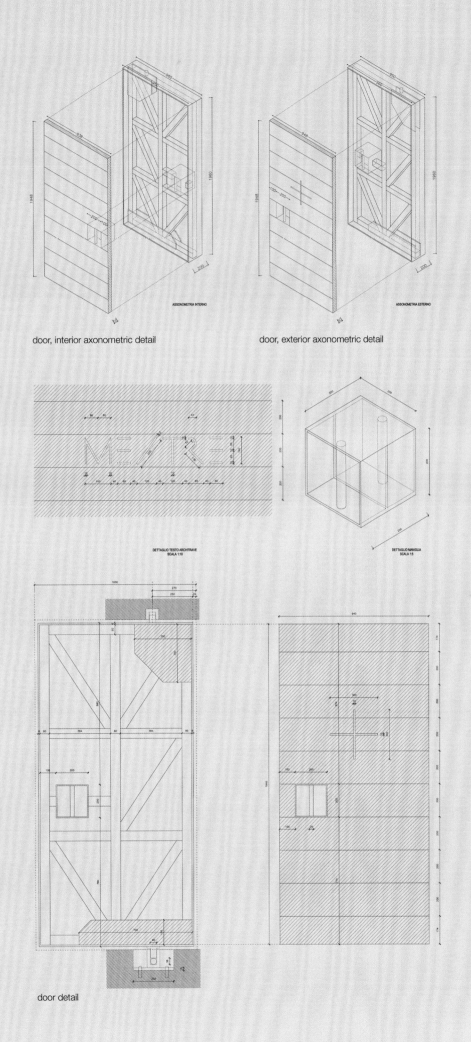

door, interior axonometric detail

door, exterior axonometric detail

door detail

Above. Exterior view. Rendering.
Right. Interior view. Rendering.

Work:
Il Cielo in Terra

Location:
San Donà di Piave, Venice, Italy

Client:
Adalberto Mestre

Project:
October 2016

Built:
November 2017–February 2019

Building Area:
9 m²

Collaborators:
Adalberto Mestre, Tommaso Campiotti,
Ignacio Aguirre López, Alejandro Cervilla García,
María Pérez de Camino Díez, Elena Jiménez
Sánchez, Alfonso Guajardo-Fajardo Cruz,
Joan Suñé, Francesc Abajo

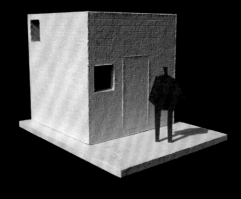

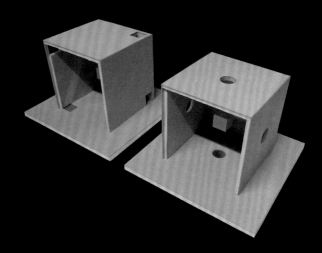

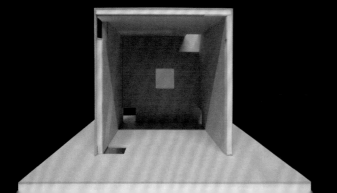

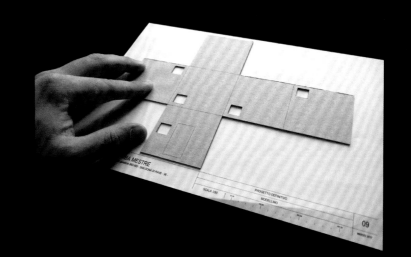

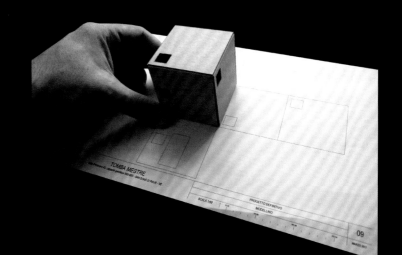

Multi-Sport Pavilion UFV

Multi-Sport Pavilion UFV
Madrid, 2017

Designed for the campus of the Francisco de Vitoria University in Pozuelo (Madrid), the building houses a sports center and classroom complex. It includes the use of sports halls, multipurpose rooms, a gymnasium, swimming pool, physiotherapy, etc. The sports complex can also be used as a large multipurpose area and meeting hall, facilitating a range of university activities.

The design of the building is restrained and volumetric adapted to the general layout of the campus in terms of maximum height and alignment. And it is intended to clearly differentiate the sports and teaching areas in terms of volume and facade material. The fundamental element of the project is a large translucent box of light, 60 x 50 x 12 m, filtered and controlled, entering into a spatial relationship with the main square of the campus.

Two clean, well-defined boxes are joined together by a low-rise building whose roof becomes an interconnecting patio.

The sports pavilion is designed with lightness in mind, in glass fiber reinforced concrete, unlike the more closed classroom complex and low interconnecting building. In the volume of the sports complex the various sides are oriented differently, so that the facades of the southern dihedral, more exposed to sunlight, are enclosed in a prefabricated panel of glass fiber reinforced concrete, while those of the northern dihedral are in translucent glass.

The southwestern facade features a low strip of transparent glass highlighting the link with the main square of the campus. And this mechanism of transparency is repeated on the northeastern facade facing the upper patio. Thus a visual relationship is created between the square and the sports complex, while the southwestern facade of the classroom complex becomes a backdrop to the complex as a whole.

Pages 92–93. Sport pavilion. Interior view.
Previous spread. Exterior view. West facade.
Above. Exterior view. North facade.
Right. Exterior view. South facade.

The structure of the pavilion is in steel: a grid of pillars and beams on the facades and trusses to resolve the great roof span. All painted in white. The remainder of the structure is in reinforced concrete, with the unique feature of wide angled beams over the basement swimming-pool area.

The result is a building of great sobriety and formal restraint.

Extraordinary Light

On the Francisco de Vitoria University Multi-Sport Pavilion in Madrid, designed and built by the architect Alberto Campo Baeza.

I have been well acquainted with the work of

Alberto Campo Baeza for a very long time now and have written about it on numerous occasions. I contributed to the very first monograph on him published in 1996 by Munilla Lería. But I must confess that his recently completed work, the sports pavilion for the Francisco de Vitoria University in Madrid, has once again taken me by surprise. So much so, in fact, that I have decided to write about it.

I think that this space so full of light, a marvelous light that is achieved by means of a great interior translucent dihedral, is hard to beat.

Here we have a box of light, or as he himself described it in a dissertation on the project, a *boîte á lumière*.

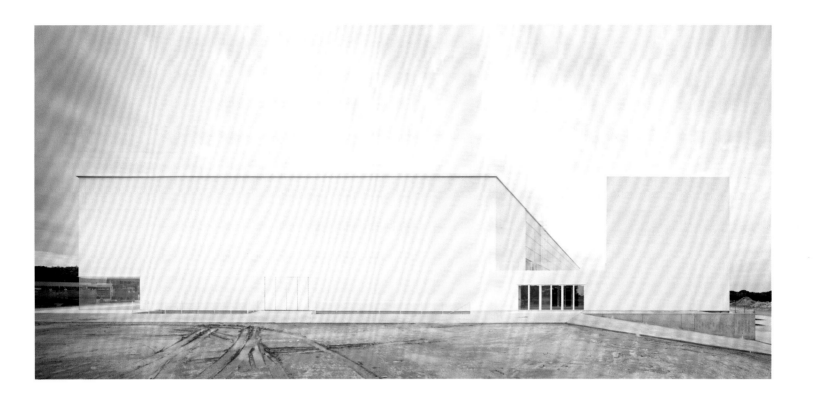

Already in a little work of his, Moliner House, built in 2008, in Zaragoza, our architect had devised a library where he used a simple, but similar, light mechanism: the north facade, entirely glazed with translucent white glass, caused light to become the protagonist of that gleaming white interior. The result was very beautiful.

In this case, not one but two enormous translucent northern walls provide this space with an extraordinary light. And all the rest of the space is white, multiplying the luminous effect. Also white is the stand covered with large, white, perfect ceramic panels, which are the very same as those covering the plinth.

Everything simple, very simple, everything white, very white, everything luminous, very luminous. Once again our architect has embodied his own stated proposals that light is more and *Architectura sine luce nulla Architectura est*, which are so much more than fine literary phrases.

When we repeatedly say and write that Alberto Campo Baeza is the architect of light, it is because we believe it and because it is confirmed in his works, as it is here. Alberto Campo Baeza fends off such assertions, arguing that this is a universal theme, inherent to architecture itself, which nobody could possibly take ownership of, least of all himself.

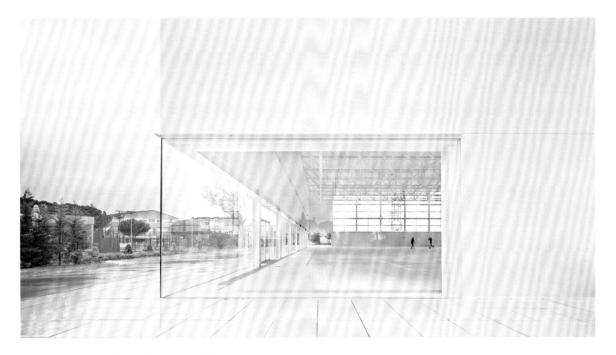

Previous spread. North facade. Partial view with the entrance.
Above. Detail south facade. Only glass corner.
Below. Sport pavilion. Interior view.
Right. Partial interior view. Glass corner.

Previous spread. Sport pavilion. Interior view.
Left. Partial view. Translucent glass north facade.
Above and below. Interior view. Southwest only glass corner.

Previous spread. Partial interior view. Northeast translucent glass corner.
Above. Partial exterior night view. North facade.
Right. Interior night view from the west. Transparency.

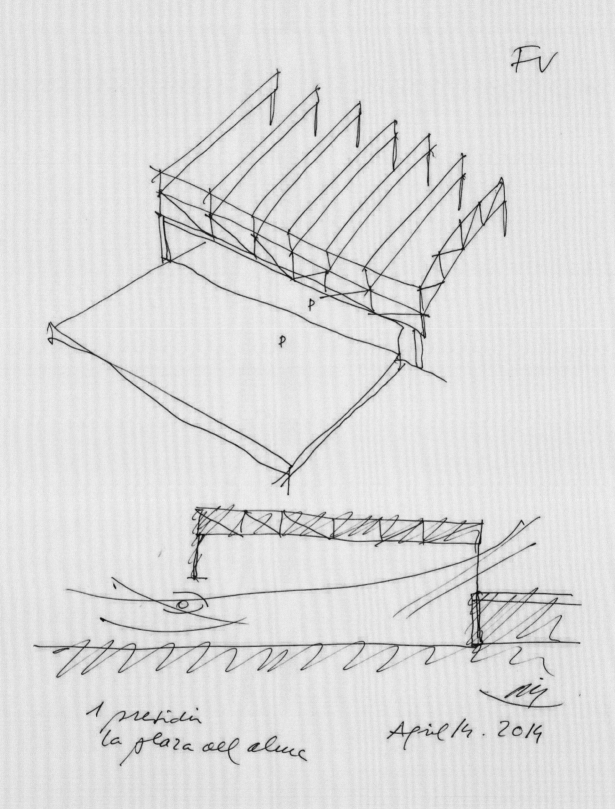

FV

P

P

1 presidio
la plaza del alma

April 14. 2014

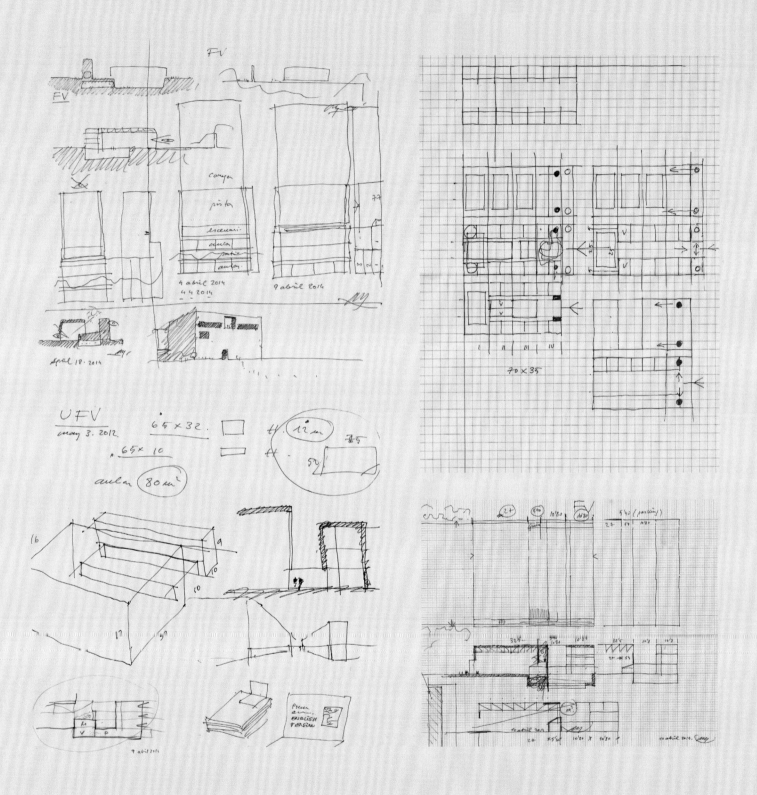

FV

UFV
may 3. 2012   65 × 32.

65 × 10

aula 80 m²

70 × 35

M-40

M-40

site plan

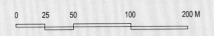

0   25   50   100   200 M

N

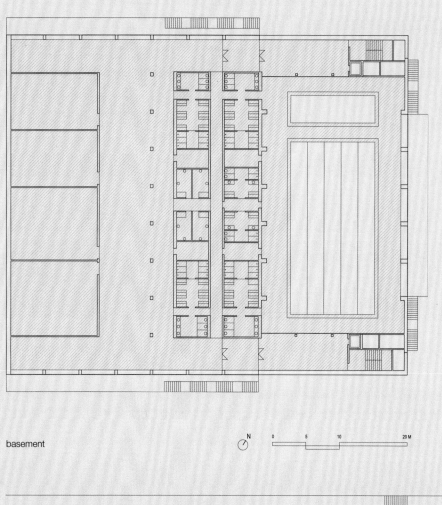

basement

N

0   5   10   20 M

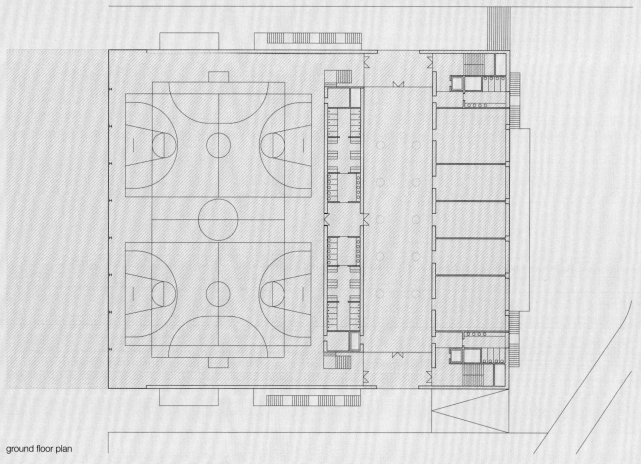

ground floor plan

first floor plan

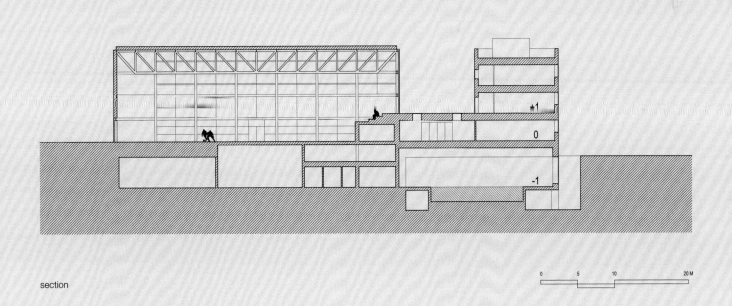

section

0   5   10   20 M

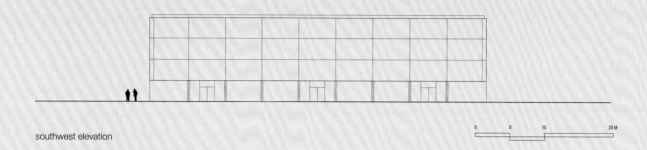

southwest elevation

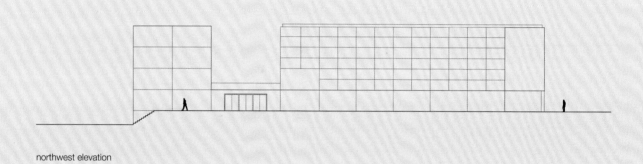

northwest elevation

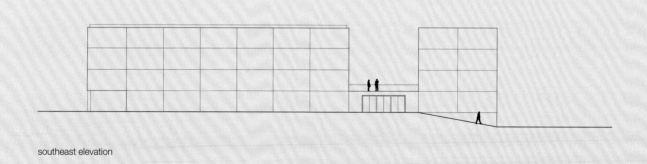

southeast elevation

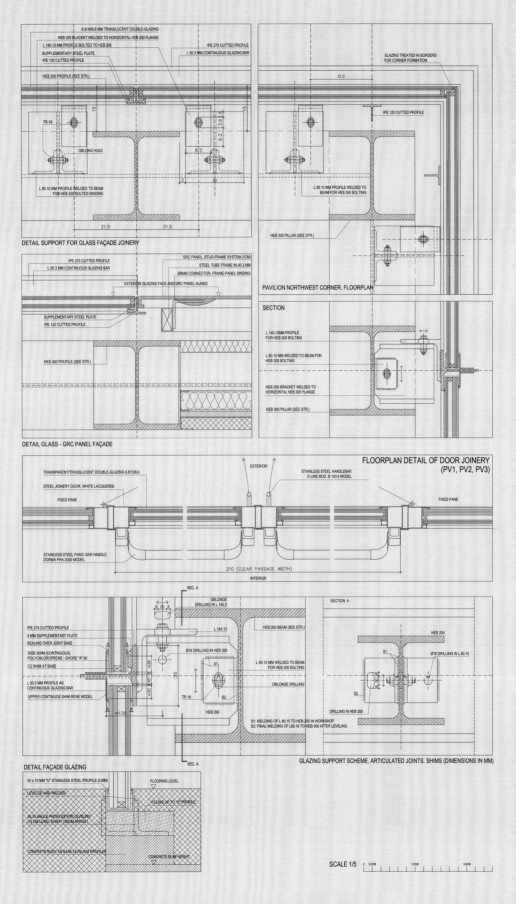

DETAIL SUPPORT FOR GLASS FAÇADE JOINERY

6.6/16/6.8 MM TRANSLUCENT DOUBLE-GLAZING
HEB 200 BRACKET WELDED TO HORIZONTAL HEB 300 FLANGE
L 140.13 MM PROFILE BOLTED TO HEB 200
SUPPLEMENTARY STEEL PLATE
IPE 120 CUTTED PROFILE
HEB 300 PROFILE (SEE STR.)
TR-16
OBLONG HOLE
L 80.10 MM PROFILE WELDED TO BEAM FOR HEB 200 BOLTED BINDING

IPE 270 CUTTED PROFILE
L 50.3 MM CONTINUOUS GLAZING BAR

GLAZING TREATED IN BORDERS FOR CORNER FORMATION
IPE 120 CUTTED PROFILE
L 80.10 MM PROFILE WELDED TO BEAM FOR HEB 200 BOLTING
HEB 300 PILLAR (SEE STR.)

PAVILION NORTHWEST CORNER. FLOORPLAN

DETAIL GLASS - GRC PANEL FAÇADE

IPE 270 CUTTED PROFILE
L 50.3 MM CONTINUOUS GLAZING BAR
EXTERIOR GLAZING FACE AND GRC PANEL ALINED
SUPPLEMENTARY STEEL PLATE
IPE 120 CUTTED PROFILE
HEB 300 PROFILE (SEE STR.)

GRC PANEL; STUD-FRAME SYSTEM (1CM)
STEEL TUBE FRAME 80.40.2 MM
Ø8MM CONNECTOR; FRAME-PANEL BINDING

SECTION

L 140.13MM PROFILE FOR HEB 200 BOLTING
L 80.10 MM WELDED TO BEAM FOR HEB 200 BOLTING
HEB 200 BRACKET WELDED TO HORIZONTAL HEB 300 FLANGE
HEB 300 PILLAR (SEE STR.)

FLOORPLAN DETAIL OF DOOR JOINERY
(PV1, PV2, PV3)

TRANSPARENT/TRANSLUCENT DOUBLE-GLAZING 6.6/12/6.6
STEEL JOINERY DOOR, WHITE LACQUERED
FIXED PANE
STAINLESS STEEL PANIC BAR HANDLE, DORMA PHA 2000 MODEL

EXTERIOR
STAINLESS STEEL HANDLEBAR
D LINE MOD. B 103.0 MODEL
FIXED PANE

210 (CLEAR PASSAGE WIDTH)
INTERIOR

DETAIL FAÇADE GLAZING

SEC. A
OBLONGE DRILLING IN L 140.3
IPE 270 CUTTED PROFILE
8 MM SUPPLEMENTARY PLATE
SEALING OVER JOINT BASE
SIDE SHIM (CONTINUOUS) POLYCHLOROPRENE - SHORE "A" 60
C2 SHIM AT BASE
L 50.3 MM PROFILE AS CONTINUOUS GLAZING BAR
UPPER CONTINUOS SHIM RENE MODEL
L 140.13
Ø16 DRILLING IN HEB 200
TR 16
HEB 200

HEB.300 BEAM (SEE STR.)
L 80.10 MM WELDED TO BEAM FOR HEB 200 BOLTING
OBLONGE DRILLING

SECTION A
HEB 200
Ø16 DRILLING IN L 80.10
DRILLING IN HEB 200

S1: WELDING OF L 80.10 TO HEB-200 IN WORKSHOP
S2: FINAL WELDING OF L80.10 TO HEB-300 AFTER LEVELING

GLAZING SUPPORT SCHEME. ARTICULATED JOINTS. SHIMS (DIMENSIONS IN MM)

SEC. A

50 x 70 MM "U" STAINLESS STEEL PROFILE (5 MM)
LEVELED AND WELDED
80.10 ANGLE PROFILES FOR LEVELING (10 CM LONG; EVERY 15CM APPROX.)
CONCRETE BODY AS BASE LEVELING PROFILES

FLOORING LEVEL
FILLING UP TO "U" PROFILE
CONCRETE SLAB HEIGHT

SCALE 1/5   0   0.3CM   1.8CM   3.6CM

detail section

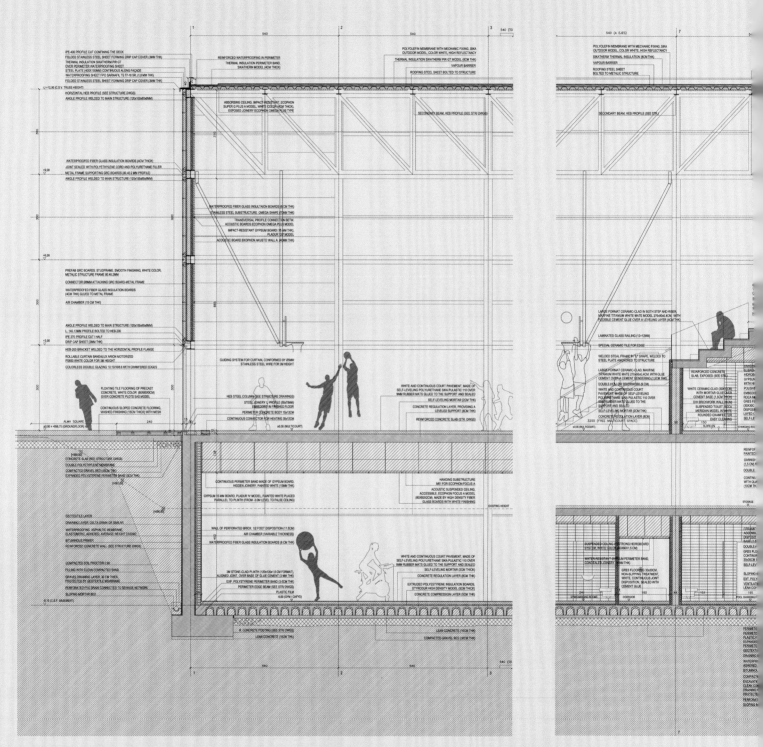

detail section

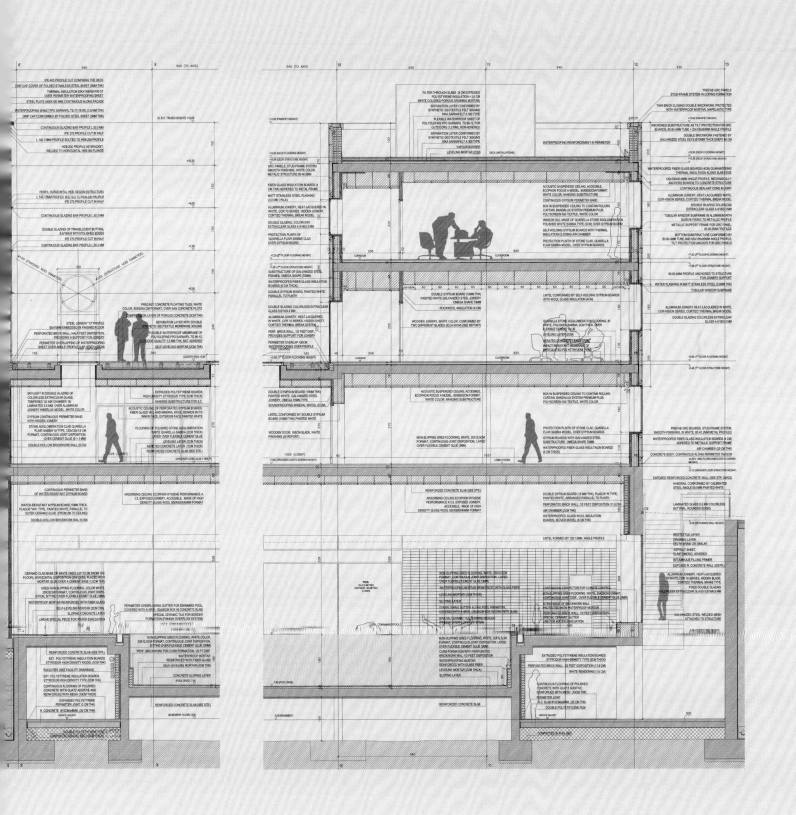

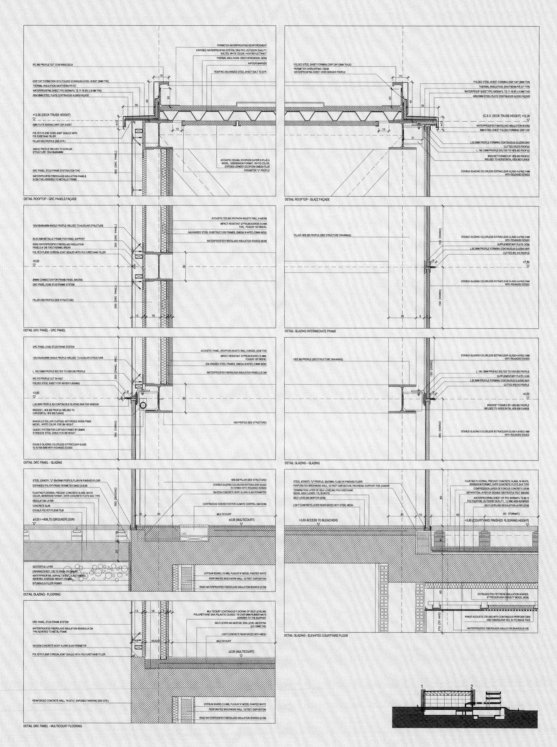

detail section

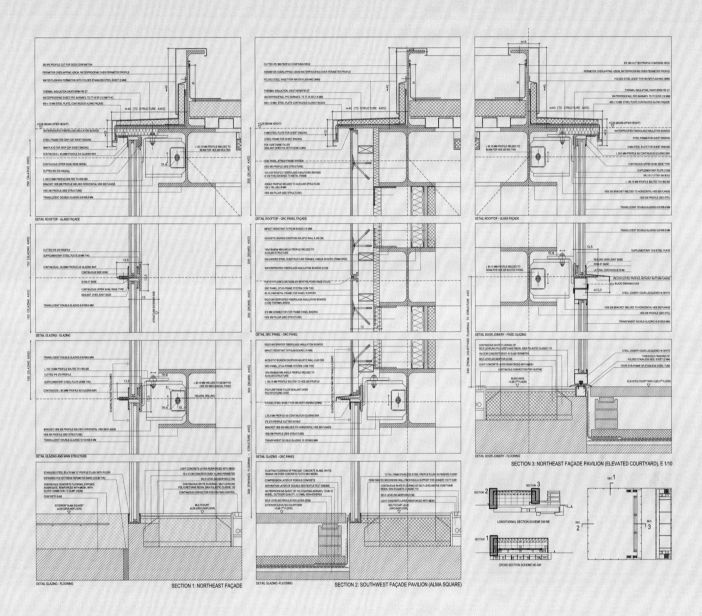

DETAIL ROOFTOP - GLASS FAÇADE

DETAIL GLAZING - GLAZING

DETAIL GLAZING AND MAIN STRUCTURE

DETAIL GLAZING - FLOORING

DETAIL ROOFTOP - GRC PANEL FAÇADE

DETAIL GRC PANEL - GRC PANEL

DETAIL GLAZING - GRC PANEL

DETAIL GLAZING - FLOORING

SECTION 1: NORTHEAST FAÇADE

SECTION 2: SOUTHWEST FAÇADE PAVILION (ALMA SQUARE)

DETAIL ROOFTOP - GLASS FAÇADE

DETAIL DOOR JOINERY - FIXED GLAZING

DETAIL DOOR JOINERY - FLOORING

SECTION 3: NORTHEAST FAÇADE PAVILION (ELEVATED COURTYARD), E 1/10

LONGITUDINAL SECTION SCHEME SW-AE

CROSS SECTION SCHEME NE-SW

detail section

Work:
Multi-Sport Pavilion UFV

Location:
Carretera. Pozuelo-Majadahonda km 1.800,
Pozuelo de Alarcón, Madrid, Spain

Client:
Universidad Francisco de Vitoria

Function:
Sports center and classrooms

Project:
2012

Built:
2017

Building Area:
9,000 m²

Collaborators:
Ignacio Aguirre López, Alejandro Cervilla García,
María Pérez de Camino, Tommaso Campiotti,
Miguel Ciria Hernández, Elena Jiménez Sánchez,
Imanol Iparraguirre, María Moura

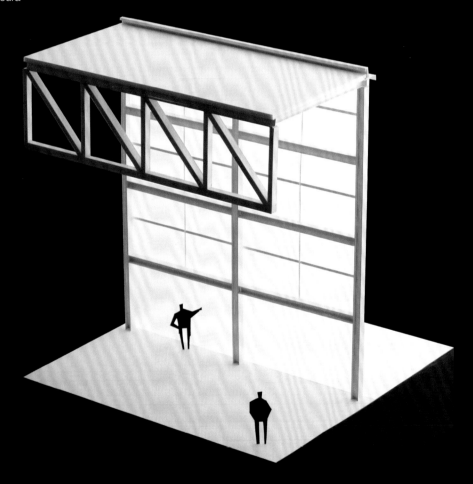

Guadalajara International Book Fair

Guadalajara, 2016

THERE WILL BE LIGHT

AN AGORA FULL OF LIGHT

We wanted to make the most beautiful pavilion in the world to represent MADRID at the Guadalajara International Book Fair 2017 in Mexico.

The idea at the heart of the project is to create a recognizable space that all the attendees at this major fair will have to pass through. We envisaged an AGORA full of LIGHT, of LIGHT that brings wisdom through books.

It consists of a white cylinder 21 m in diameter (7 x 3), and 14 m high (7 x 2), with a ceiling full of light.

We built white tiered seating all around the inside of this large white cylinder, a grandstand, creating an amphitheater, a true AGORA, crowned with a band of shelves containing books. The cylindrical space is accessed via four openings at its four cardinal points. People will pass through, or they will climb up, take down books, and sit down to read them in the seating area. The four openings will allow people to pass through and move freely.

Previous spread. Interior view.
Right. Exterior view.

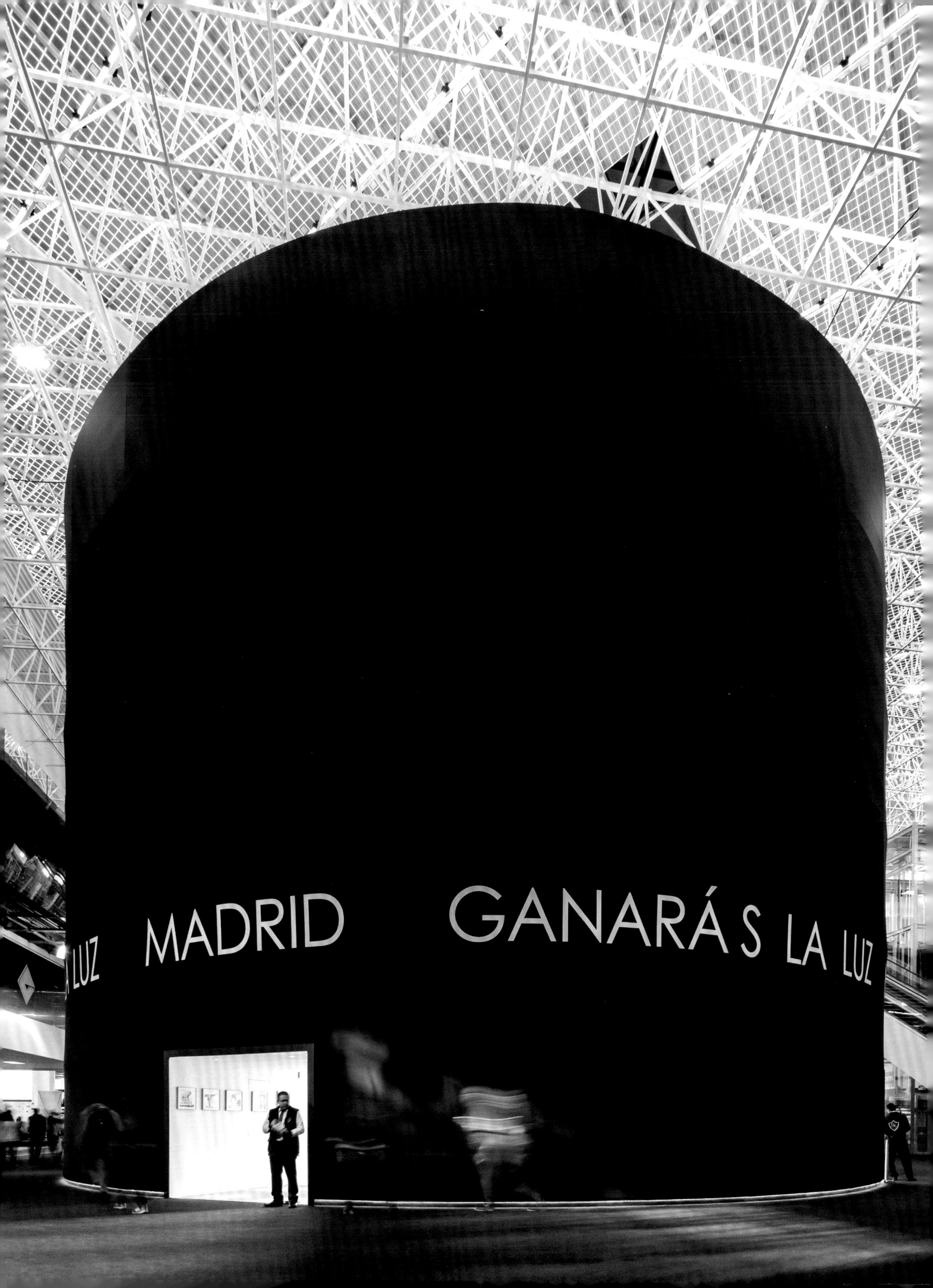
LUZ
MADRID
GANARÁS LA LUZ

All white, very white, bright, shining bright, brilliant. Floating in the air above, like a firmament of small stars, many tiny pieces of mirror in motion and in different positions produce interesting reflections that will create elements of tension, tangibly defining that space. Some pieces will be letters, making up words like MADRID, CERVANTES, or QUIJOTE, OCTAVIO PAZ, and JUAN RULFO.

And, as if they had fallen from the sky, little fragments of mirror on the white floor and letters composing the same words: MADRID, CERVANTES, PEACE, RULFO. All those little pieces with their reflections will make visible the LIGHT coming from above.

Between the cylinder and the space of the building in which it is contained, in the *intrados*, in what we might call the pendentive spaces, we envisage everything painted black, in contrast with the shining white interior of the large cylinder. These preceding areas in black will not only serve to create a positive "wow effect" on entering and leaving the white, more luminous central space, but will also contain spaces for a literary café, small offices, tourist promotion, and various activities such as exhibitions or a children's play area, as well as smaller areas programmed for the pavilion.

Not only will the central space serve as a true AGORA for the MADRID Pavilion, it will be the very heart of the fair.

Left and below. Exterior view.

Above. Partial interior views. Seating area and upper level with shelves.
Right. Interior view from the ground access level.
Following spread. Interior view from the upper level.

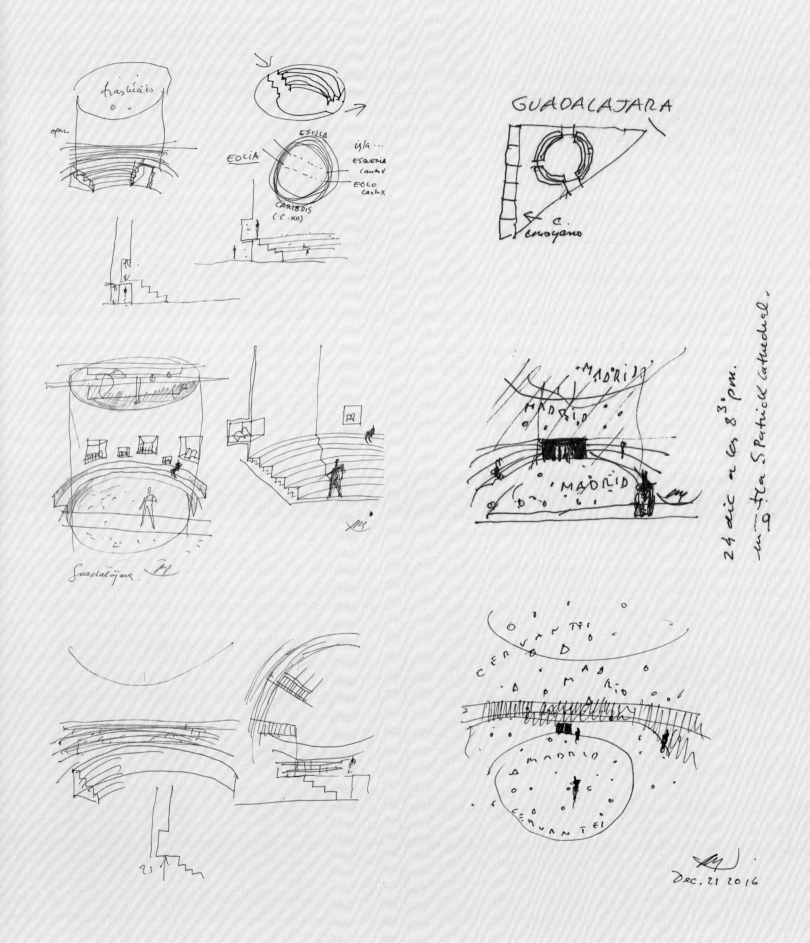

GUADALAJARA

24 dic a las 8³ pm.
en Sta S Patrick Cathedral.

Dec. 21 2016

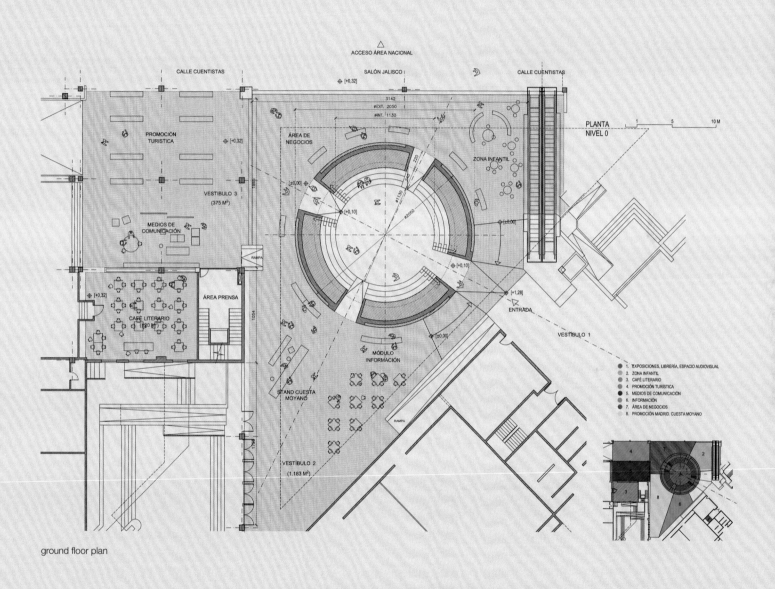

ground floor plan

PLANTA
NIVEL 0

1. EXPOSICIONES, LIBRERÍA, ESPACIO AUDIOVISUAL
2. ZONA INFANTIL
3. CAFÉ LITERARIO
4. PROMOCIÓN TURÍSTICA
5. MEDIOS DE COMUNICACIÓN
6. INFORMACIÓN
7. ÁREA DE NEGOCIOS
8. PROMOCIÓN MADRID. CUESTA MOYANO

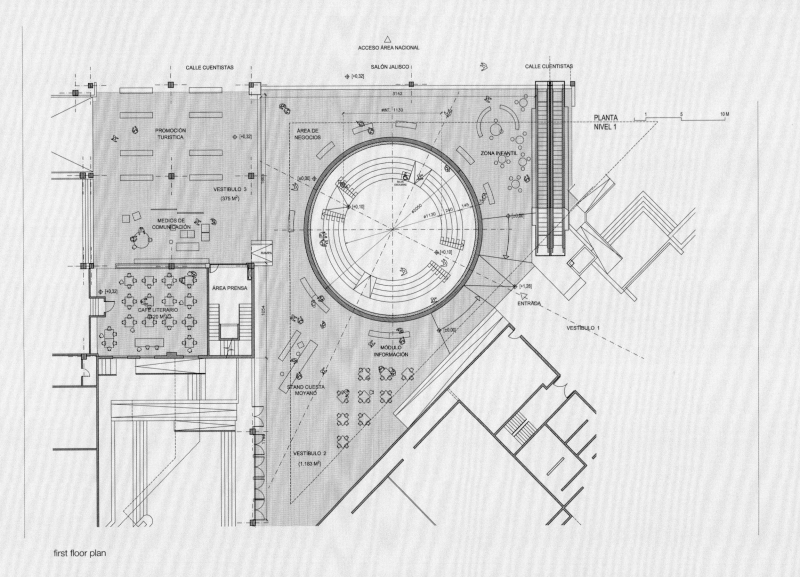

ACCESO ÁREA NACIONAL

CALLE CUENTISTAS

SALÓN JALISCO

CALLE CUENTISTAS

PLANTA
NIVEL 1

PROMOCIÓN
TURÍSTICA

ÁREA DE
NEGOCIOS

ZONA INFANTIL

VESTÍBULO 3
(375 M²)

MEDIOS DE
COMUNICACIÓN

SALIDA
ESCALERAS

ÁREA PRENSA

CAFÉ LITERARIO
(120 M²)

ENTRADA

VESTÍBULO 1

MÓDULO
INFORMACIÓN

STAND CUESTA
MOYANO

VESTÍBULO 2
(1.183 M²)

first floor plan

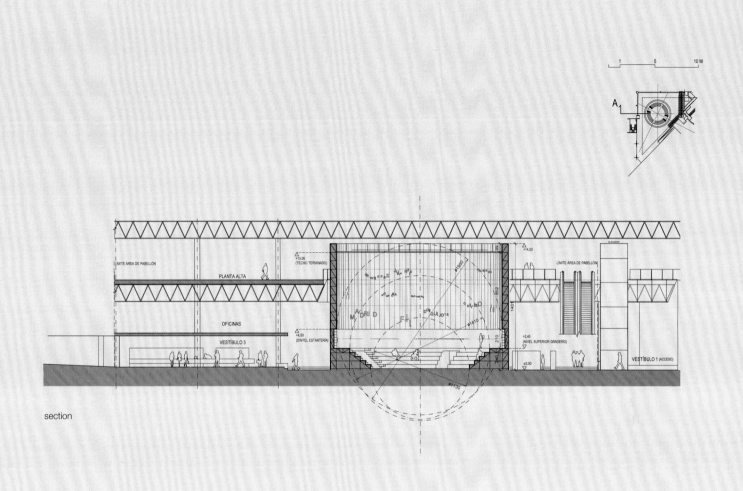

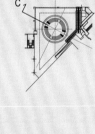

section

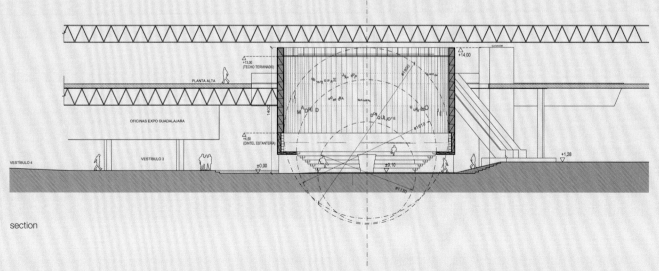

section

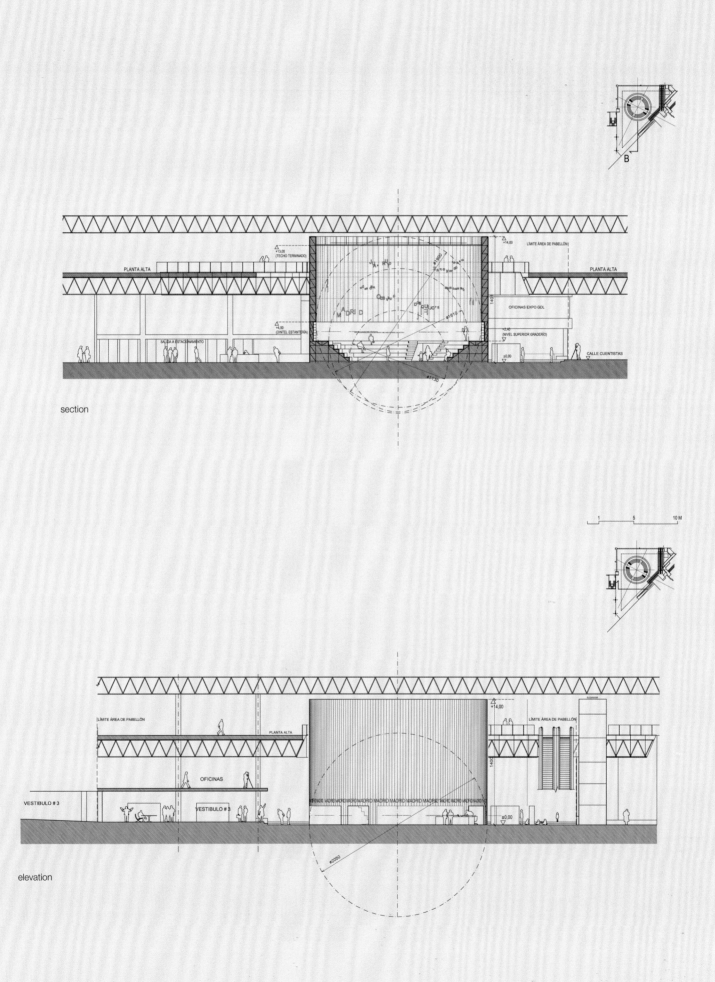

section

elevation

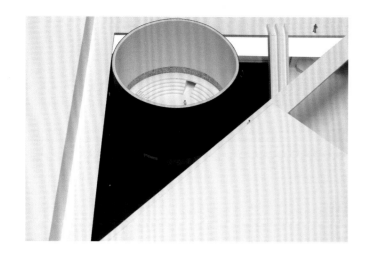

Work:
Guadalajara International Book Fair

Location:
Guadalajara, México

Client:
Ayuntamiento de Madrid

Project:
2016

Built:
2017

Area:
350 m²

Collaborators:
Alejandro Cervilla García, Ignacio Aguirre López,
Teresa Sanchis, Elena Jiménez Sánchez,
Tommaso Campiotti

Domus Aurea

Domus Aurea
Monterrey, 2016

In collaboration with Gilberto L. Rodríguez

For a Spanish architect to build a house in Mexico is a privilege. To build a house in Monterrey is a gift. To build the TEC lottery house in Monterrey is amazing. And, logically, I did my utmost to ensure that this house would be the most beautiful in the world. That is my stated intent with every new project that falls into my hands.

And of course, if Barragán is always present in all my architecture, he is even more in this case, which is why I decided that not only would my house be flooded with light, but that it would be the golden light of Barragán.

With this in mind, after creating a diagonal space resulting from concatenating two spaces of double height, I decided to gild the high vertical wall on which all the southern light would fall and fill it with this much-coveted golden hue.

Accordingly this light-filled house would be literally flooded with golden light, and thus become a veritable DOMUS AUREA.

In functional terms, the house is divided into three planes. On the ground floor the most public areas. Continuity to the garden will be through verandas and shaded areas. On the upper floor, the bedrooms and living area overlook the lower floor. At the higher rooftop level, the more private areas will be located, including the swimming pool.

We dream of a white house, serene, full of light, a golden light, where its inhabitants will be happy.

Previous spread. Northwest facade. Partial view.
Right. Northeast facade. Main access.

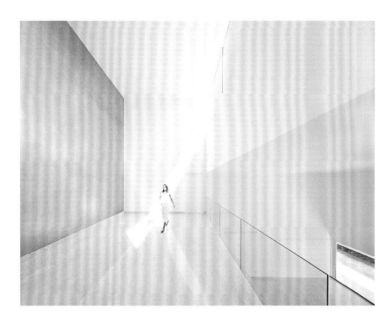

Top, above, and right. Interior views from the upper level.

Previous spread. Interior view from the upper level. Diagonal space and golden light.
Above. Interior view from the ground level.
Right above and below. Interior view from the upper level.

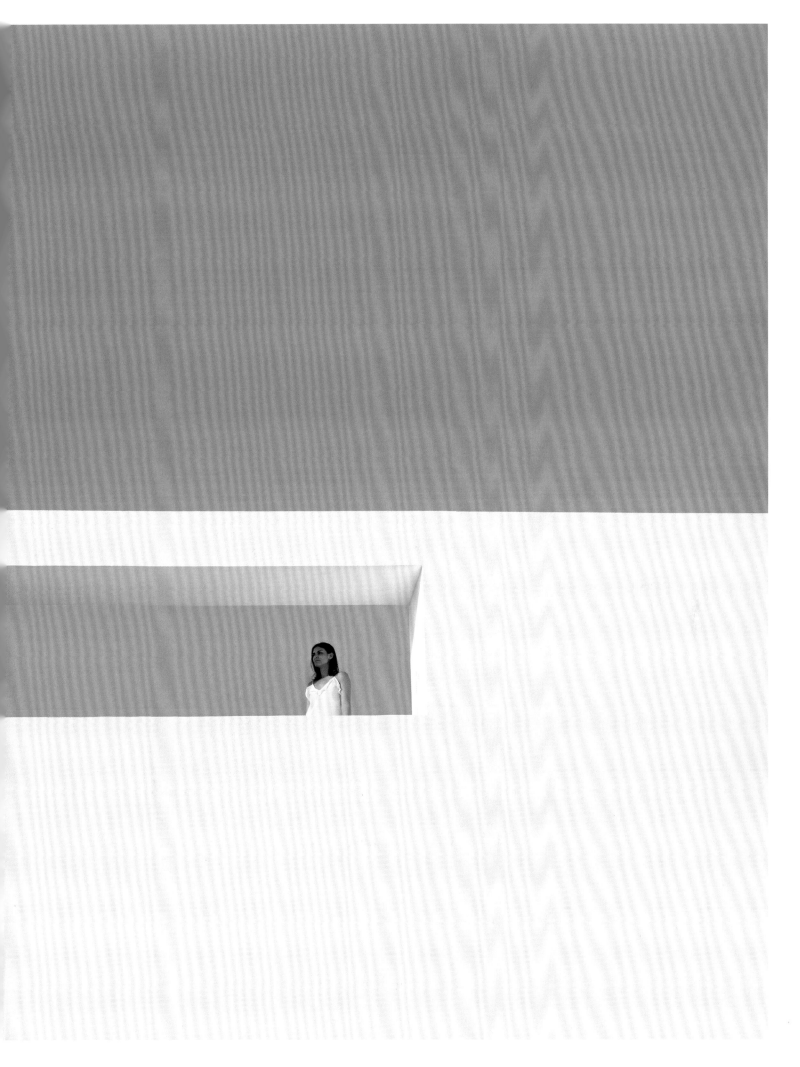

Previous spread. Detail facade. Horizontal window in the rooftop level.
Left. Rooftop level. Swimming pool and horizontal window.
Above. Rooftop level. View of the surrounding landscape.

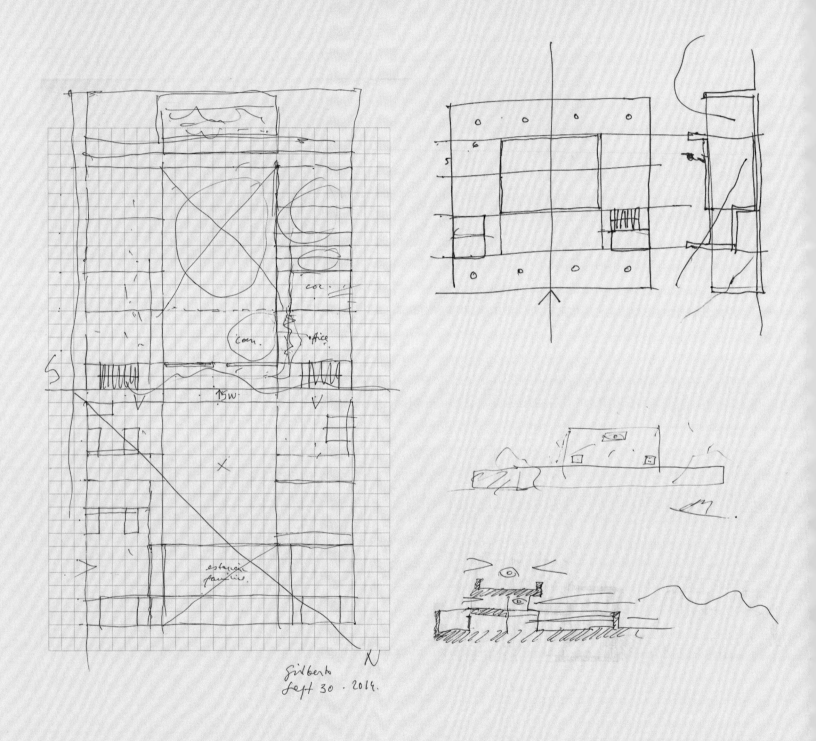

Gilberto
Sept 30 · 2014.

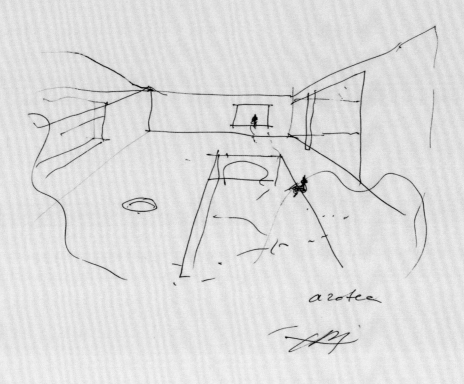

azotea

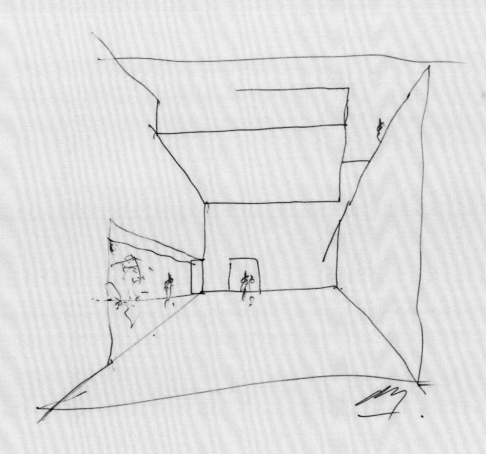

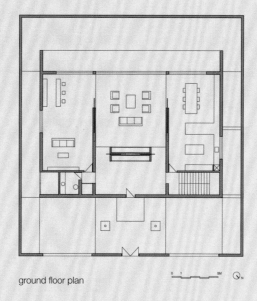

ground floor plan

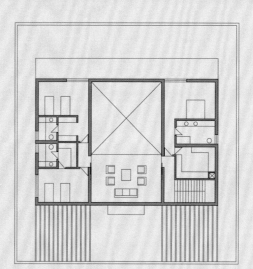

first floor plan

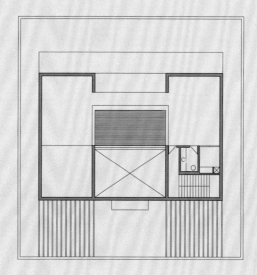

roof plan

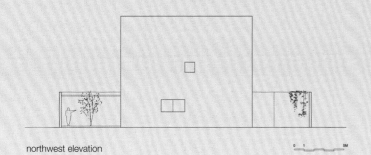

northwest elevation

0 1   5M

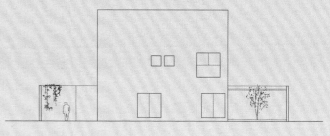

southeast elevation

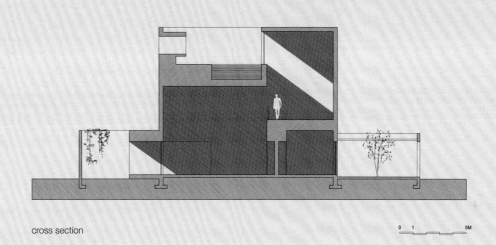

cross section

0 1   5M

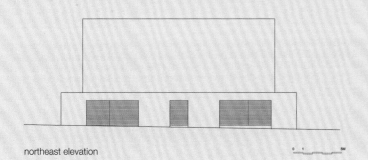

northeast elevation

0 1   5M

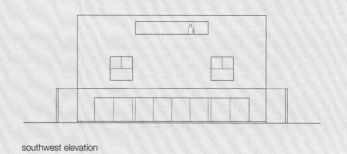

southwest elevation

Work:
Domus Aurea

Location:
Monterrey, México

Client:
Sorteos TEC –
Instituto Tecnológico de Monterrey

Project:
2014

Built:
2016

Area:
500 m²

Collaborators:
María Pérez de Camino Díez, Pamela Díaz de
León, Alejandro Cervilla García, Ignacio Aguirre
López, David Alatorre, Viviana Ortíz, Mauricio
Bárcenas, Katia Radilla, Guillermo Durán, Elena
Jiménez Sánchez, Tommaso Campiotti, Imanol
Iparraguirre Barbero

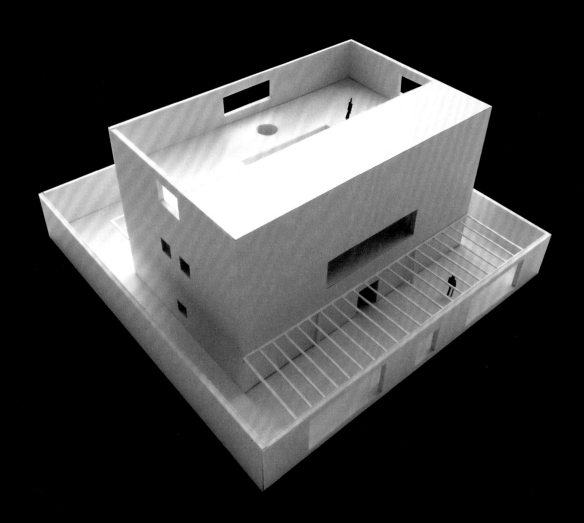

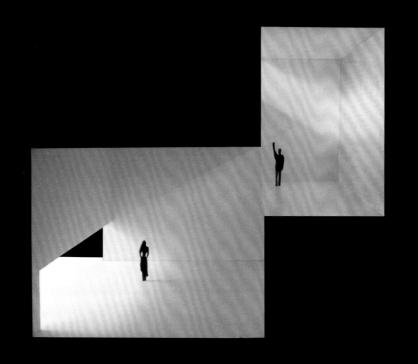
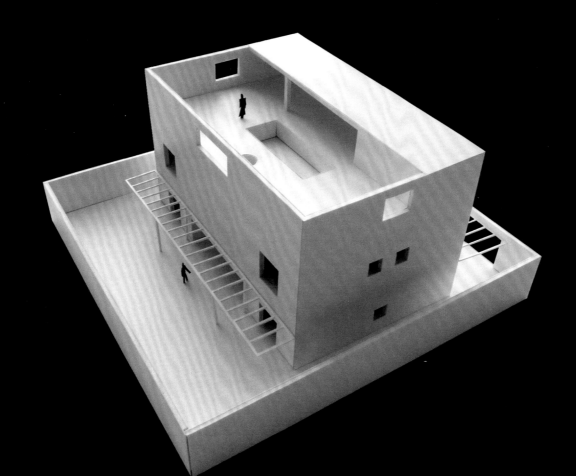

Cala House

Cala House
Madrid, 2015

2+2+2 IS MUCH MORE THAN JUST 6.

The house is located on a sloping plot with a landscape of distant horizon none other than Madrid's western mountain range. At ground level it doesn't appear to be anything special, but as we go up we feast our eyes on a panoramic view of the urban landscape of the east of Madrid. From the four towers to the left to the Madrid tower to the right. Beautiful and also curious. Logically the more public parts of the house will be at the upper levels to frame and enjoy the stunning views. Complying with prevailing regulations we are required to work with a square ground plan of 12 x 12 m that is divided into four 6 x 6 m squares. Following this pattern, the ground planes are raised, square by square, with a simple helicoidal movement. The spaces are of double height and intersect with one another, producing diagonality that is also helicoidal. The result explains very well the proposal we set out with, namely that 2+2+2 is more than just 6.

Thus in this house a known spatial mechanism is employed, the Raumplan, with the concatenation of spiraling double spaces. Each two double spaces are connected by vertical displacement so that a diagonal space is created. If, as we go up, we turn 90 degrees and connect it with the other two, and if we continue to go up turning a further 90 degrees, we get an amazing spatial structure: the concatenation of three spiraling diagonal spaces, just like a corkscrew, which further explains our statement that 2+2+2 is much more than 6. Once the house is built and the appropriate openings are made, just like those of a musical instrument, so that it is filled with light, and once that instrument is tuned, we can highlight the movement of the solid light of the sun throughout the day. The rooftops planted with jasmine and vines will be a delightful feature, their large spaces framing this strange Madrid landscape. Similarly framed with vines and jasmines will be the porches below that open onto the garden.

Previous spread. Exterior view. North facade.
Right. Exterior view from the surrounding landscape.

Previous spread. Exterior view. East facade.
Above. Exterior view. South facade.
Below. Exterior view of the main entrance.
Right. Exterior view from the northwest.

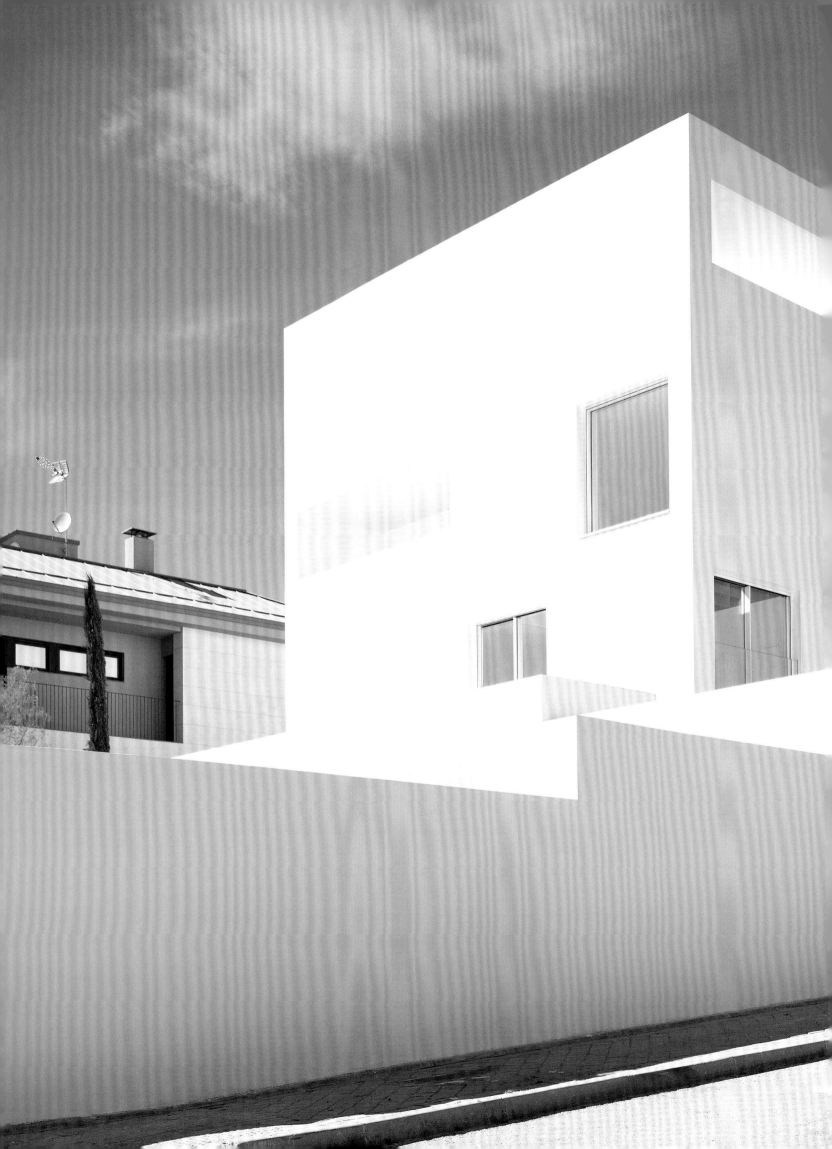

Previous spread. Exterior view from the northeast.
Above. Interior view from the library.
Right. Interior view. Spiraling double spaces.

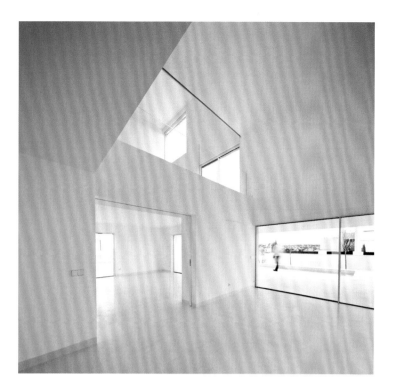

Top. Interior view from the ground level.
Above. Interior view from the first level.
Right. Interior view from the upper level.

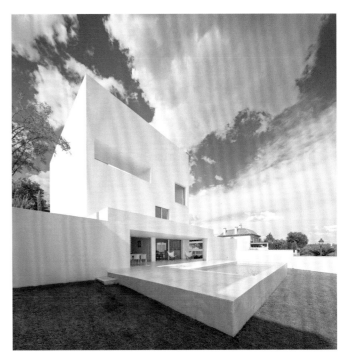

Left. Exterior view. Terrace and garden. Panoramic view of Madrid.
Above. Exterior view from the southwest.

Right. Exterior terraces.
Following spread. Panoramic view. Horizontal window with canopy.

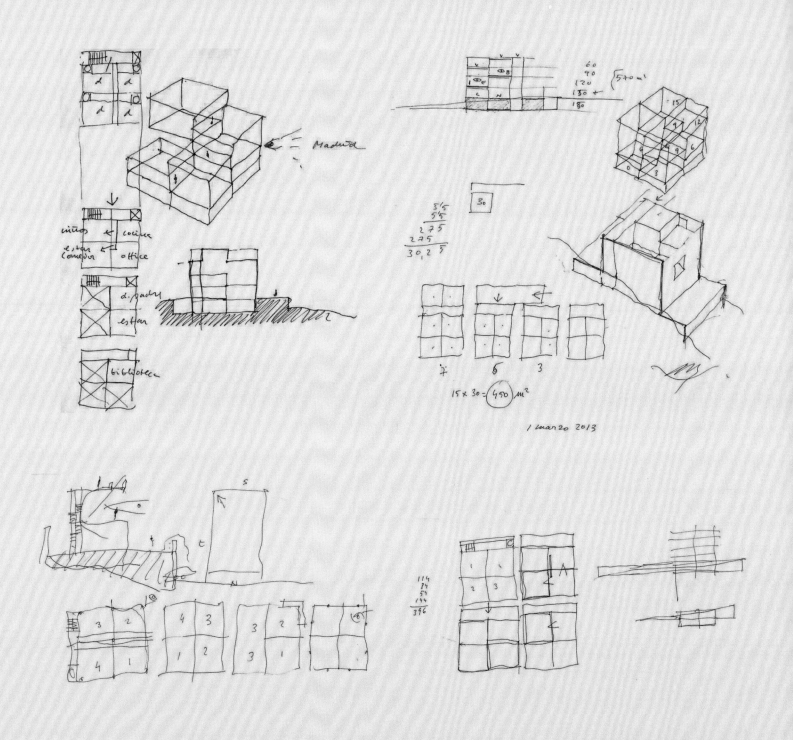

Madrid

niños   cocina
estar   office
comedor

d. padres
estar

biblioteca

60
90
120
150 +
180   570 m²

30

3'5
5'5
2 7 5
2 7 5
30,2 5

15 x 30 = (450) m²

1 marzo 2013

114
84
54
144
396

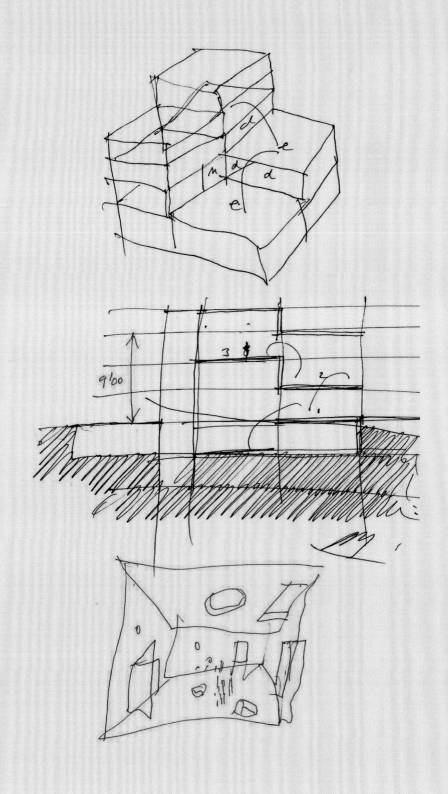

191

first floor plan

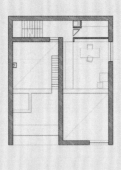

second floor plan

terrace plan

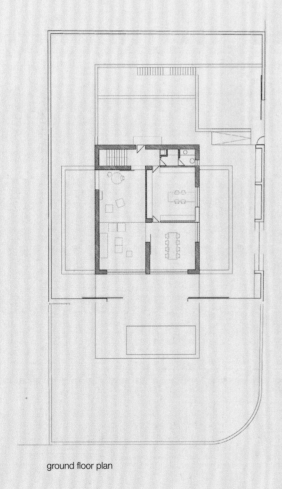

ground floor plan

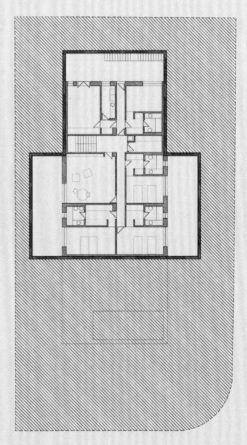

basement plan

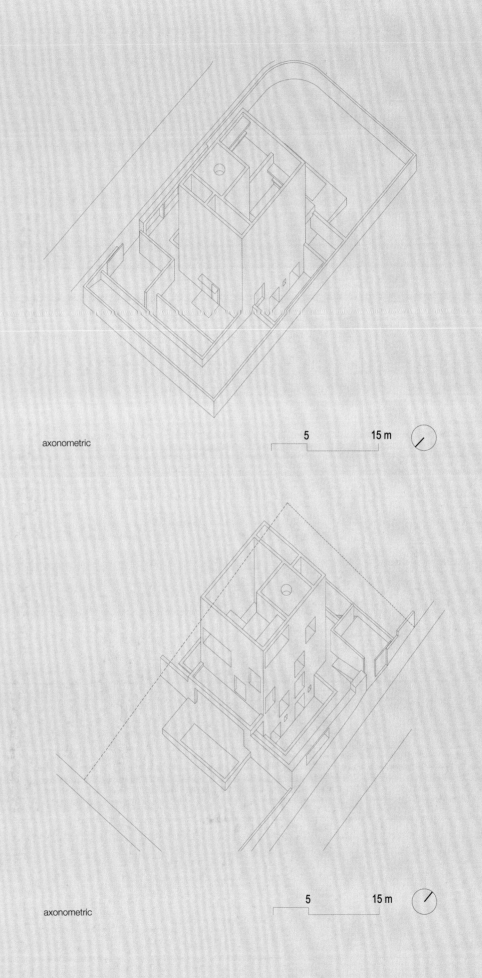

axonometric   5   15 m

axonometric   5   15 m

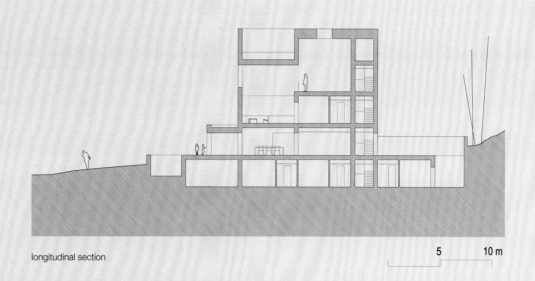

longitudinal section

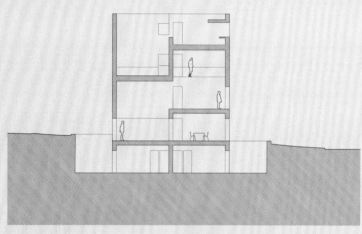

cross section

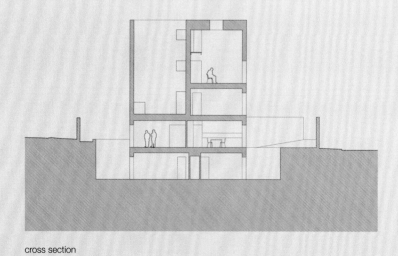

cross section

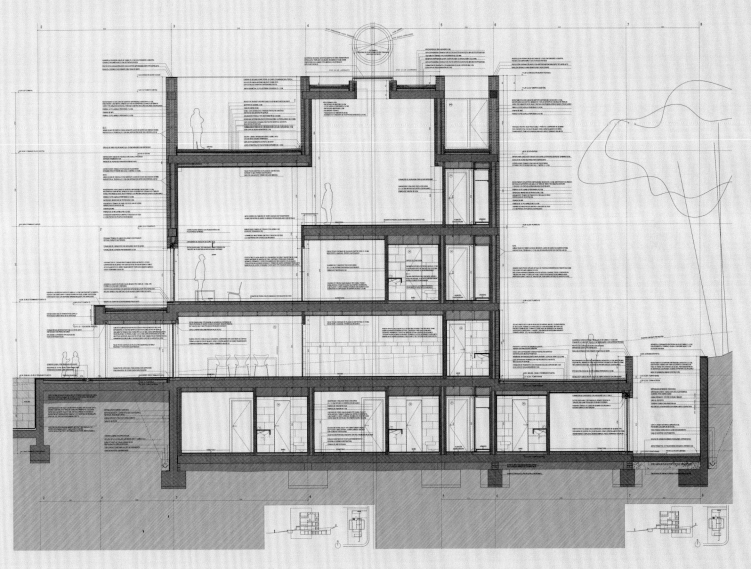

detail section

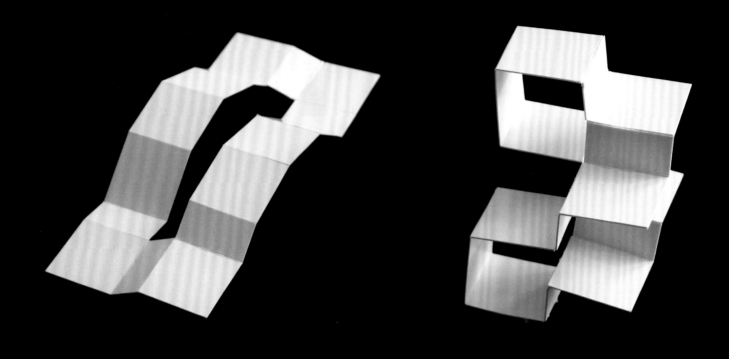
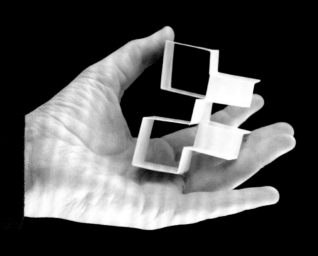

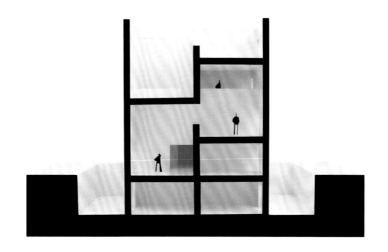

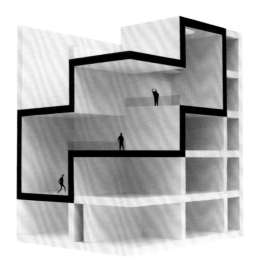

Work:
Cala House

Location:
Aravaca, Madrid, Spain

Client:
Private

Project:
2013

Built:
2015

Area:
500 m²

Collaborators:
Ignacio Aguirre López, Alejandro Cervilla García,
Alfonso Guajardo-Fajardo, Manel Barata, Jesús
Aparicio Alfaro, María Pérez de Camino Díez,
Tommaso Campiotti, Maria Moura

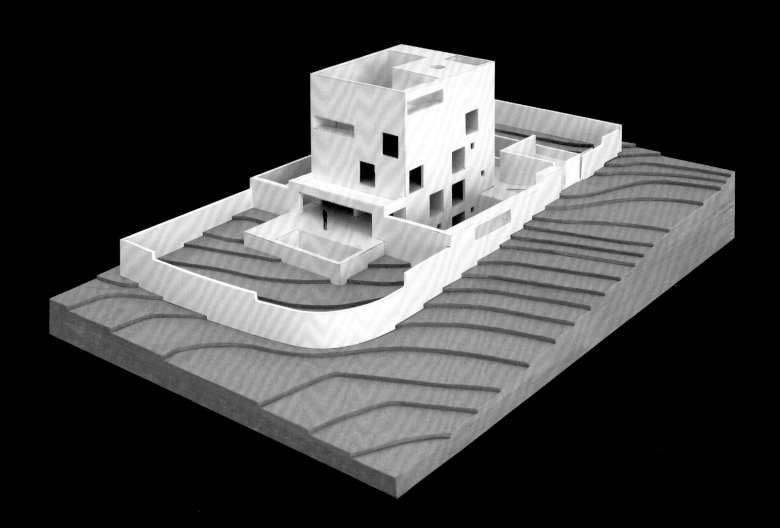

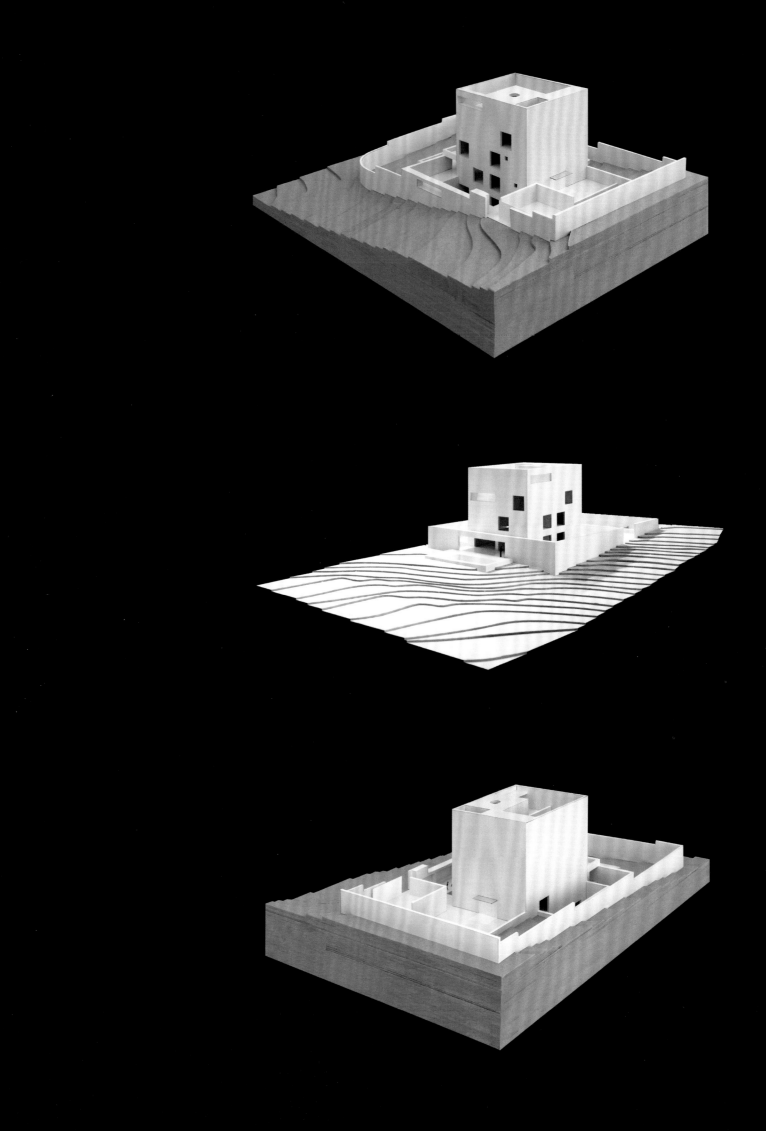

House of the Infinite

House of the Infinite

Cádiz, 2014

INFINITE PLANE FACING THE INFINITE SEA

We have built the most radical house we have
ever made, an infinite plane facing the infinite sea.

A house facing the Atlantic Ocean, at the water's edge on a beach of Cádiz, like a piece of
earthly paradise, where the Romans once lived
in nearby Bolonia.

We built a powerful podium in Roman travertine whose upper horizontal plane becomes
the protagonist of the space. Inside the podium, underneath this platform like a temenos,
is the house.

Above and behind the stony platform, we have
erected stone walls to protect us from the strong
prevailing winds.

As if it were an acropolis. A temenos where the
gods descend to converse with humans and
toast with sherry on this plane on high looking
out onto the infinite sea.

The house of the infinite.

Previous spread. Exterior view looking at the sea.
Right. Exterior view from the south and the surrounding landscape.

Previous spread. Exterior view. South facade.
Above. Exterior view from the northeast.
Right. Front view to the sea.

Above. Partial view. North facade.
Below. West facade.
Right. Partial view. South facade.

Top and above. Interior view of first level.
Right. Partial view of first level. Transparency.

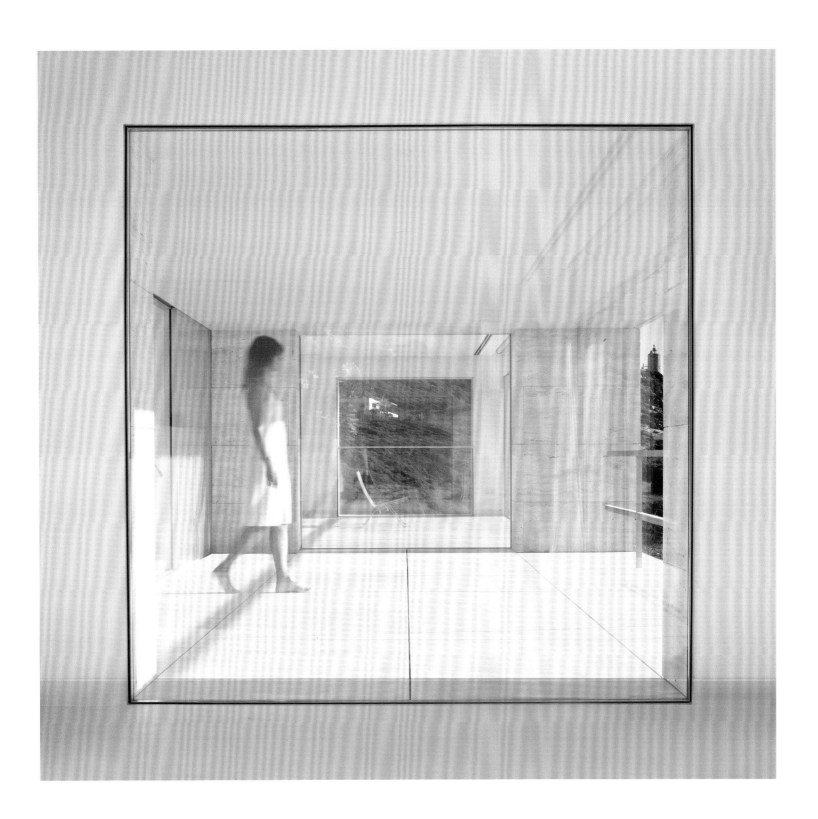

Previous spread. First level. Terrace.
Above. First level. Interior view of living room.

Above. Detail view of the staircase.
Below. Ground level. Living room.
Right. First level. Entrance.

Left. Exterior view. Horizontal plane looking at the sea.
Above. Access level. Roof plan.
Below. Roof plan. Partial view with the carved stairs and stands.
Following spread. Roof plan. Partial view.

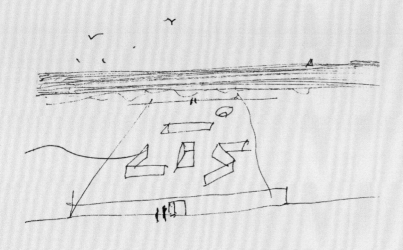

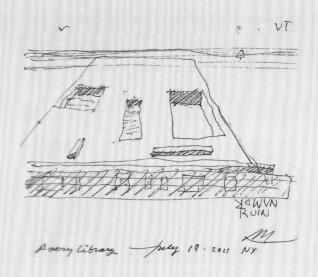

TOWN RUIN

Avery Library — July 19 · 2011 NY

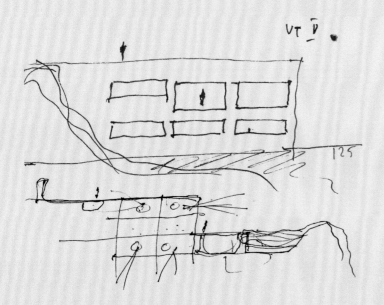

VT D

125

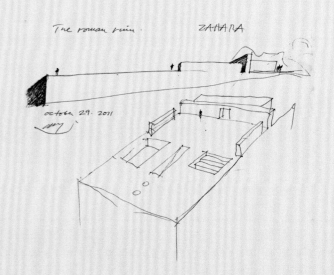

The roman ruin · ZAHARA

october 29 · 2011

V.T.

1 de noviembre de 2012

223

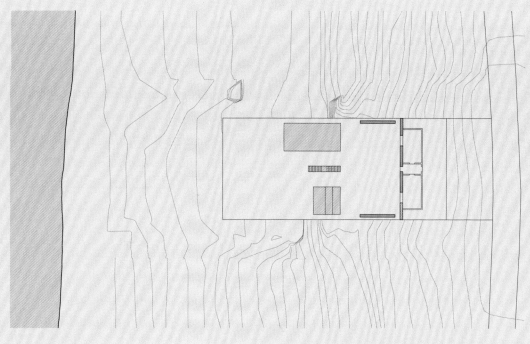

viewpoint platform

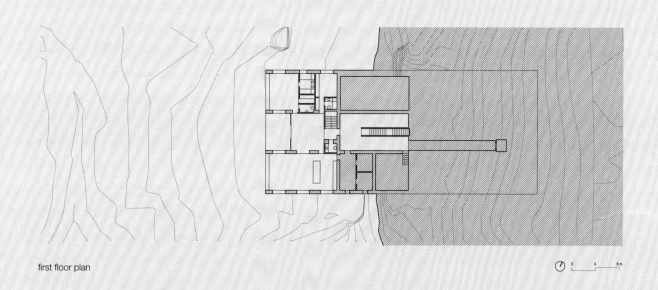

first floor plan

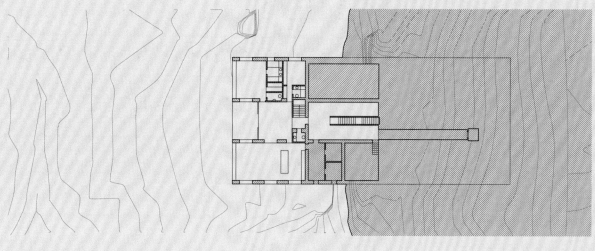

ground floor plan

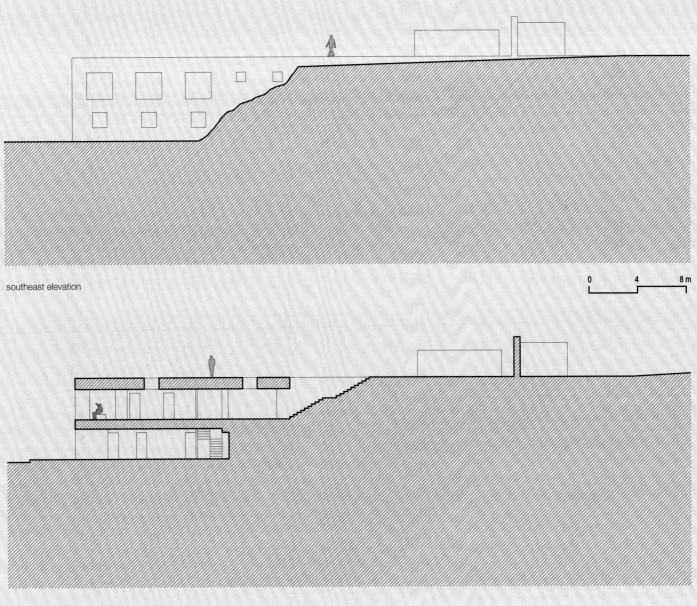

southeast elevation

0 4 8 m

longitudinal section

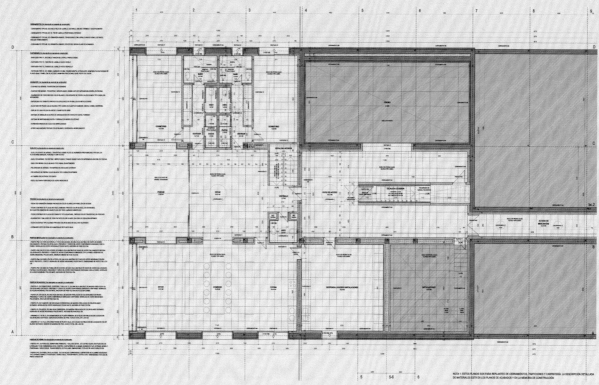

detail plan

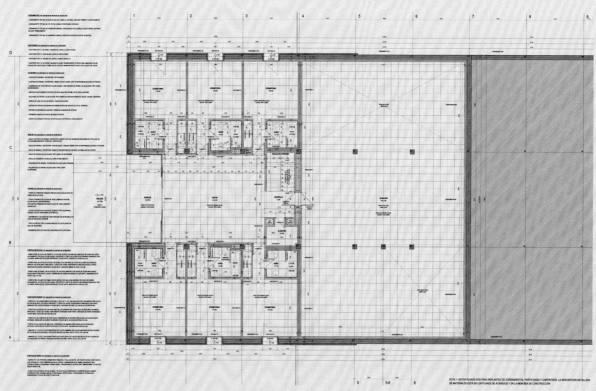

detail plan

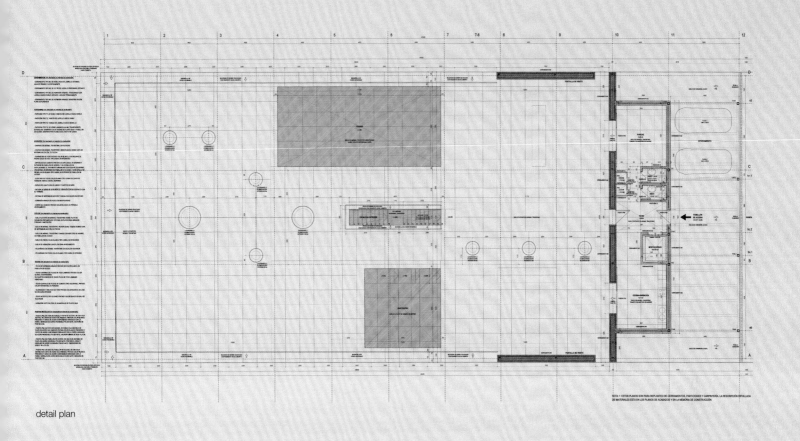

detail plan

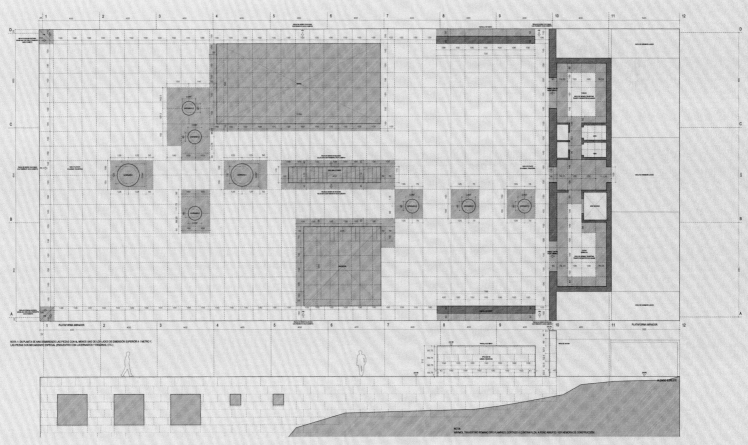

detail stone

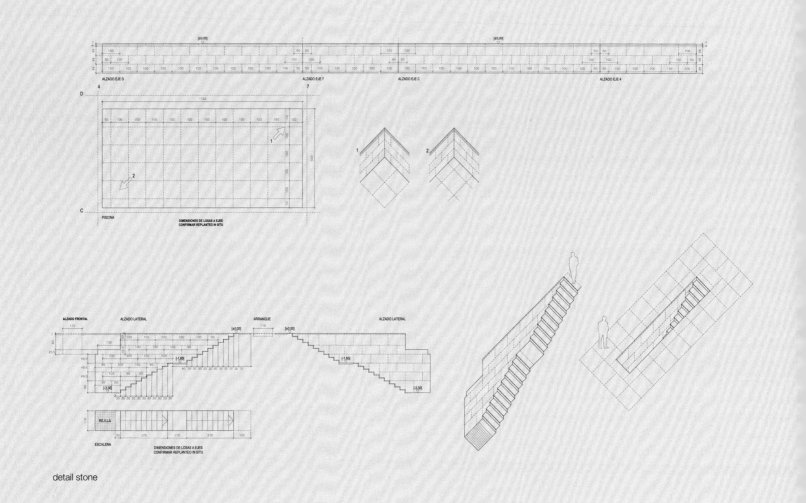

detail stone

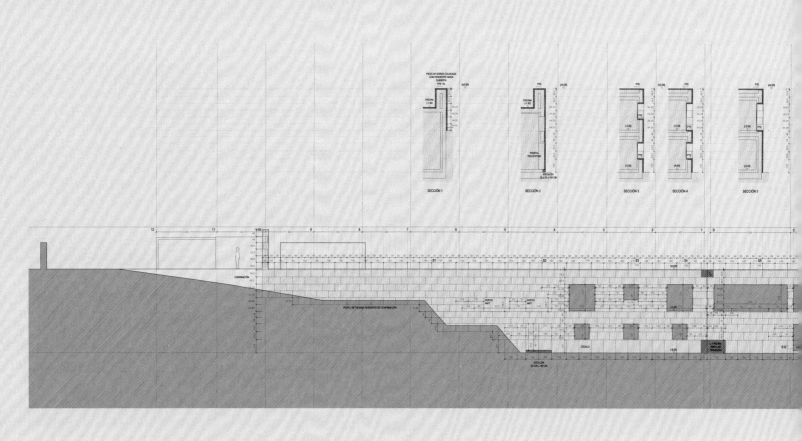

detail stone

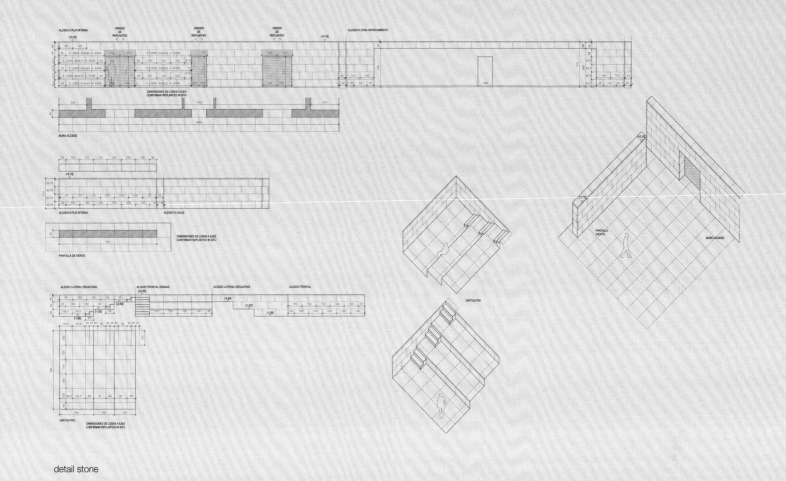

detail stone

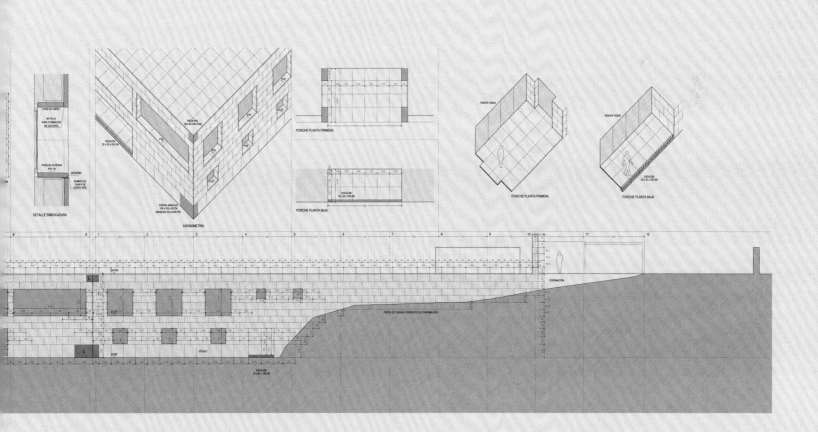

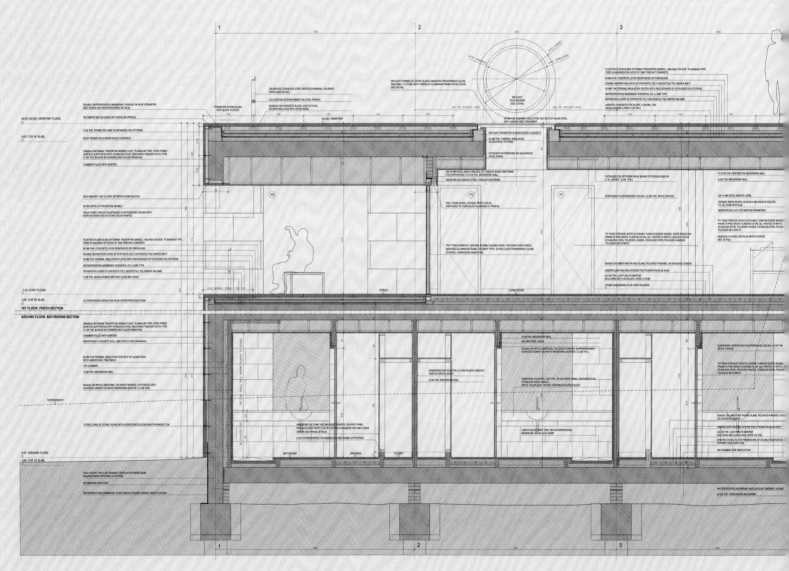

detail section

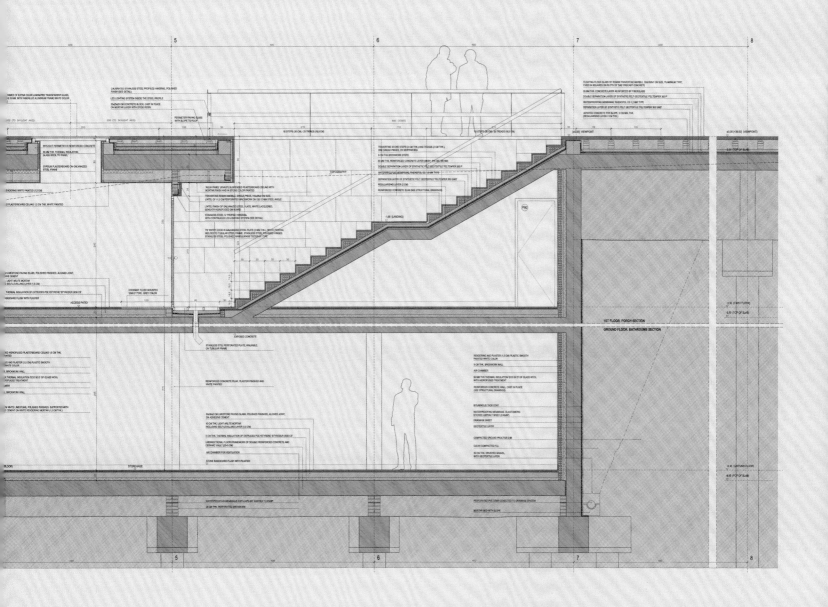

1ST FLOOR, PORCH SECTION

GROUND FLOOR, BATHROOMS SECTION

Work:
House of the Infinite

Location:
Cádiz, Spain

Client:
Private

Project:
2012

Built:
2014

Area:
900 m²

Collaborators:
Tomás Carranza (codirector of construction),
Javier Montero (codirector of construction),
Alejandro Cervilla García, Ignacio Aguirre López,
Gaja Bieniasz, Agustín Gor, Sara Oneto

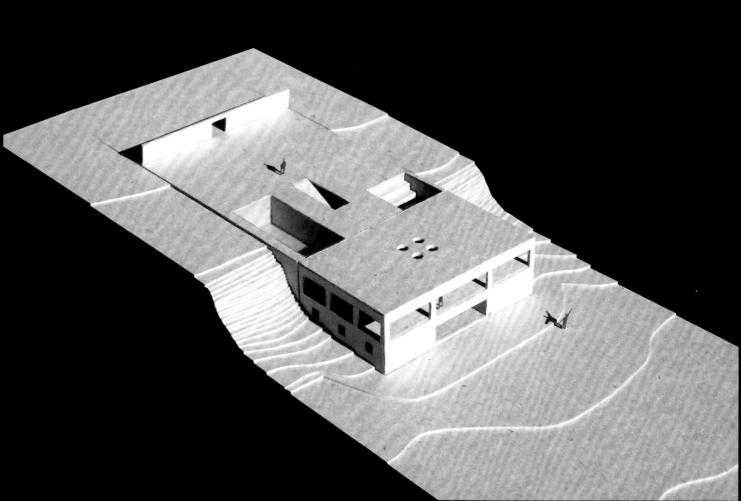

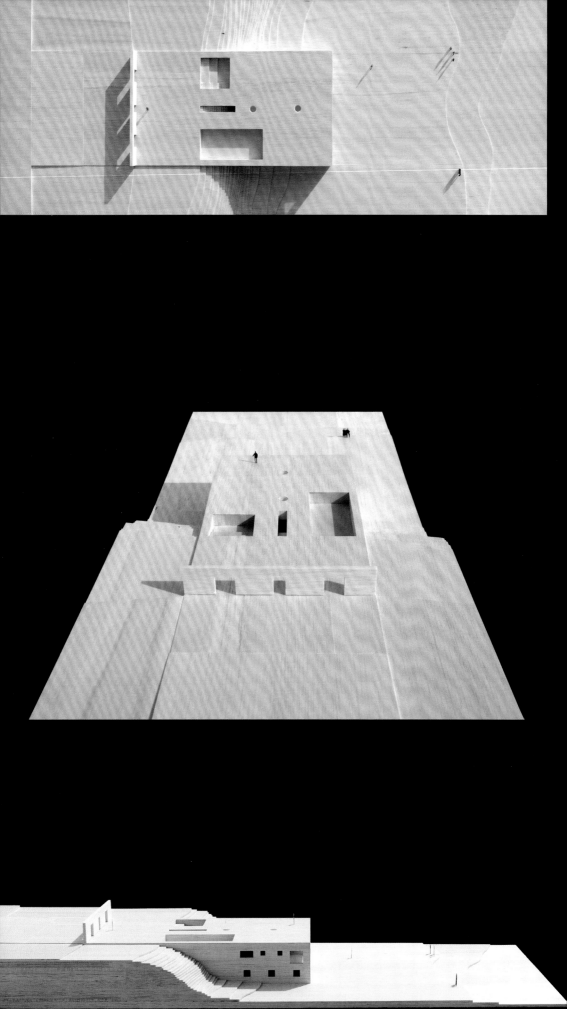

Junta de Castilla y León Offices

Junta de Castilla y León Offices
Zamora, 2008–2012

In collaboration with Pablo Fernández Lorenzo,
Pablo Redondo Díez, Alfonso González Gaisán,
and Francisco Blanco Velasco.

BUILDING WITH AIR

To build with air, the abiding dream of every architect:

Facing the cathedral and following the outline of
the former convent's kitchen garden, we erect a
strong stone wall box open to the sky. Its walls
and floors made entirely of stone. The very same
stone as the cathedral. A real hortus conclusus.
In the corner facing the cathedral, a massive
stone measuring 250 x 150 x 50 cm, a veritable
cornerstone. And chiseled on that stone:

HIC LAPIS ANGULARIS MAIO MMXII POSITO

Within the stone box, a glass box, only glass.
Like a greenhouse. With a double facade similar
to a Trombe wall. The external skin of the facade
is made of glass, each single sheet measuring
600 x 300 x 12 cm and all joined together simply
with structural silicone and hardly anything else.
As if entirely made of air.

The trihedral upper angles of the box are
made completely with glass, thus even further
accentuating the effect of transparency. Precisely
what Mies was looking for in his Friedrichstrasse
tower. The trihedron built with air, a true glass
corner. And engraved in acid on the glass:

HOC VITRUM ANGULARIS MAIO MMXII POSITO

Previous spread. Glass box. Northeast corner.
Right and following spread. Exterior view from cathedral.

Above. Exterior view. South facade.
Above right. Exterior view. South facade.
Below right. Exterior view. Corner to Cathedral Plaza.

Above left. Exterior view. Facade to Cathedral Plaza.
Above right. Entrance.
Following spread. West facade.

The stone box made from memory. With its cornerstone deeply rooted in the soil.

The glass box made for the future. With its glass corner blending into the sky.

To build with air, the abiding dream of every architect.

—

Left. Southwest corner.
Above. West facade.

Above. Northwest corner.
Below. Southeast corner.
Right. South facade.
Following spread. Roof. View to the cathedral.

Above. **Hall.**
Right. **Hall and stair.**
Following spread. **Hall.**

Top. Glass box. Southeast corner.
Above. Transparency. Open offices.
Right. Northwest corner. Transparency.

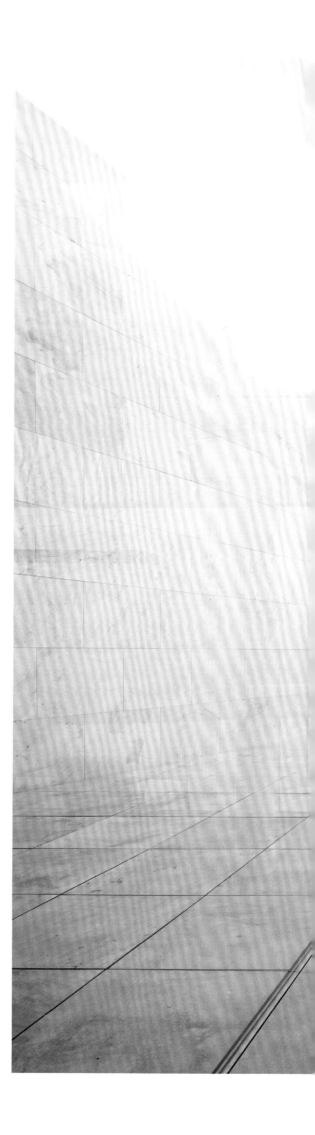

Above. East facade. Night view.

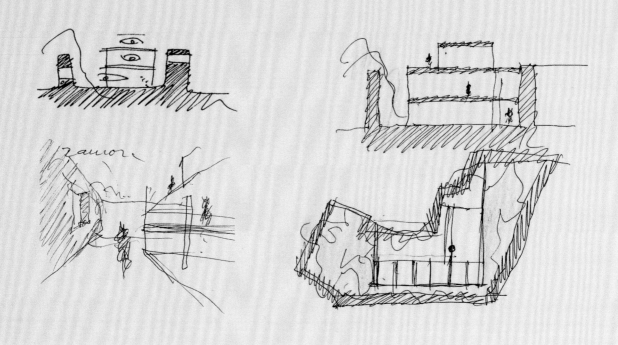

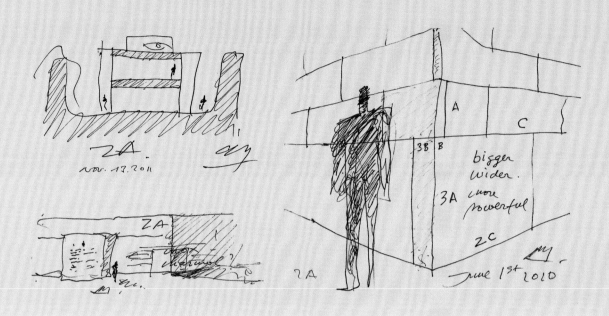

2A
nov. 17. 2011

bigger
wider.

3A more
powerful

A

C

3B B

2C

2A

June 1st 2010

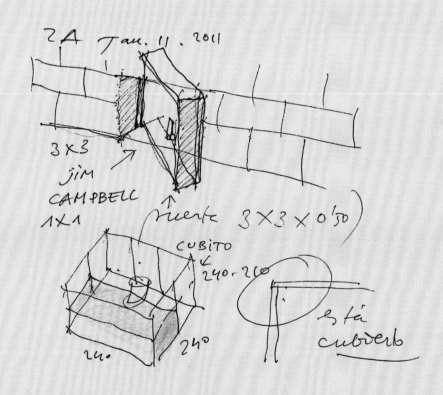

2A   Jan. 11. 2011

3×3
JIM
CAMPBELL
1×1

fuerte 3×3×0'50)

CUBITO
240 - 2?0

240   240

está
cubierto

zamora's historical center

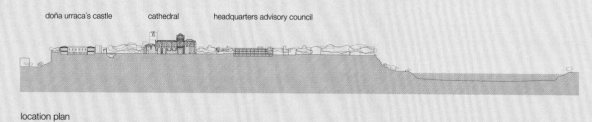

doña urraca's castle   cathedral   headquarters advisory council

location plan

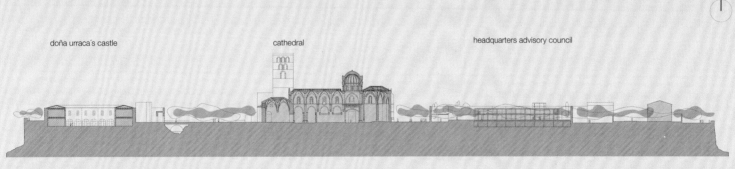

doña urraca´s castle   cathedral   headquarters advisory council

site plan

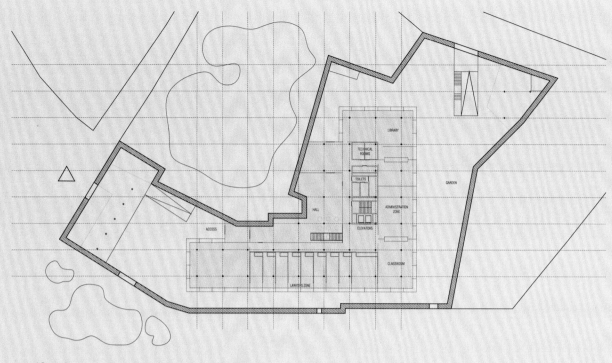

ground floor plan

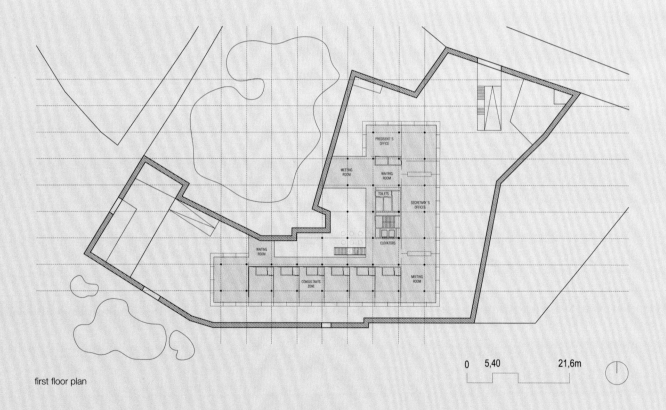

first floor plan

```
0    5,40        21,6m
```

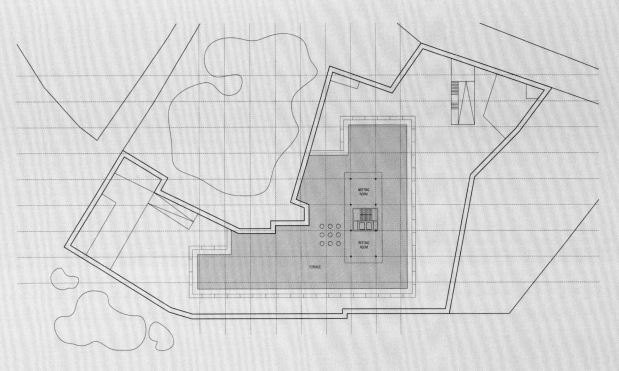

roof floor plan

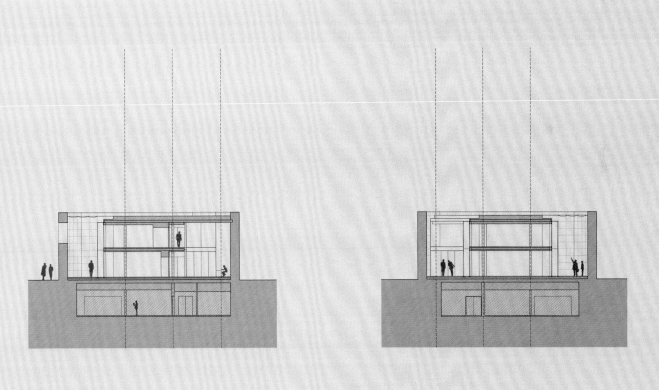

cross sections

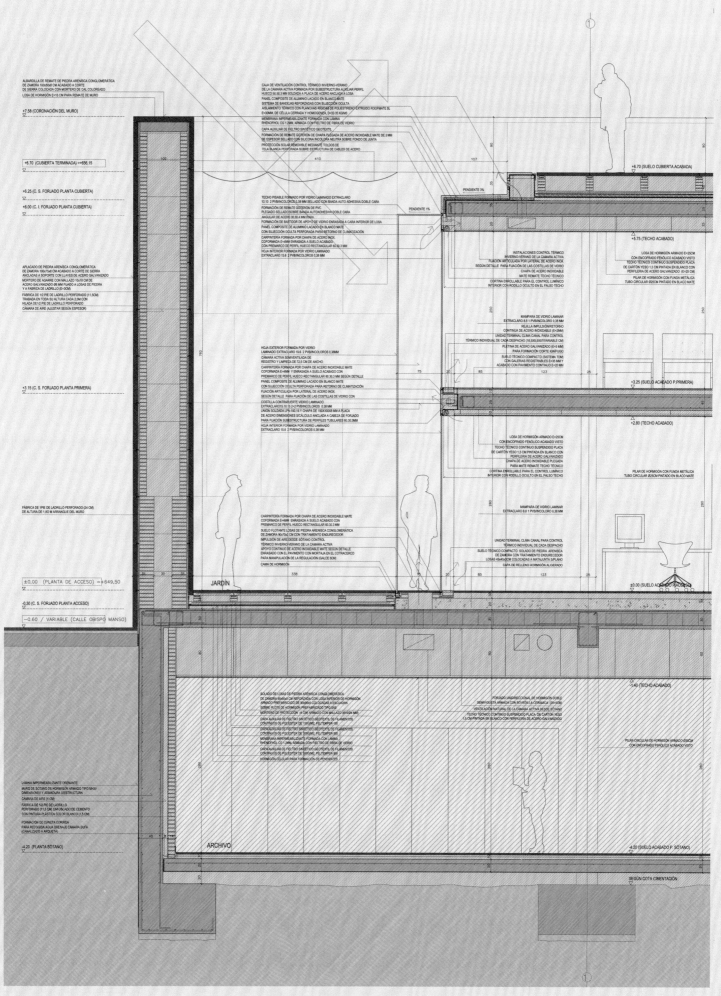

detail section

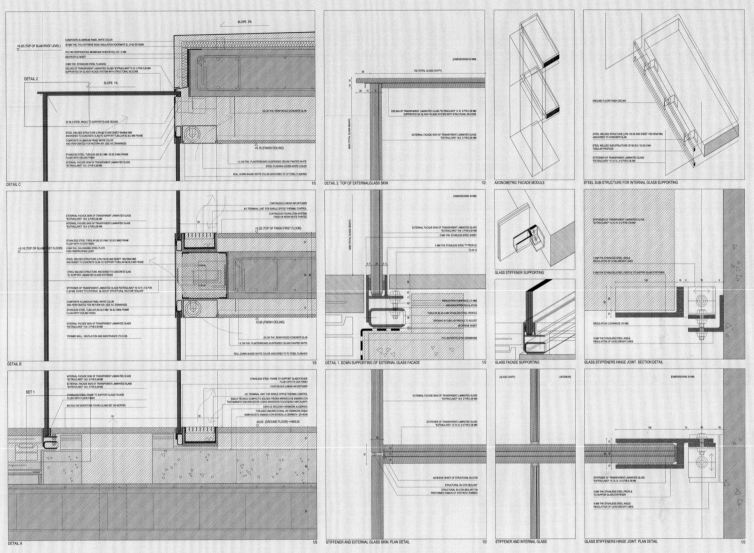

facade section

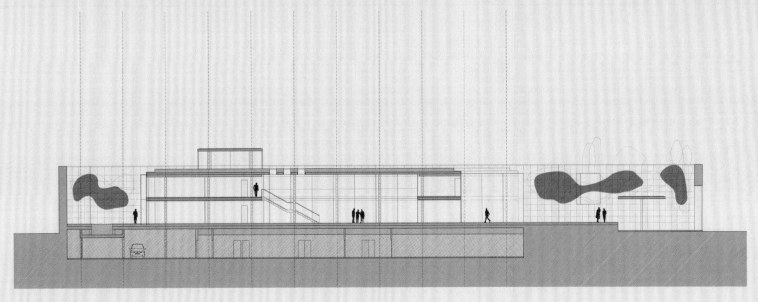

longitudinal section

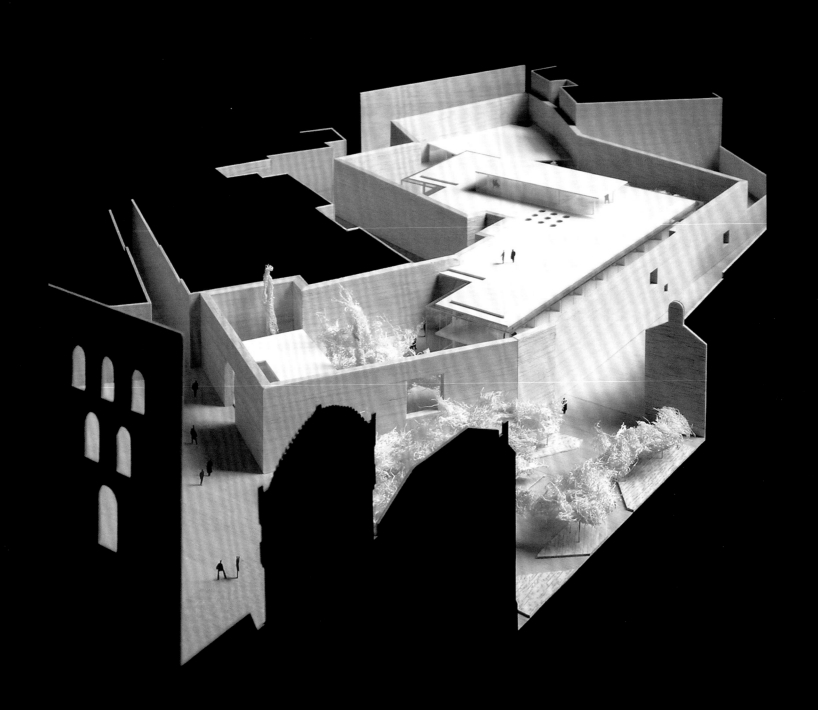

Work:
Junta de Castilla y León Offices

Location:
Obispo Manso, 1, Zamora, Spain

Client:
Junta de Castilla y León.
Consejería de Hacienda

Project:
2006

Built:
2012

Area:
12,100 m^2

Collaborators:
Ignacio Aguirre, Miguel Ciria

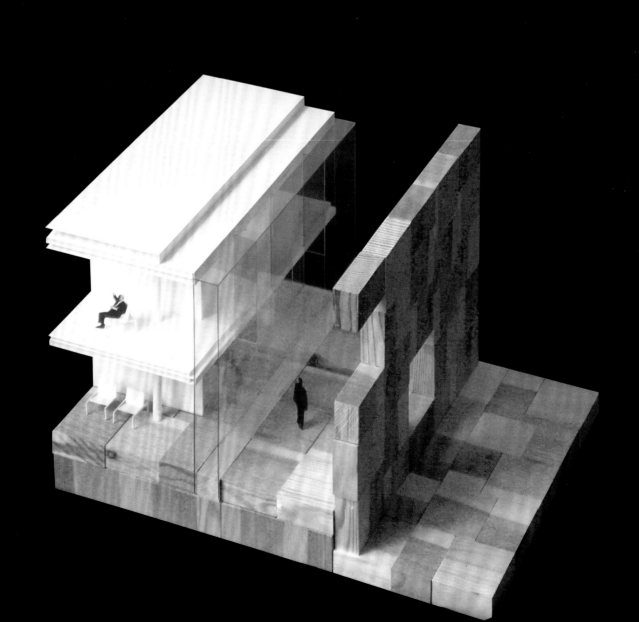

Between Cathedrals

Between Cathedrals
Cádiz, 2010

The project "Between Cathedrals" seeks to create an intervention worthy of the most significant location in the history of Cádiz, the oldest city of the West: the empty space facing the sea located between the Old and New Cathedrals.

The basic premise is to cover and protect an archaeological excavation. Additionally, this new plane serves as a base for a space facing the ocean, a raised public space providing clear views unobstructed by cars passing on the circle road.

A light, white platform is thus conceived, poised over the excavation as if on tiptoe, and reached by a side ramp. Over this plane, a huge canopy structure is built to provide protection from the sun and rain.

Constructed as if it were a ship, it is painted completely white to accentuate its lightness. The paved area is carpeted in white marble.

In the construction of the base: the memory of ships. In that of the shade structure, as if it were a baldachin: the memory of a Holy Week procession.

We sought to make a beautiful piece of architecture, worthy of this wonderful place, and worthy of being part of the collective memory of Cádiz.

Previous spread. View to the sea from the canopy.
Right. Cathedrals and public square. View from Campo del Sur.
Following spread. View from Campo del Sur. Platform and canopy.

Above. Ground plan level. Archaeology.

Left. Canopy. View to the sea.
Above. View to the sea.

The project's objectives are to cover and protect the archaeological excavation. Additionally, we would like this covering plane to serve as the base for a public area facing the sea, at a height that provides a clear view, so the cars on the access highway cannot be seen.

—

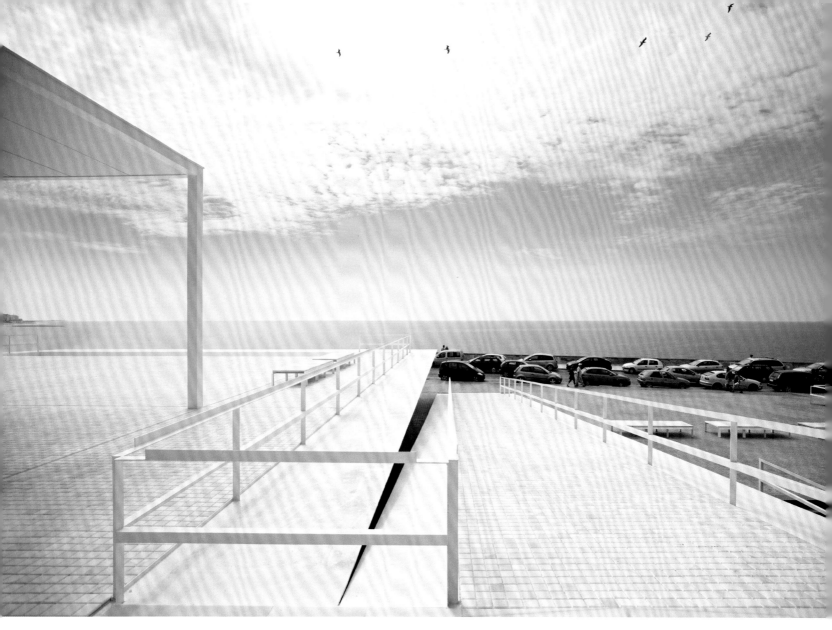

Above. Ramp to the platform.
Above right. Platform edge and ramp.

Above. View to the sea. Public space.

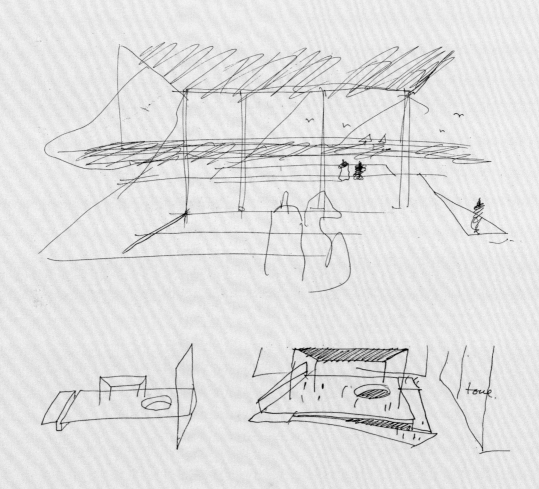

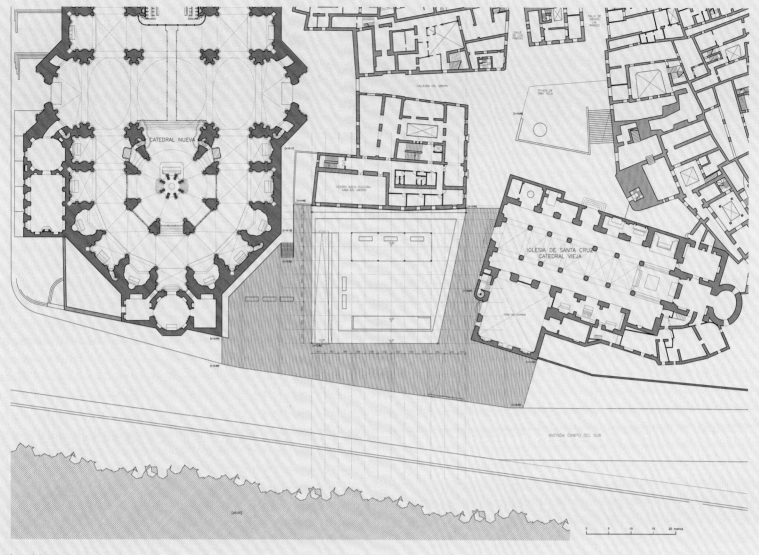

lower plan

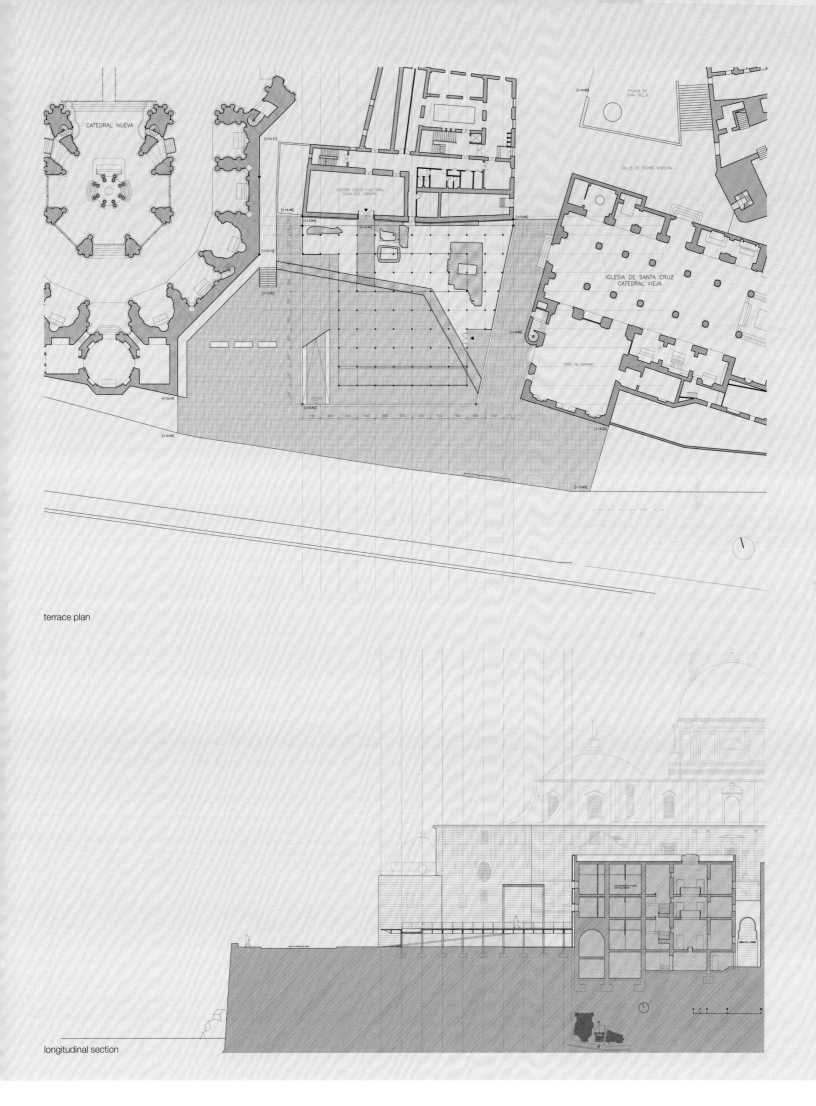

terrace plan

longitudinal section

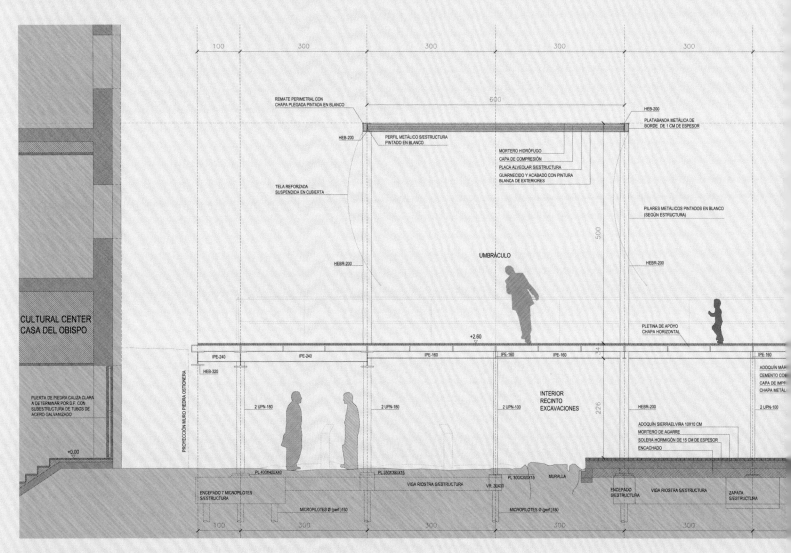

CULTURAL CENTER
CASA DEL OBISPO

PUERTA DE PIEDRA CALIZA CLARA
A DETERMINAR POR D.F. CON
SUBESTRUCTURA DE TUBOS DE
ACERO GALVANIZADO

+0,00

REMATE PERIMETRAL CON
CHAPA PLEGADA PINTADA EN BLANCO

PERFIL METÁLICO S/ESTRUCTURA
PINTADO EN BLANCO

HEB-200

TELA REFORZADA
SUSPENDIDA EN CUBIERTA

HEBR-200

UMBRÁCULO

+2,60

HEB-200

PLATABANDA METÁLICA DE
BORDE DE 1 CM DE ESPESOR

MORTERO HIDRÓFUGO
CAPA DE COMPRESIÓN
PLACA ALVEOLAR S/ESTRUCTURA
GUARNECIDO Y ACABADO CON PINTURA
BLANCA DE EXTERIORES

PILARES METÁLICOS PINTADOS EN BLANCO
(SEGÚN ESTRUCTURA)

HEBR-200

PLETINA DE APOYO
CHAPA HORIZONTAL

600

500

PROYECCIÓN MURO PIEDRA OSTIONERA

IPE-240   IPE-240   IPE-160   IPE-160   IPE-160   IPE-160

HEB-320

2 UPN-180   2 UPN-180   2 UPN-100   INTERIOR
                                                      RECINTO
                                                      EXCAVACIONES

HEBR-200

ADOQUÍN MAR
CEMENTO CO
CAPA DE IMPR
CHAPA METÁL

2 UPN-100

ADOQUÍN SIERRAELVIRA 10X10 CM
MORTERO DE AGARRE
SOLERA HORMIGÓN DE 15 CM DE ESPESOR
ENCACHADO

226

PL 400X400X40   PL 350X350X15   PL 300X300X15   MURALLA

ENCEPADO 7 MICROPILOTES
S/ESTRUCTURA

VIGA RIOSTRA S/ESTRUCTURA   VR 30X30

MICROPILOTES Ø (perf.)150

ENCEPADO
S/ESTRUCTURA

VIGA RIOSTRA S/ESTRUCTURA

ZAPATA
S/ESTRUCTURA

MICROPILOTES Ø (perf.)150

100   300   300   300   300

100   300   300   300   300

constructive section

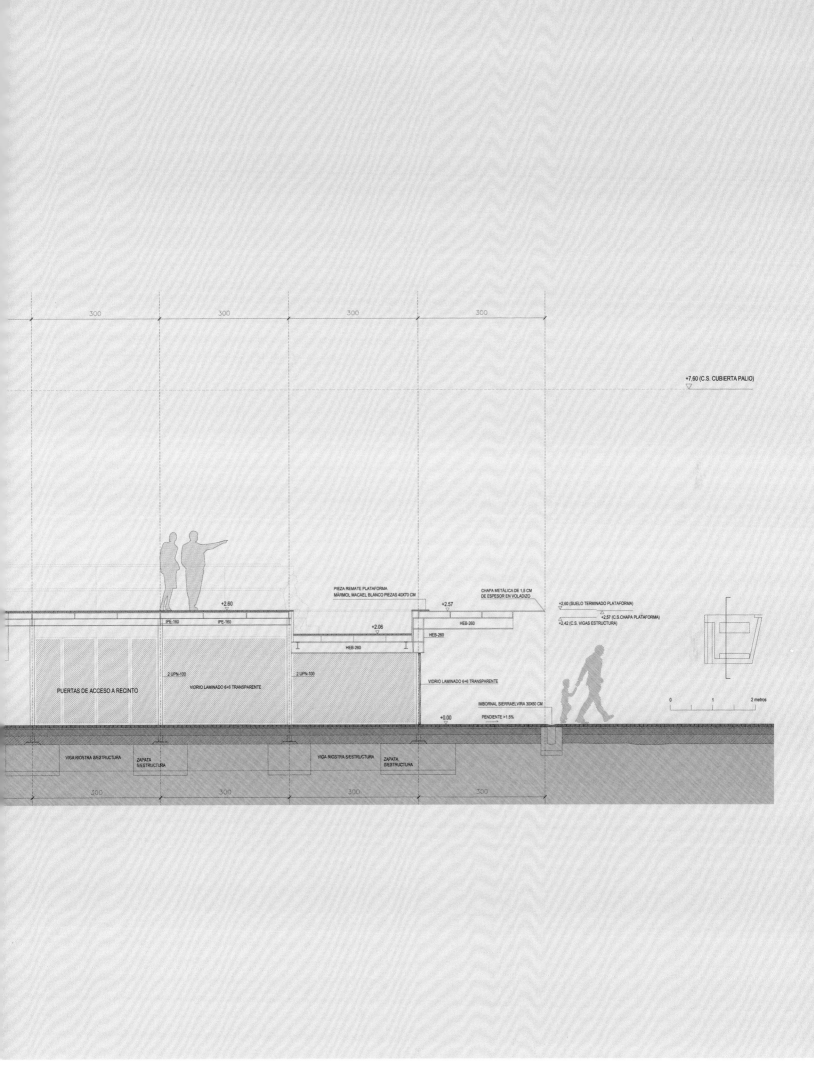

300   300   300   300

+7,60 (C.S. CUBIERTA PALIO)

PIEZA REMATE PLATAFORMA
MÁRMOL MACAEL BLANCO PIEZAS 40X70 CM

CHAPA METÁLICA DE 1,5 CM
DE ESPESOR EN VOLADIZO

+2,60 (SUELO TERMINADO PLATAFORMA)
+2,57 (C.S.CHAPA PLATAFORMA)
+2,42 (C.S. VIGAS ESTRUCTURA)

+2,60

+2,57

IPE-160   IPE-160

HEB-260

+2,06

HEB-260

HEB-260

2 UPN-100

2 UPN-100

PUERTAS DE ACCESO A RECINTO

VIDRIO LAMINADO 6+6 TRANSPARENTE

VIDRIO LAMINADO 6+6 TRANSPARENTE

IMBORNAL SIERRAELVIRA 30X60 CM

+0,00

PENDIENTE >1,5%

VIGA RIOSTRA S/ESTRUCTURA

ZAPATA
S/ESTRUCTURA

VIGA RIOSTRA S/ESTRUCTURA

ZAPATA
S/ESTRUCTURA

300   300   300   300

0   1   2 metros

Work:
Between Cathedrals

Location:
Avenida Campo del Sur - Barrio del Pópulo,
Cádiz, Spain.

Client:
Ayuntamiento de Cádiz

Project:
2006

Built:
2010

Area:
1,000 m²

Collaborators:
Ignacio Aguirre, Emilio Delgado

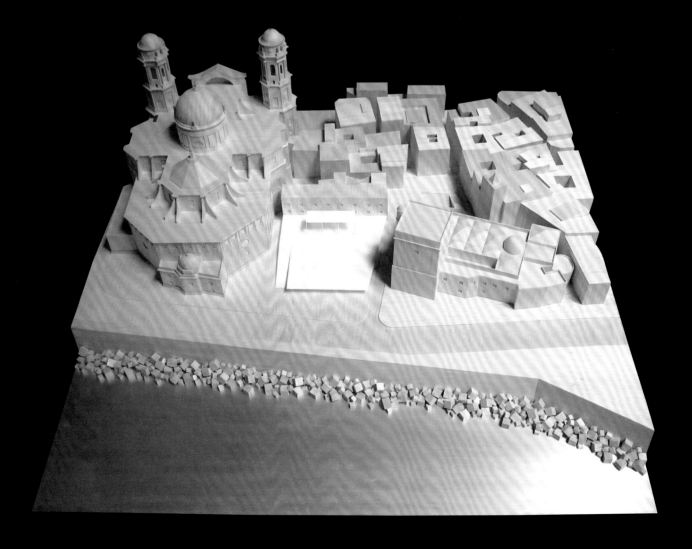

Andalucía
Mu

Andalucía's Museum of Memory

Granada, 2009

SPREADING THE MESSAGE

We would like to make "the most beautiful building" for the Museo de la Memoria de Andalucía (Andalucía's Museum of Memory) in Granada.

The MA. A museum that wishes to transmit the entire history of Andalucía. As early as Roman times, Strabo described the inhabitants of Andalucía as "the most cultivated of the Iberians, who have laws in verse."

Our project for the MA is a building in line with the central headquarters of the Caja Granada Savings Bank that we finished in 2001. We propose a podium building measuring 60 x 120 m and rising three stories, so that its upper floor coincides with the podium of the main Caja Granada building and its facade as well. Everything is arranged around a central courtyard, in elliptical form—in which circular ramps rise, connecting the three levels and creating a very interesting spatial tension. The dimensions of the elliptical courtyard have been taken from the courtyard of the Palace of Charles V in the Alhambra.

And to crown it all, as if it were a gate to the city, a strong vertical piece emerges, the same height and width as the main building of the Caja Granada Savings Bank. It thus appears before the highway that circles Granada as a screen-facade that sends messages over the large plasma screens that will cover it entirely. Like Piccadilly Circus in London or Times Square in New York.

Previous spread. Patio and ramp.
Right. Exterior view with Sierra Nevada in the background.
Following spread. Patio and ramp.

And to finish the entire operation, a large horizontal platform all the way to the river, the MA's open field that will serve as a public space in that new area of the city of Granada.

—

Above. Screen building. South facade.
Below. Southwest facade. Caja Granada Savings Bank on the right.

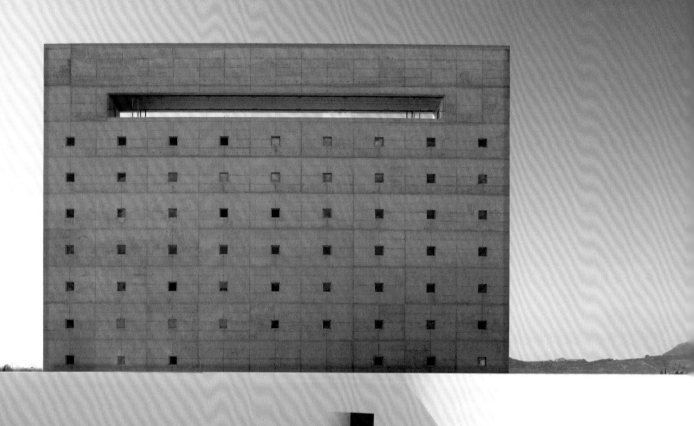

The new building, silent in its forms, is resounding in its elements, to communicate the messages of the new millennium in which we are already immersed.

—

Left. Patio. Screen building in the background.
Below. Screen building in the background.
Following spread. Patio and ramp. Caja Granada Savings Bank building in the background.

Above. Panoramic restaurant in screen building.
Right. Screen building. Northwest facade.

Above. Panoramic restaurant in screen building.

Above left. Museum. Exit to the patio.
Above right. Theater.
Below. Museum. Window to the patio.
Following spread. Museum. Exhibition area.

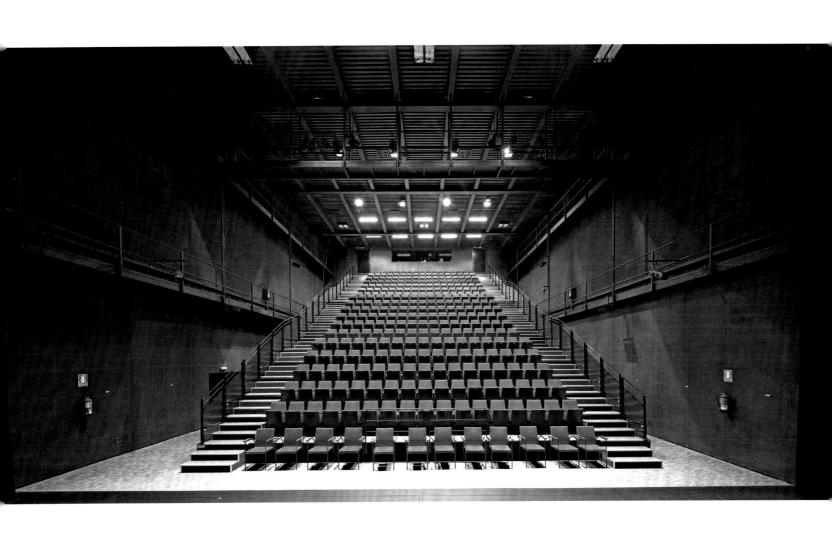

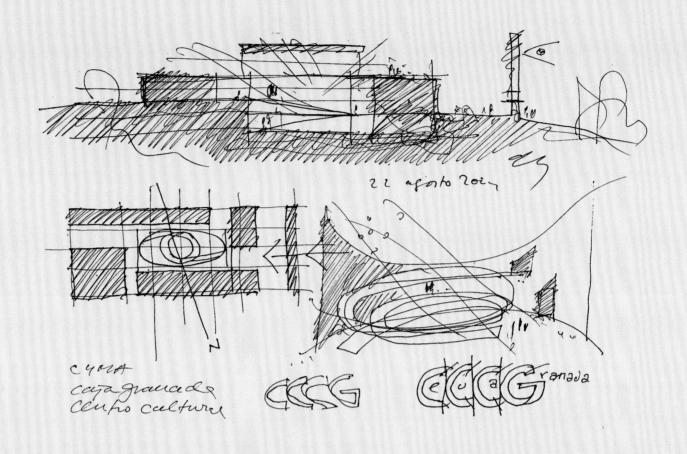

22 agosto 2024

CYQZA
caja granada
Centro Cultural

CCCG

CCCG Granada

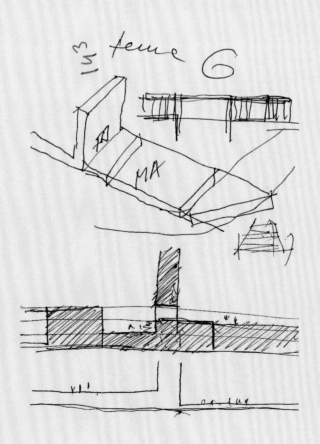

tema 6

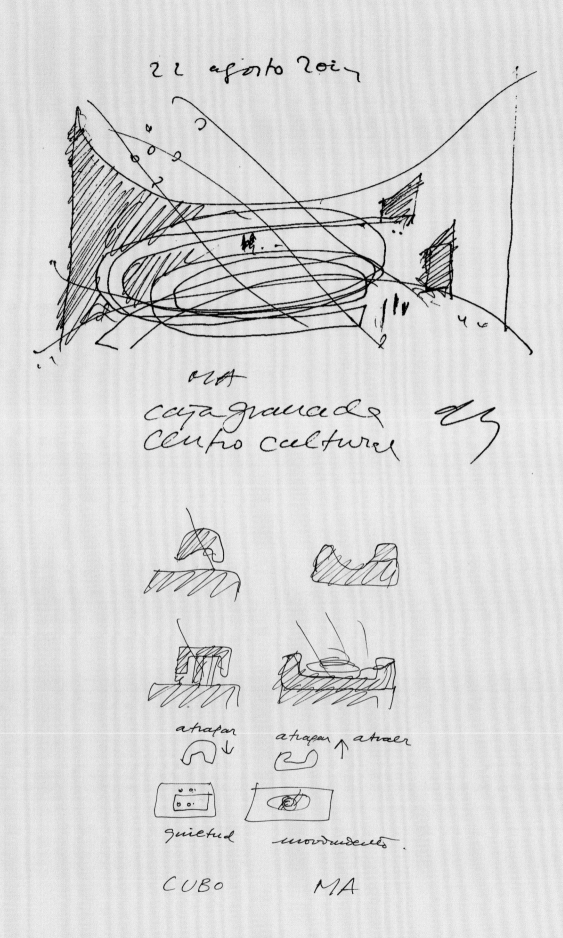

22 agosto 2014

CAJA
caja granada
centro cultural

atrapar   atrapar   atraer

quietud   movimiento

CUBO   MA

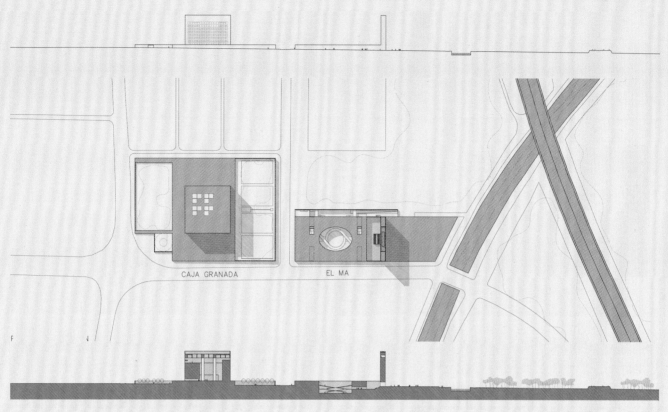

site plan

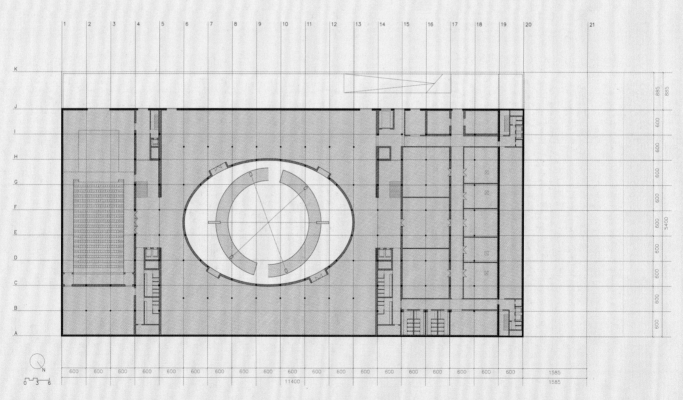

landscape floor plan

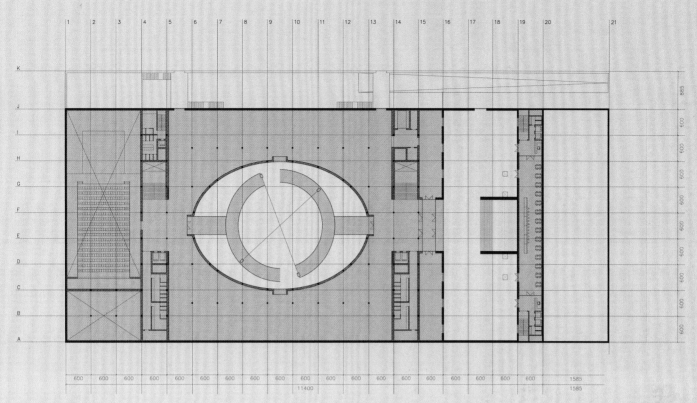

ground floor plan

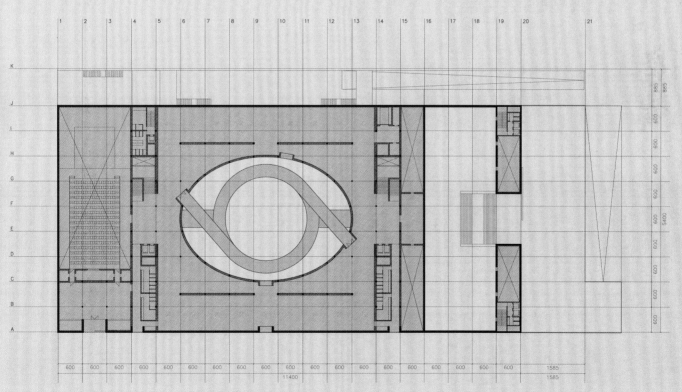

first floor plan

321

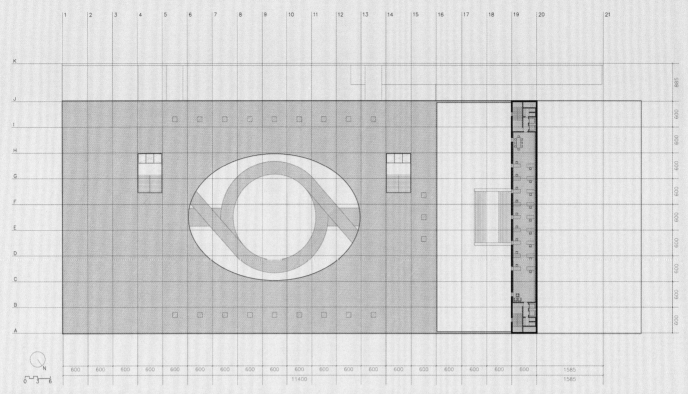

roofed podium plan

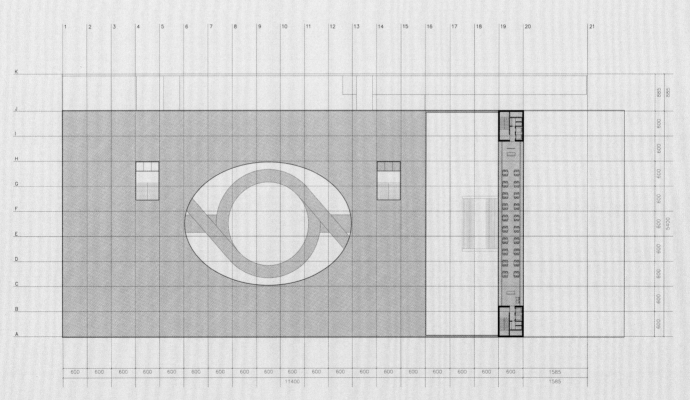

observation level plan

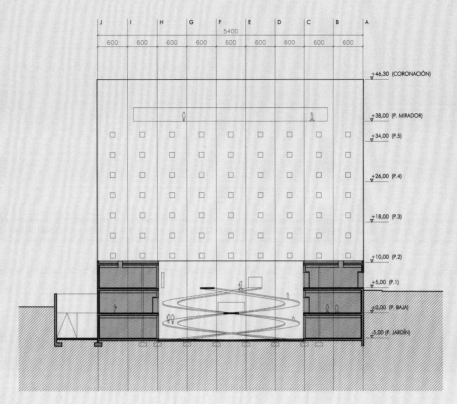

cross section

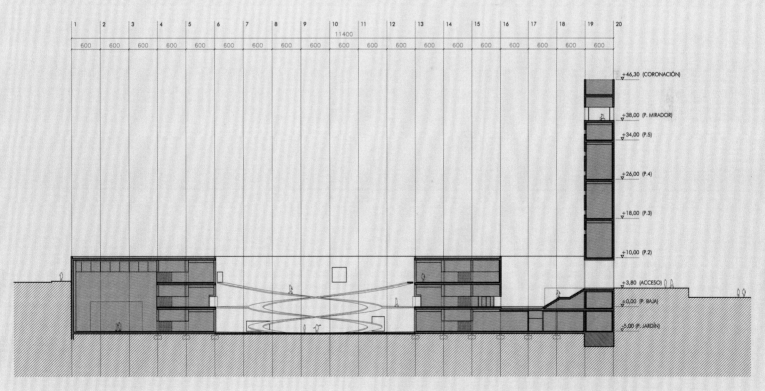

longitudinal section

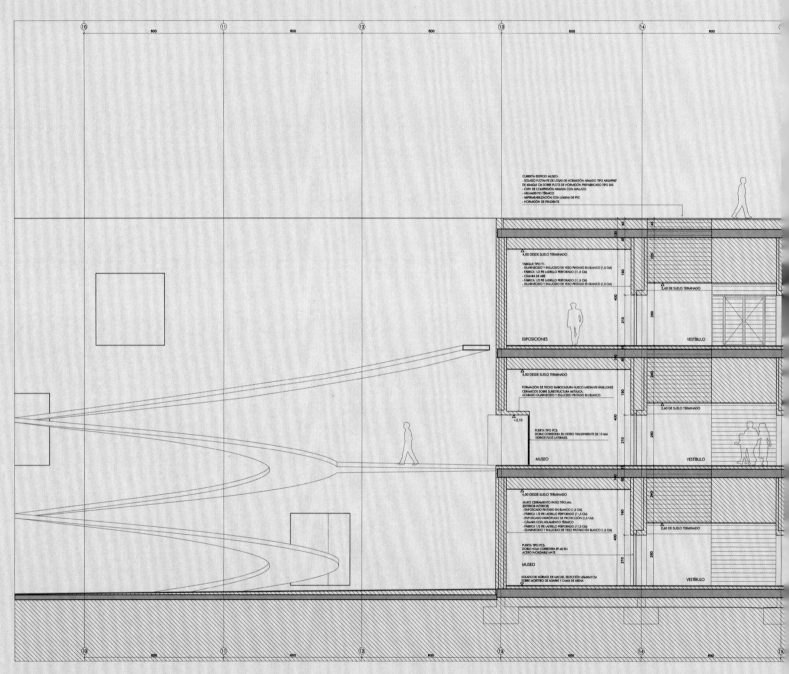

longitudinal section

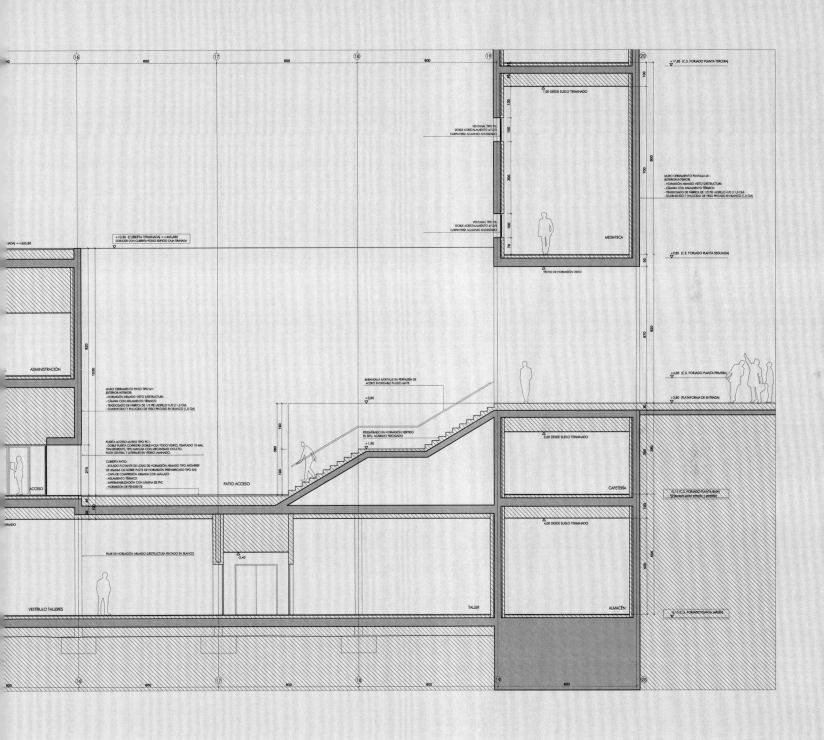

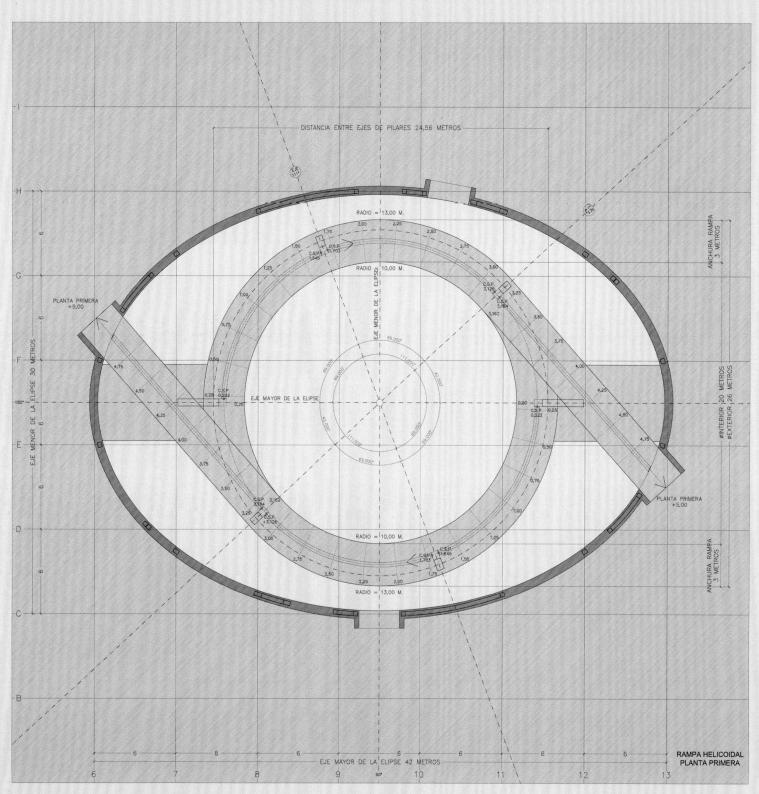

DISTANCIA ENTRE EJES DE PILARES 24,56 METROS

RADIO = 13,00 M.

RADIO = 10,00 M.

EJE MENOR DE LA ELIPSE

EJE MAYOR DE LA ELIPSE

PLANTA PRIMERA +5,00

PLANTA PRIMERA +5,00

RADIO = 10,00 M.

RADIO = 13,00 M.

EJE MENOR DE LA ELIPSE 30 METROS

ANCHURA RAMPA 3 METROS

ANCHURA RAMPA 3 METROS

ØINTERIOR 20 METROS
ØEXTERIOR 26 METROS

EJE MAYOR DE LA ELIPSE 42 METROS

**RAMPA HELICOIDAL
PLANTA PRIMERA**

first floor ramp plan

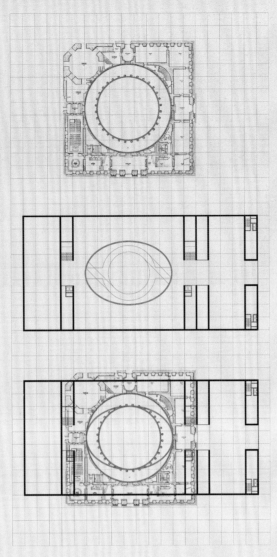

MA museum and Palace of Charles V (Alhambra)

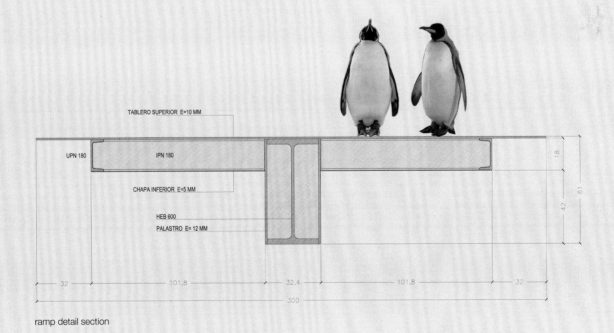

TABLERO SUPERIOR E=10 MM

UPN 180   IPN 180

CHAPA INFERIOR E=5 MM

HEB 600
PALASTRO E= 12 MM

32   101,8   32,4   101,8   32

300

ramp detail section

Work:
Andalucía's Museum of Memory

Location:
Avenida de las Ciencias, s/n, Granada, Spain

Client:
Caja Granada

Project:
2006

Built:
2009

Area:
15,000 m²

Collaborators:
Alejandro Cervilla, Ignacio Aguirre

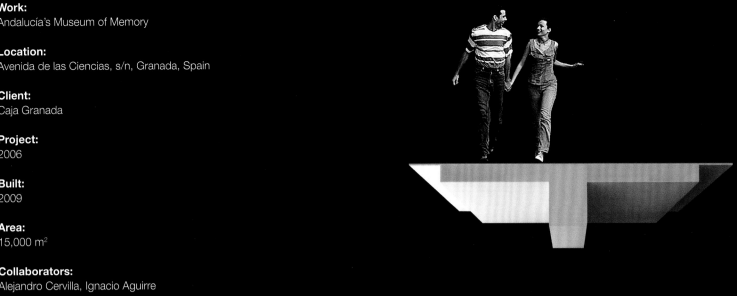

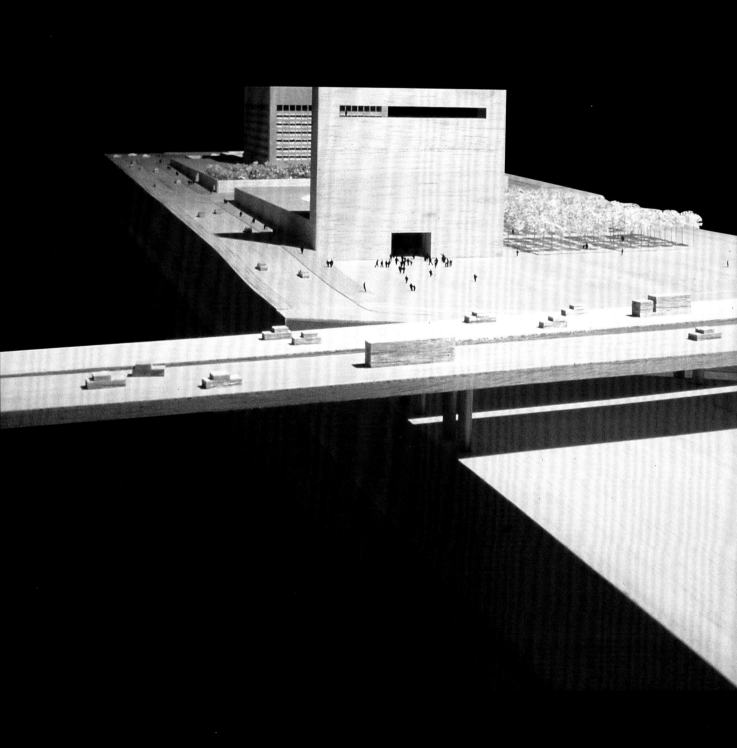

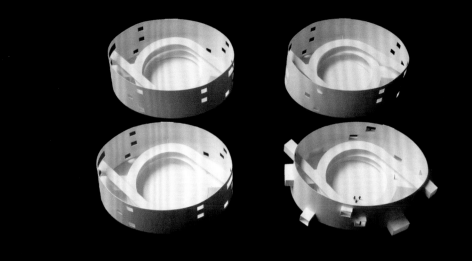

Rufo House

Rufo House
Toledo, 2010

The brief was to build a house on a hilltop outside of the city of Toledo. The hill faces southwest and offers interesting views of the distant horizon, reaching the Gredos Mountains to the northeast. The site measures 60 x 40 m and has a 10-meter slope.

At the highest point, we established a longitudinal podium, 6 m wide and 3 m high, that extends the entire length of the site from side to side. All of the house's functions are developed inside of this long box, the length of concrete creating a long horizontal platform up high, as if it were a jetty that underlines the landscape with tremendous force.

This long concrete box is perforated and cut into, conveniently creating objects and voids to appropriately accommodate the requested functions (courtyard + covered courtyard, kitchen, living room, dining room, hall, bedroom, courtyard + courtyard, bedroom, garage, swimming pool, bedroom, courtyard).

In this distribution, the living-dining room opens to the garden while the bedrooms face onto courtyards open to the sky and garden, affording them the necessary privacy. The stairway connecting the upper floor is situated in the area behind the living-dining room.

Previous spread. Partial view from the southwest.
Right. Exterior view from the south.
Below. Snow-covered view of the building.
Following spread. Partial view from the northeast.

Below left. Exterior view of the front.
Below right. View of the surrounding landscape with the swimming pool in the foreground.

On top of the podium and aligned with it, is a canopy:
ten concrete columns with a square section supporting
a simple flat roof, as if it were a table with ten legs.
Under this roof, behind the columns, is a delicate glass
box. To protect the views of the house from the back,
a simple row of poplars was planted.

—

Above. View from the garden.
Right above. View from the rear patio.
Right below. View from the rear patio with the garden-access door opened.

Above. Interior view with the landscape in the background.

Above. Glass box.
Below. Glass box with the stairs in the foreground.
Right. Interior view of the glass box.

Above. Exterior view of the glass box.

Above. Exterior view from the northeast.
Below. Exterior view of the rear.

Once again, the theme of the hut on top of the cave.
Once again, the theme of a tectonic architecture over
a stereotomic architecture.

___

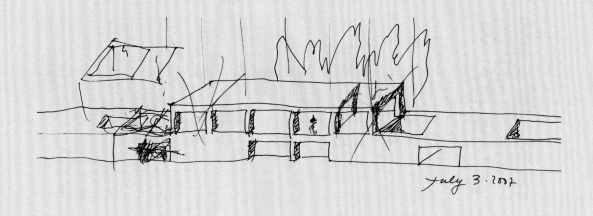

July 3 . 2007

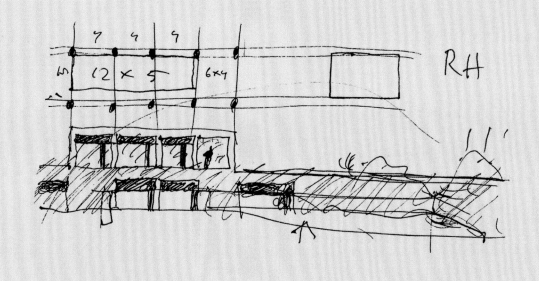

RH

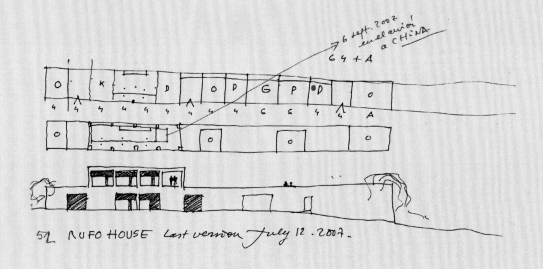

52 RUFO HOUSE Last version July 12 . 2007.

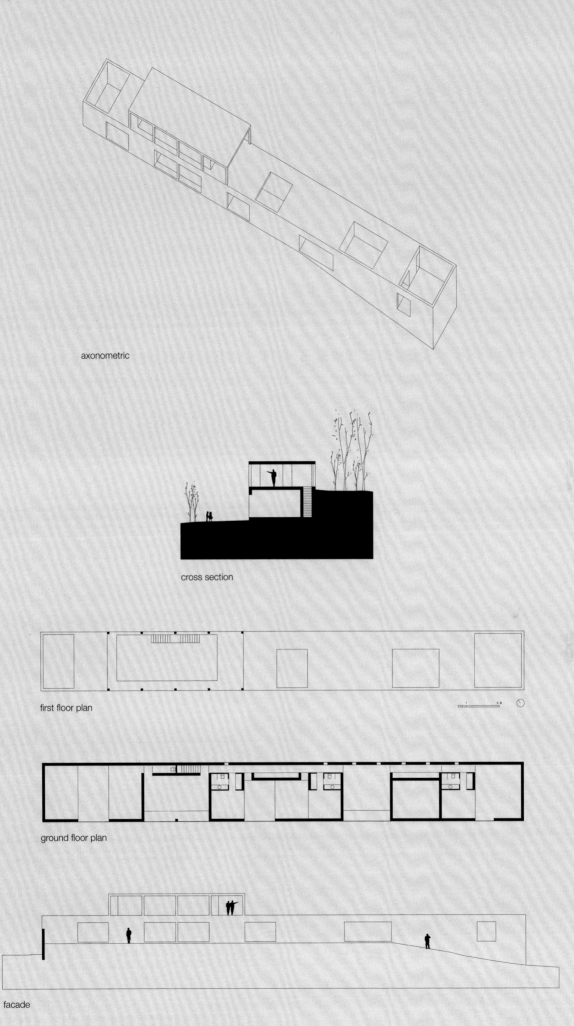

axonometric

cross section

first floor plan

ground floor plan

facade

Work:
Rufo House

Location:
Brezo, parcela 158, Urb. Montesión,
Toledo, Spain

Client:
Rufino Delgado Mateos

Project:
2008

Built:
2009

Area:
200 m²

Collaborators:
Raúl Martínez, Petter Palander

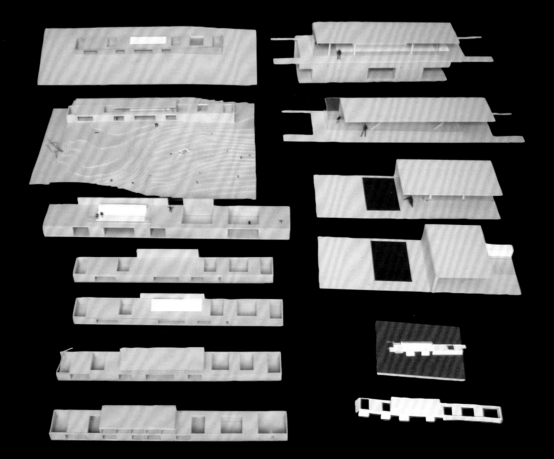

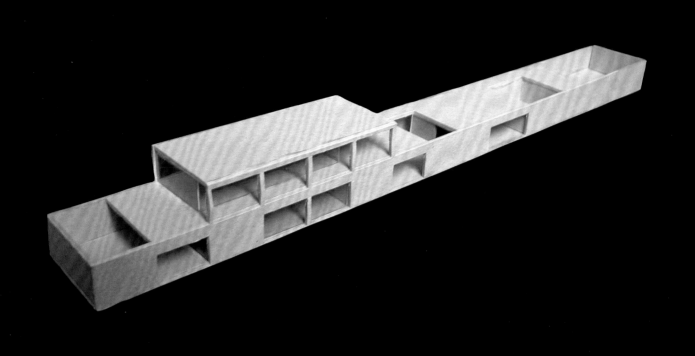

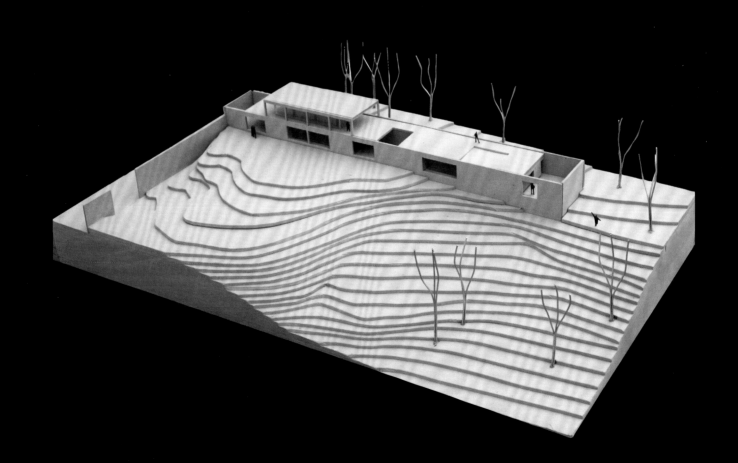

Olnick Spanu House

Olnick Spanu House

Garrison, New York, 2008

GILDING THE LILY

This is a place of profound tranquility where, after a day of rain and fog, an intense light reflects in the stilled mirror of the majestic Hudson River's deep waters.

A place where twilights are a thousand colors as the water breaks into a thousand reflections. A place where the air is clean and calm and mild. One could say a place that is very close to heaven.

In this impressive place, we establish a plane, a platform that underlines the landscape before us, seeking to enhance it.

A large long box is thus built, 37 m long by 17 m wide by 4 m high, with sturdy concrete walls that accentuate its relationship to the land. The roof of this box is flat, paved in stone, travertine, so that we may use it.

And to protect ourselves from the sun and rain, over the stone plane we raise a light roof 30 m long by 12 m wide by 3 m tall, held by 10 cylindrical steel pillars that are arranged according to a 6 x 6 m grid. This roof cantilevers 3 m along all of its sides. And to make this space habitable, we put a glass box under the roof, an enclosure measuring 28 m long by 7 m wide. This glass box contains the back row of columns within it and leaves the front columns outside, in order to further accentuate its transparency.

Previous spread. Exterior view of the glass box from the northeast.
Right. Main access.

Above. Exterior view with the platform.
Below. External view from the southwest.
Right. View of the house with the surrounding landscape.

Below. Interior view with the surrounding woods.
Following spread. Interior view with the platform and the landscape.

This construction on the platform resembles a large table with ten legs. Three areas are created within it, divided by two white boxes that do not reach the ceiling, containing the stairs and service spaces.

—

Below, the bedrooms and baths are housed inside the cement box. In its central vestibule, connecting the main entrance and the access to the garden, a gallery has been created where pieces of Arte Povera and other contemporary Italian art are displayed, in addition to other areas around the house.

In all, once again, the hut over the cave. The tectonic piece on top of the stereotomic piece.

Left above. Interior view of the dining room.
Left. Interior view of the living room.
Above. Interior view of a corner of the glass box.
Right. Interior view.
Following spread. Night view from the northeast.

PIECE OF ART.   June 6 ⑧
2003.

Saber fire del PAOLINI.

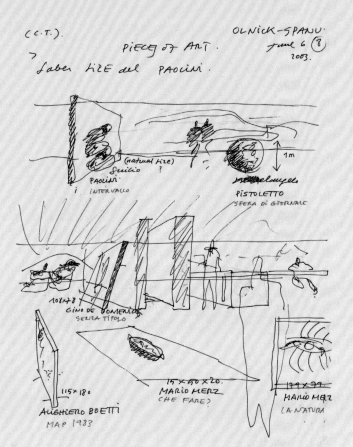

(natural fire)
Guilio ?
PAOLINI
i   INTERVALLO

1m

PISTOLETTO
SFERA DI GIORNALE

108×78
GINO DE DOMENIO
SENZA TITOLO

115×180

15×60×20.
MARIO MERZ
(CHE FARE)

177×77
MARIO MERZ
LA NATURA

ALIGHIERO BOETTI
MAP 1983

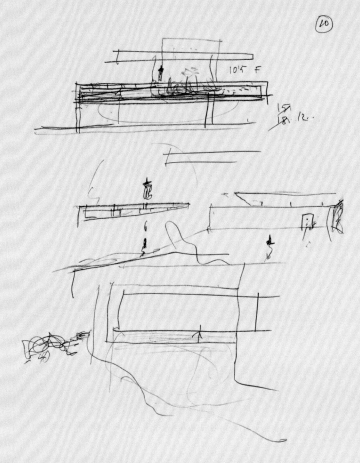

10'5 F

15
18 12.

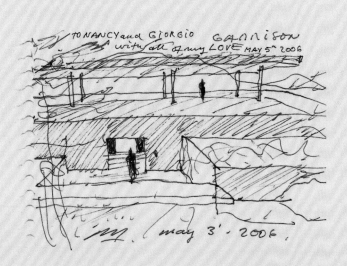

TO NANCY and GIORGIO GARRISON
with all of my LOVE MAY 5th 2006

M. may 3'. 2006.

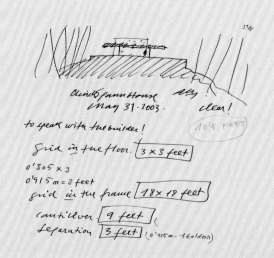

Olnick Spanu House
May 31. 2003.   clear!
                        10'5 FEET

to speak with the builder!

grid in the floor. 3 × 3 feet
0'305 × 3
0'915 m = 3 feet
grid in the frame 18 × 18 feet

cantilever 9 feet

separation 3 feet (0'915m - 16 aldon)

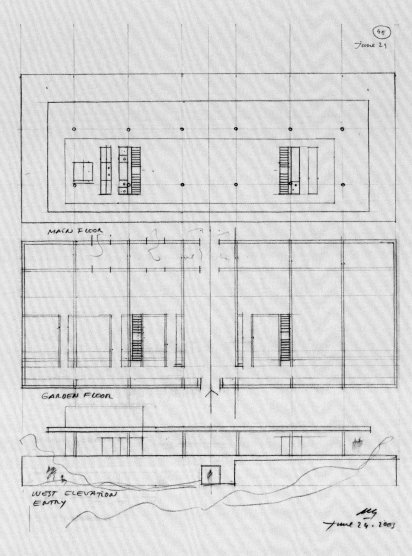

MAIN FLOOR

GARDEN FLOOR

WEST ELEVATION
ENTRY

June 24 . 2003

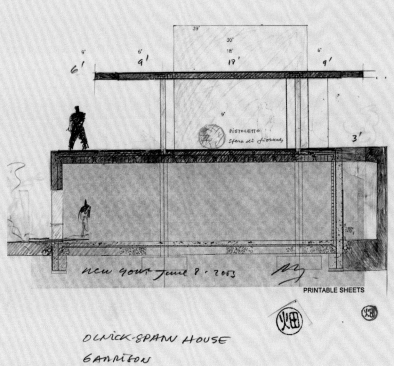

39'
30'
18'
9'
6'
9'   18'   9'
6'

PISTOLETTO
Sfera di Giornale

3'

New York June 8 . 2003

PRINTABLE SHEETS

OLNICK-SPANN HOUSE
GARRISON

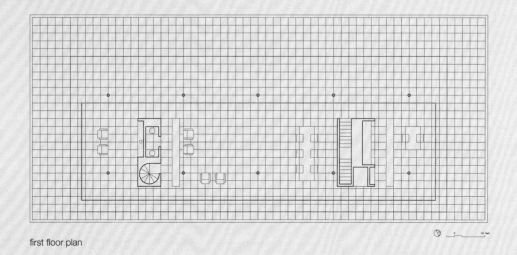

first floor plan

ground floor plan

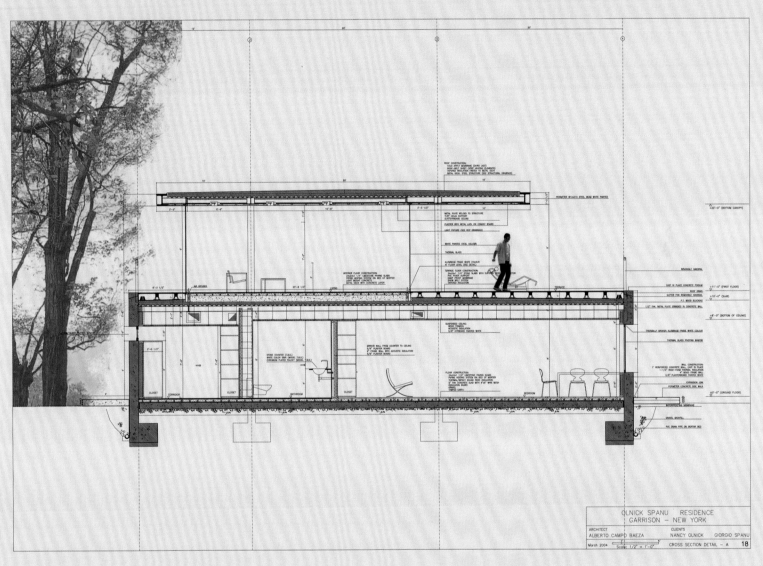

constructive section

OLNICK SPANU   RESIDENCE
GARRISON — NEW YORK

ARCHITECT   CLIENTS
ALBERTO CAMPO BAEZA   NANCY OLNICK   GIORGIO SPANU

March 2004   Scale: 1/2" = 1'-0"   CROSS SECTION DETAIL — A   18

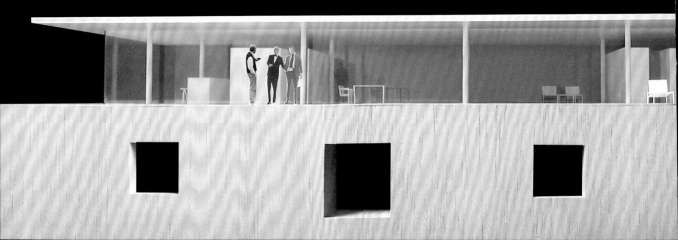

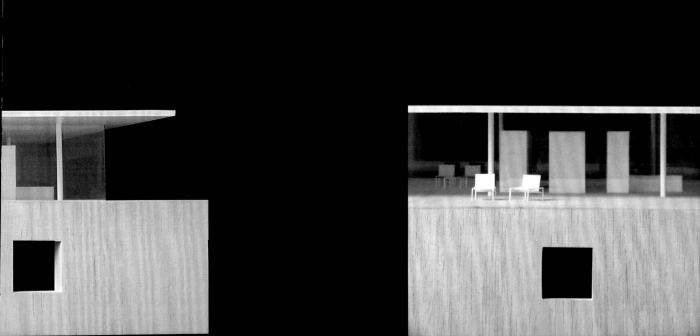

Moliner House

Moliner House

Zaragoza, 2008

To build a house for a poet. To make a house for dreaming, living, and dying. A house in which to read, to write, and to think.

We raised high walls to create a box open to the sky, like a nude metaphysical garden, with concrete walls and floor. To create an interior world. We dug into the ground to plant leafy trees.

And floating in the center, a box filled with the translucent light of the North. Three levels were established. The highest for dreaming. The garden level for living. The deepest level for sleeping.

For dreaming, we created a cloud at the highest point. A library constructed with high walls of light diffused through large translucent glass. With northern light for reading and writing, thinking and feeling.

For living, the garden with southern light, sunlight. A space that is all garden, with transparent walls that bring together inside and outside.

And for sleeping, perhaps dying, the deepest level. The bedrooms below, as if in a cave.

Once again, the cave and the cabin.

Previous spread. External view from the street.
Right. Exterior general view from the east.
Following spread. South facade.

Left. View from a corner.
Below. View of the perimeter wall curved-corner.
Following spread. North facade. Translucent light.

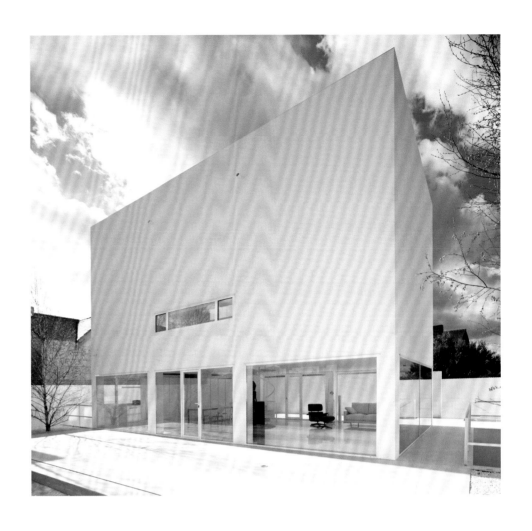

Dreaming, living, dying.
The house of the poet.

———

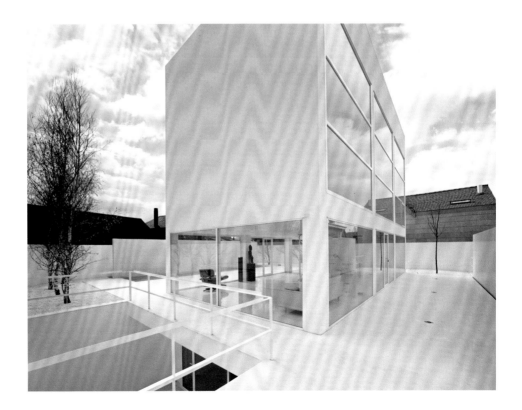

Left. View from the surrounding patio.
Right above. Exterior view. South facade.
Right. View of the northeast corner.

Above. Cross view. Transparency.
Below left. Exterior view.
Below right. View of the staircase.
Following spread. View of the library. Translucent light.

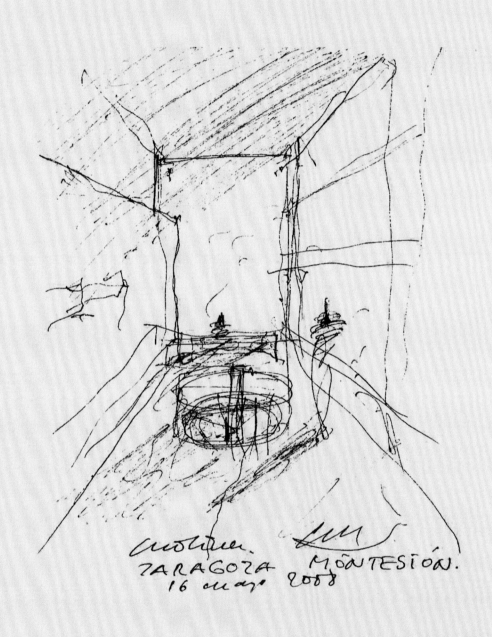

ZARAGOZA   MONTESIÓN.
16 mayo 2008

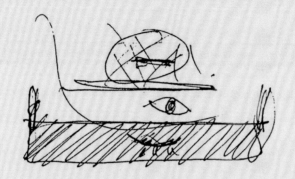

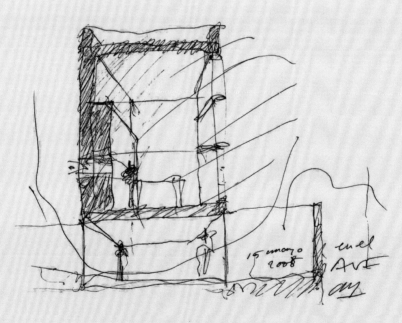

Casa Moliner en Zaragoza

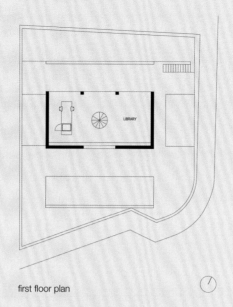

first floor plan

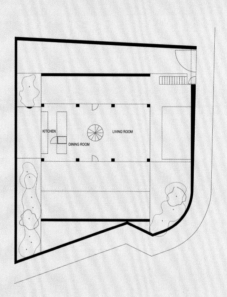

ground floor plan

basement level plan

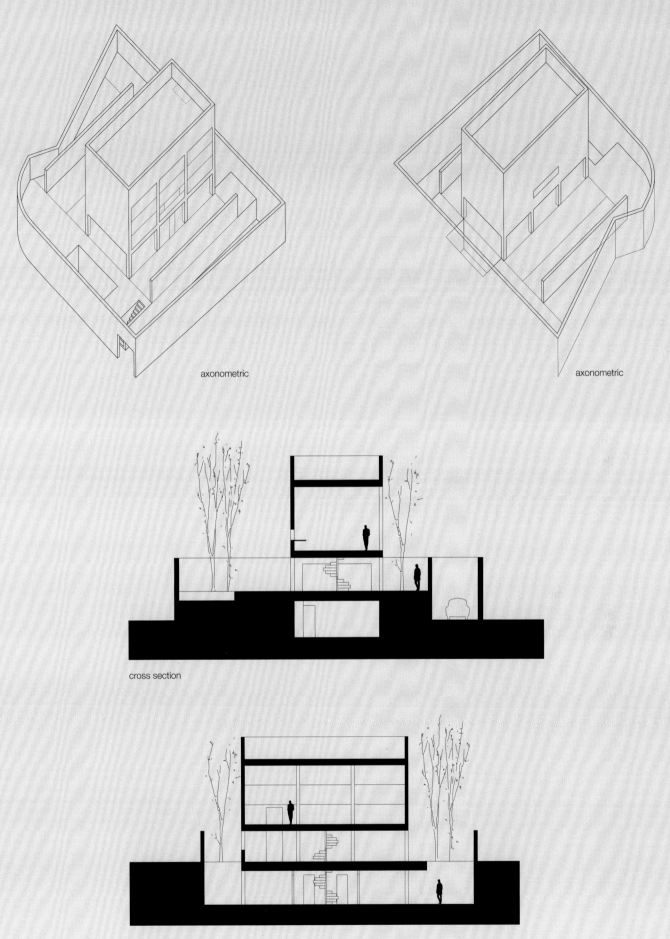

axonometric

axonometric

cross section

longitudinal section

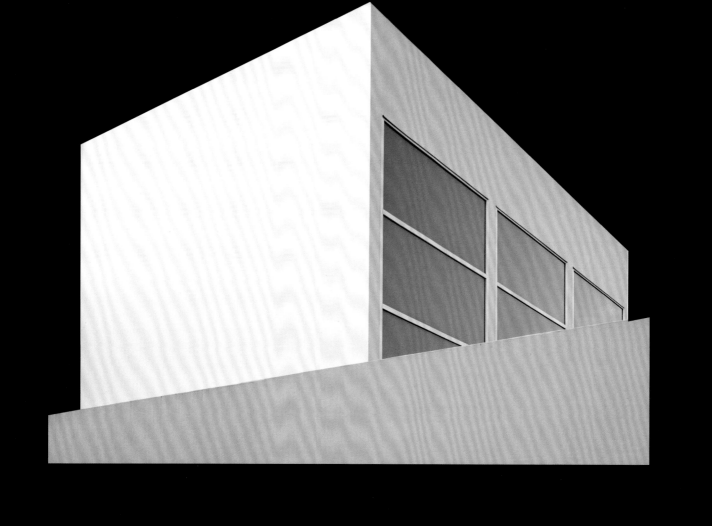

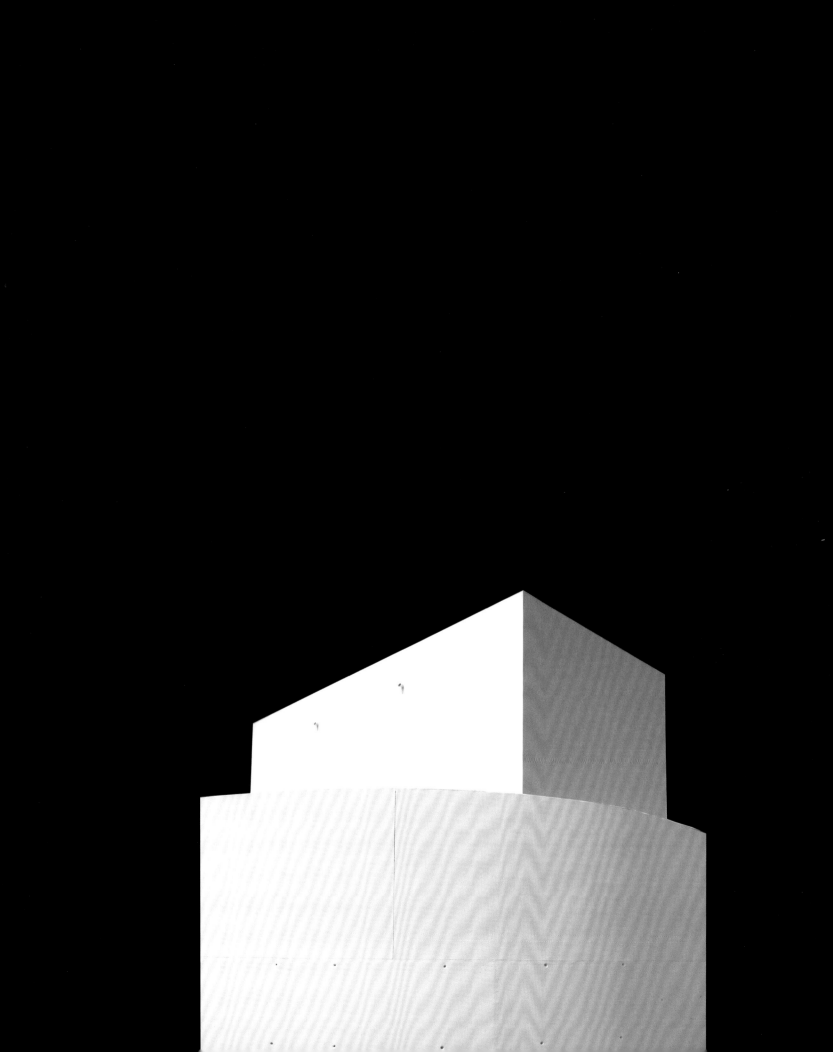

Day Care Center for Benetton

Day Care Center for Benetton

Treviso, Italy, 2007

A BOX OPEN TO THE SKY

We built a square box composed of nine smaller squares. The center square emerges to bring light from the heights of the vestibule. The classrooms are arranged in the surrounding squares.

This square structure is inscribed within a larger circular enclosure made up of double circular walls. Open to the sky, four courtyards are created that suggest the four elements: air, earth, fire, and water.

The space between the perimeter walls serves as a "secret" place for the children. The courtyard spaces, tensed between the curved and the straight walls, are particularly remarkable.

The central space, the highest and with light from above, recalls a hammam in the way it gathers sunlight through nine perforations in the ceiling and three more on each of its four facades.

The children have understood the building well, and a book of their impressions has even been published. They are happy there.

Previous spread. Exterior view with the main access.
Right. Exterior view.

Left. Patio view with sand floor. Patio view with wood floor.
Patio view with stone floor. Patio view with grass floor.
Right above. Patio view with the grass floor.
Right. Patio view with the stone floor.

Above. Patio with children playing.
Right. Exterior view.

The children have understood the building well, and a
book of their impressions has even been published.
They are happy there.

—

Above. View of the patio with the wood floor.
Below. Patio with children playing.
Right above. Exterior view. Canopy and curved wall.

The space between the perimeter walls serves as a "secret" place for the children. The courtyard spaces, tensed between the curved and the straight walls, are particularly remarkable.

—

Above. Main hall.
Below. Exterior night view.
Right. Main hall. Light from the heights.

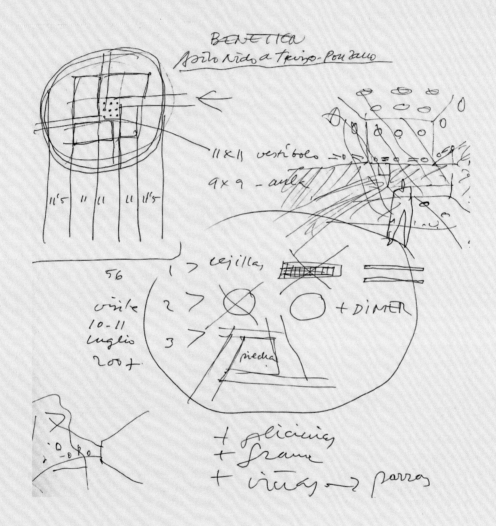

Asilo Nido a Ponzano
Maggio 2002

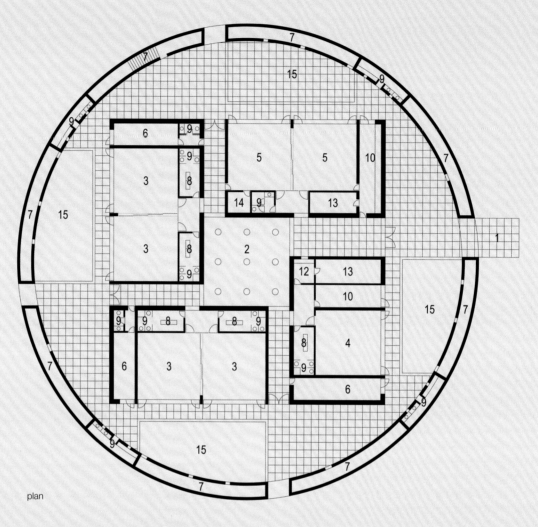

plan

1. entrance
2. hall
3. classroom
4. infants classroom
5. dining room
6. meeting room
7. storage
8. cloakroom
9. bathroom
10. kitchen
11. principal's office
12. janitor's room
13. storeroom
14. laundry
15. dormitory

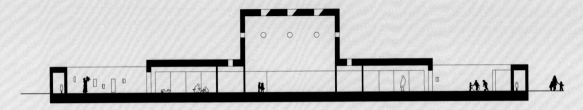

section through hall

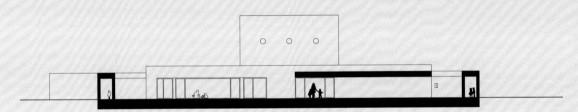

section through yard

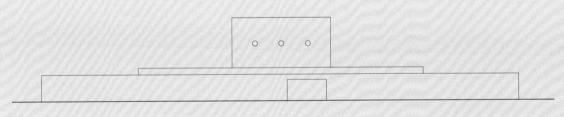

elevation

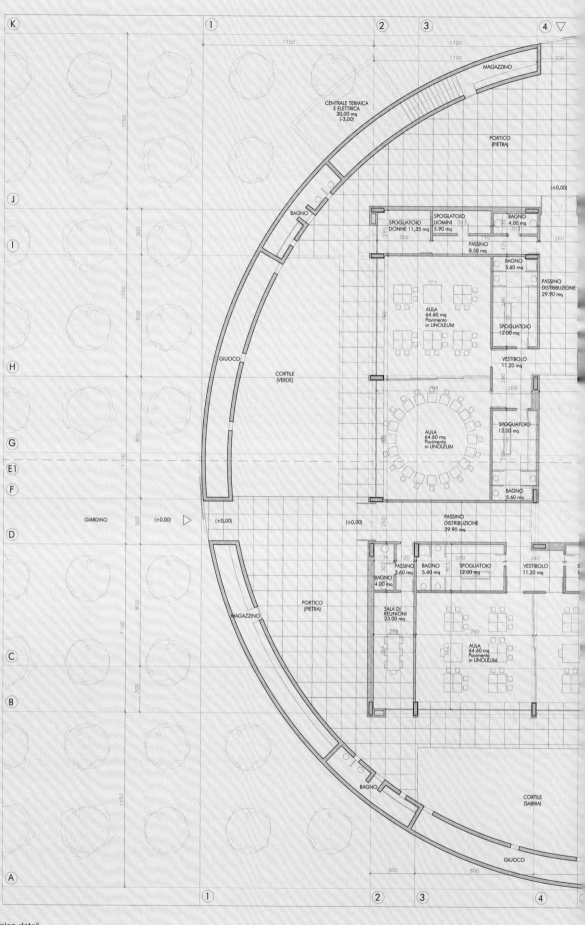

CENTRALE TERMICA
E ELETTRICA
30,00 mq
(-3,00)

MAGAZZINO

PORTICO
(PIETRA)

(±0,00)

BAGNO

SPOGLIATOIO
DONNE 11,35 mq

SPOGLIATOIO
UOMINI 5,90 mq

BAGNO
4,00 mq

PASSINO
8,50 mq

BAGNO
5,60 mq

PASSINO
DISTRIBUZIONE
29,90 mq

GIUOCO

AULA
64,60 mq
Pavimento
in LINOLEUM

SPOGLIATOIO
12,00 mq

CORTILE
(VERDE)

VESTIBOLO
11,20 mq

AULA
64,60 mq
Pavimento
in LINOLEUM

SPOGLIATOIO
12,00 mq

BAGNO
5,60 mq

GIARDINO

(±0,00)

(±0,00)

(±0,00)

PASSINO
DISTRIBUZIONE
29,90 mq

BAGNO
4,00 mq

PASSINO
3,60 mq

BAGNO
5,60 mq

SPOGLIATOIO
12,00 mq

VESTIBOLO
11,20 mq

PORTICO
(PIETRA)

SALA DI
REUNIONI
23,00 mq

MAGAZZINO

AULA
64,60 mq
Pavimento
in LINOLEUM

BAGNO

CORTILE
(SABBIA)

GIUOCO

plan detail

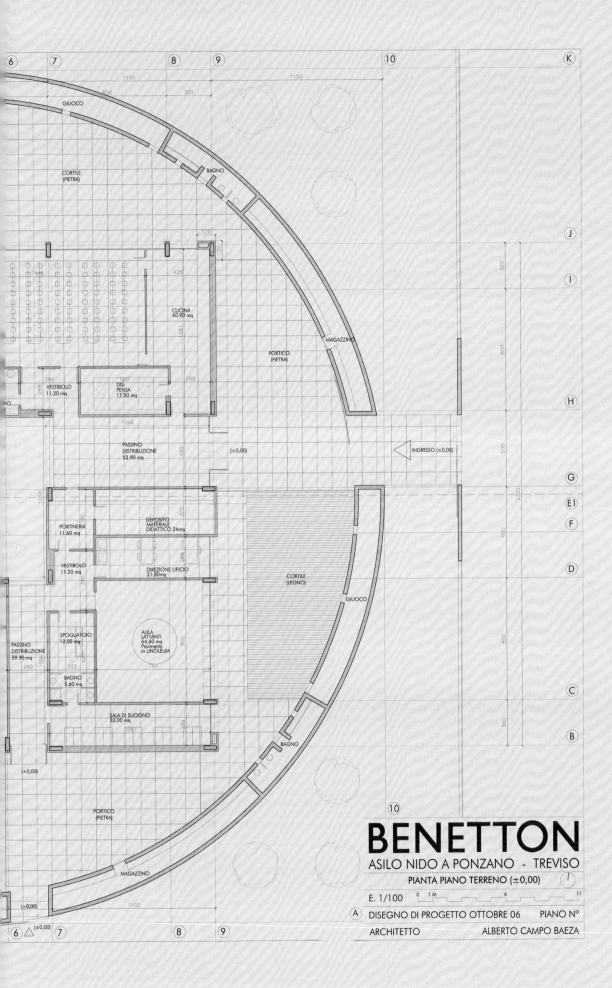

GIUOCO

CORTILE
(PIETRA)

BAGNO

CUCINA
40.90 mq

PORTICO
(PIETRA)

MAGAZZINO

VESTIBOLO
11.20 mq

DIS-
PENSA
17.50 mq

PASSINO
DISTRIBUZIONE
52.90 mq

(±0,00)

◁ INGRESSO (±0,00)

PORTINERIA
11.60 mq

DEPOSITO
MATERIALE
DIDATTICO 24 mq

VESTIBOLO
11.20 mq

DIREZIONE UFICIO
21.80 mq

CORTILE
(LEGNO)

GIUOCO

PASSINO
DISTRIBUZIONE
29.90 mq

SPOGLIATOIO
12.00 mq

AULA
LATTANTI
64.60 mq
Pavimento
in LINOLEUM

BAGNO
5.60 mq

SALA DI SUOGNO
32.00 mq

BAGNO

(±0,00)

PORTICO
(PIETRA)

MAGAZZINO

(±0,00)

△ (±0,00)

BENETTON
ASILO NIDO A PONZANO - TREVISO
PIANTA PIANO TERRENO (±0,00)

E. 1/100   0 1 M   6   11

DISEGNO DI PROGETTO OTTOBRE 06   PIANO N°

ARCHITETTO   ALBERTO CAMPO BAEZA

413

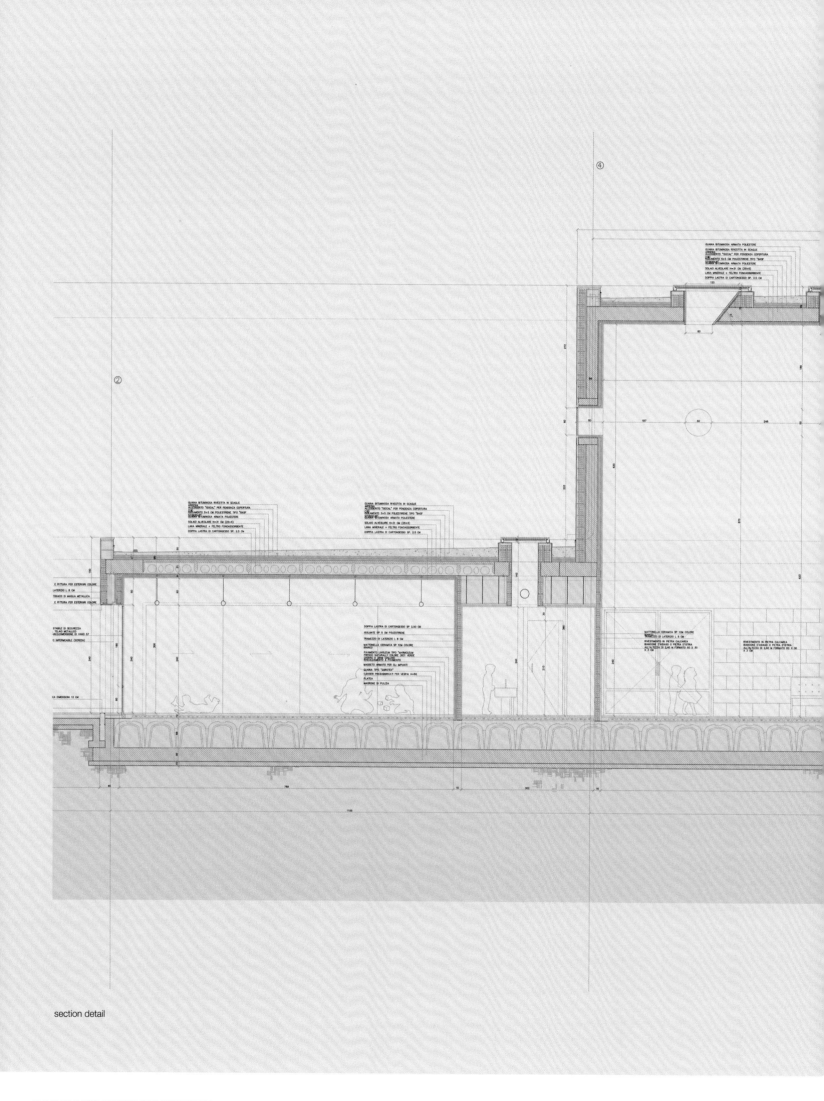

section detail

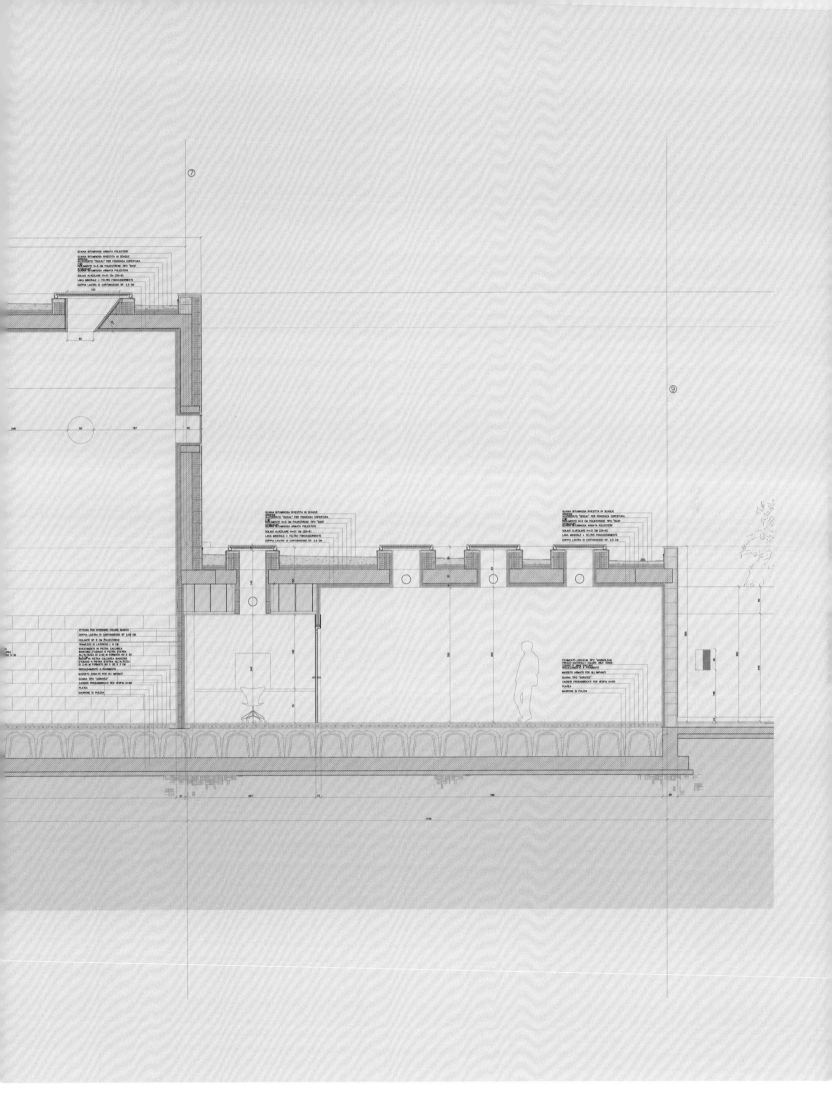

415

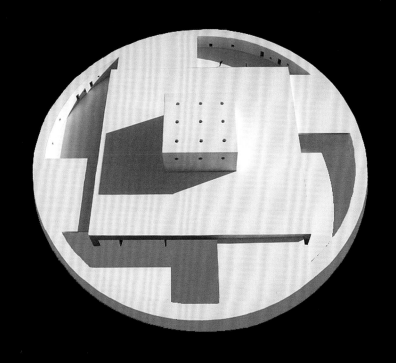
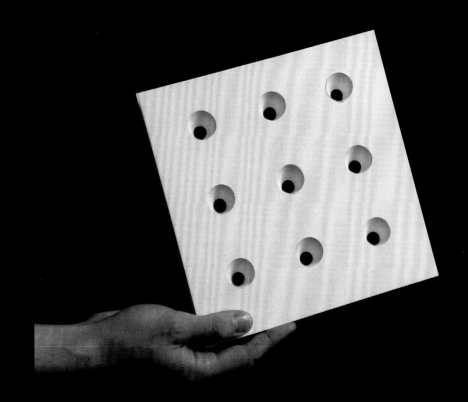

Guerrero House

Guerrero House

Vejer de la Frontera, Cádiz, 2005

To build a well-balanced house full of light and shade.

We built very tall, 8 m high walls around a 33 x 18 m rectangle, and covered the central strip, 9 x 18 m. We raised the ceiling of the 9 x 9 central square to the same height as the 8 m high outside walls. To fill this central space with shade, we opened it to the front and back, creating 3 m deep porches that protect these openings from the sun, tempering the light. To either side, bedrooms and baths.

In the front courtyard, the entrance to the house, four orange trees mark the central and main axis, flanked by low walls that hide service areas. In the back courtyard, another four orange trees are similarly aligned. And at the end, carved into the ground, a trough-like pond stretches from side to side.

Previous spread. **Exterior view.**
Below. **Exterior view.**
Right. **View from the southwest.**

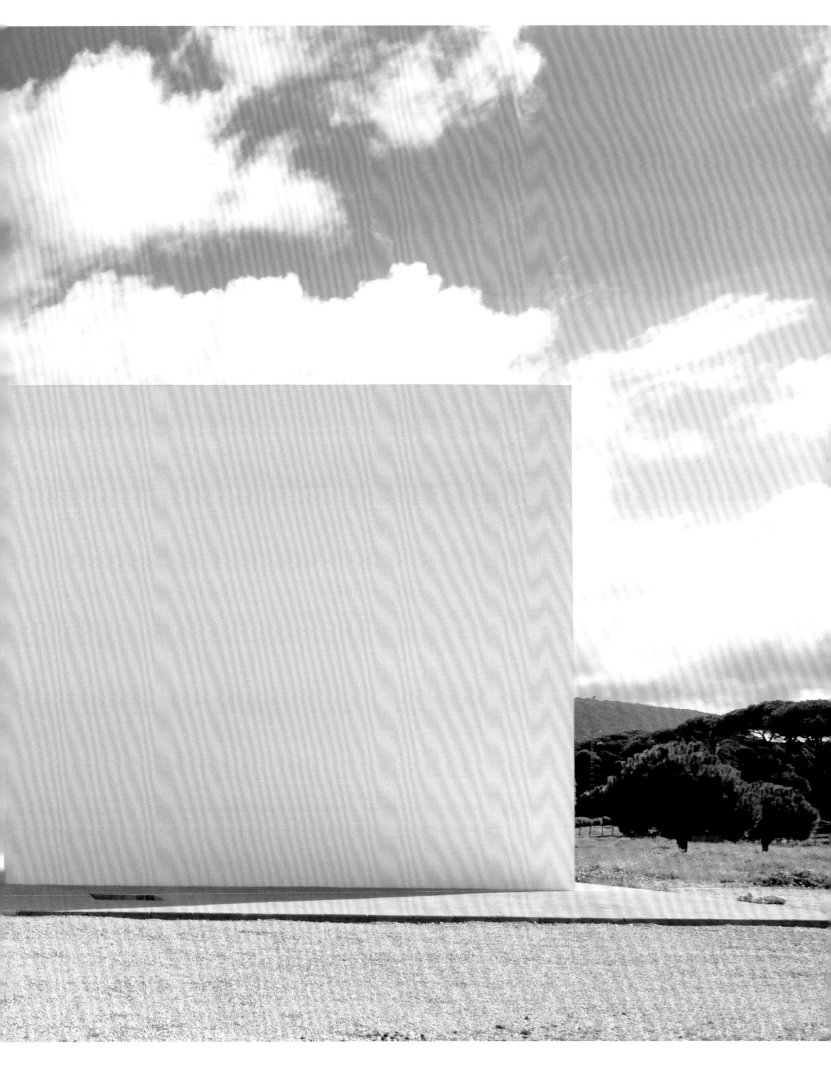

Previous spread. Exterior view with the door opened.
Above. View of the patio with the door opened.
Right. View from the patio. Transparency.

The house is the construction of a luminous shadow.

—

Above. Interior view with main space.
Below. Interior views.

Left. Patio with the orange trees.
Above. Patio exterior view.
Below. View of the main entrance.

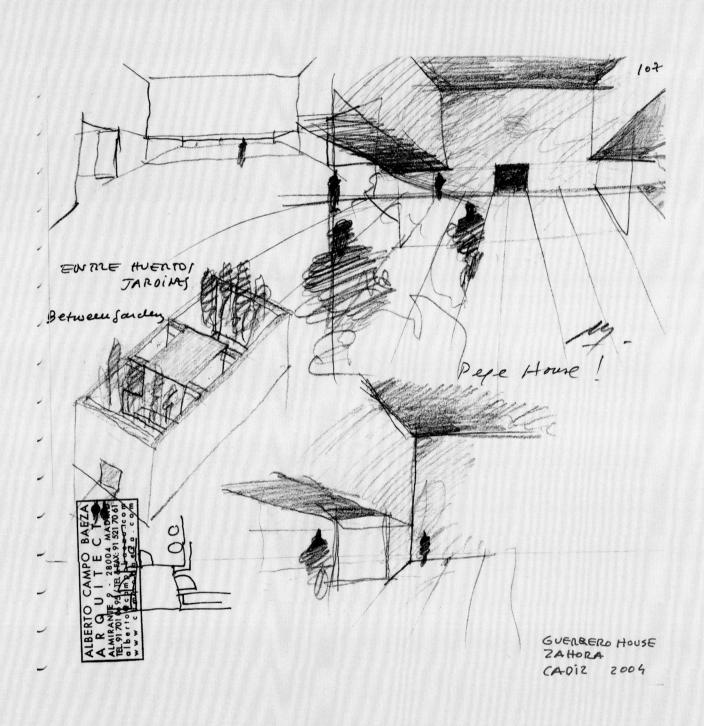

107

ENTRE HUERTOS
JARDINES

Between gardens

Pepe House!

GUERRERO HOUSE
ZAHORA
CADIZ 2004

ALBERTO CAMPO BAEZA
ARQUITECTO
ALMIRANTE 9 - 28004 MADRID
TEL 91 701 06 95 / FAX 91 521 70 61
alberto@cbarrquitectos.com
www.campobaeza.com

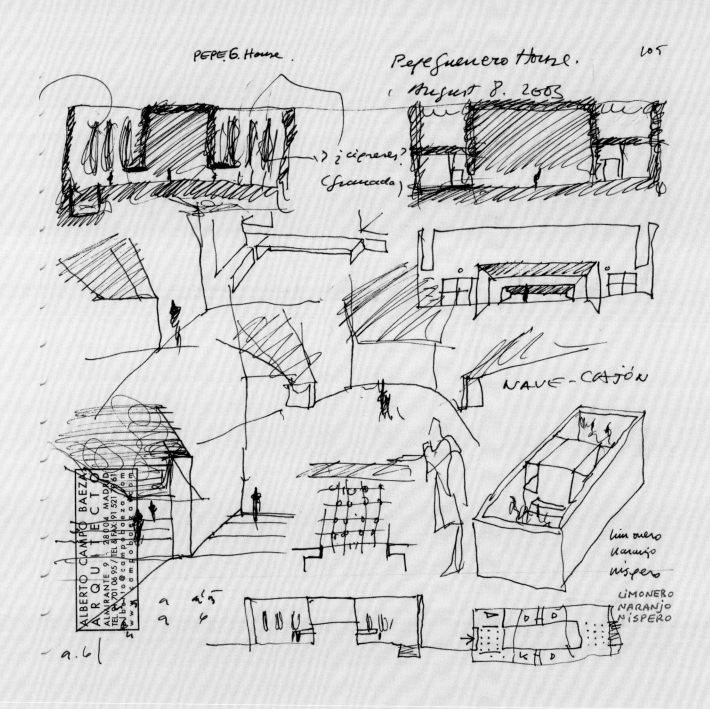

PEPE.G. House.

Pepe Guerrero House.
August 8. 2003

105

¿cipreses?
(Granada)

NAVE-CAJÓN

LIMONERO
NARANJO
NÍSPERO

ALBERTO CAMPO BAEZA
ARQUITECTO
ALMIRANTE 9 . 28004 MADRID
TEL & FAX:91 521 70 61
estudio@campobaeza.com
www.campobaeza.com

a.61

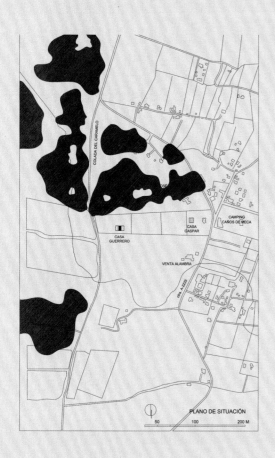

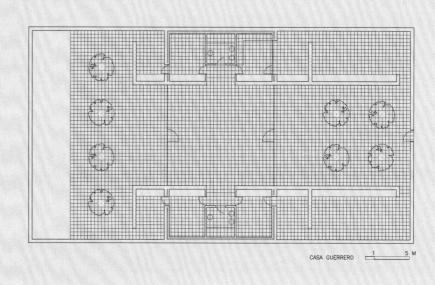

CASA GUERRERO   1   5 M

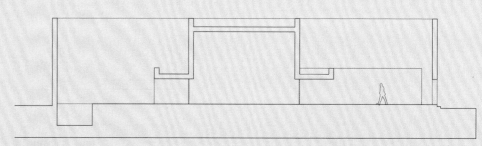

site plan   plan and section

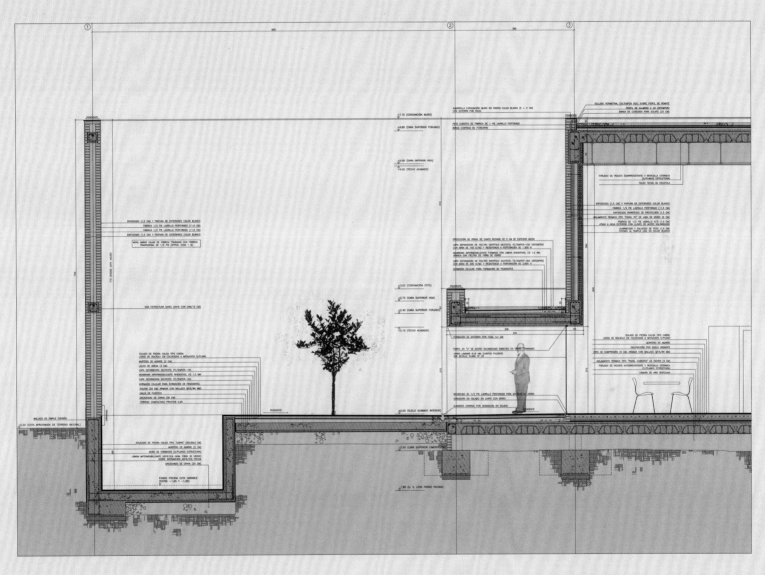

constructive section

Work:
Guerrero House

Location:
Vejer de la Frontera, Cádiz, Spain

Client:
José Guerrero Castro

Project:
2004

Built:
2005

Area:
170 m²

Collaborators:
Ignacio Aguirre, Miguel Vela

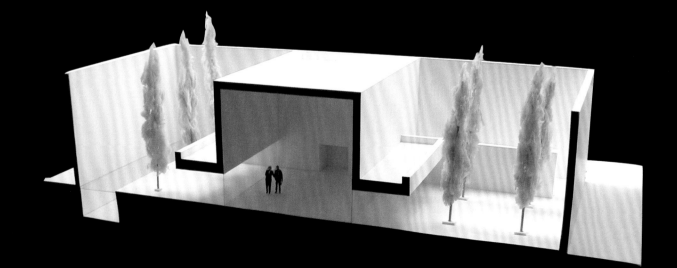

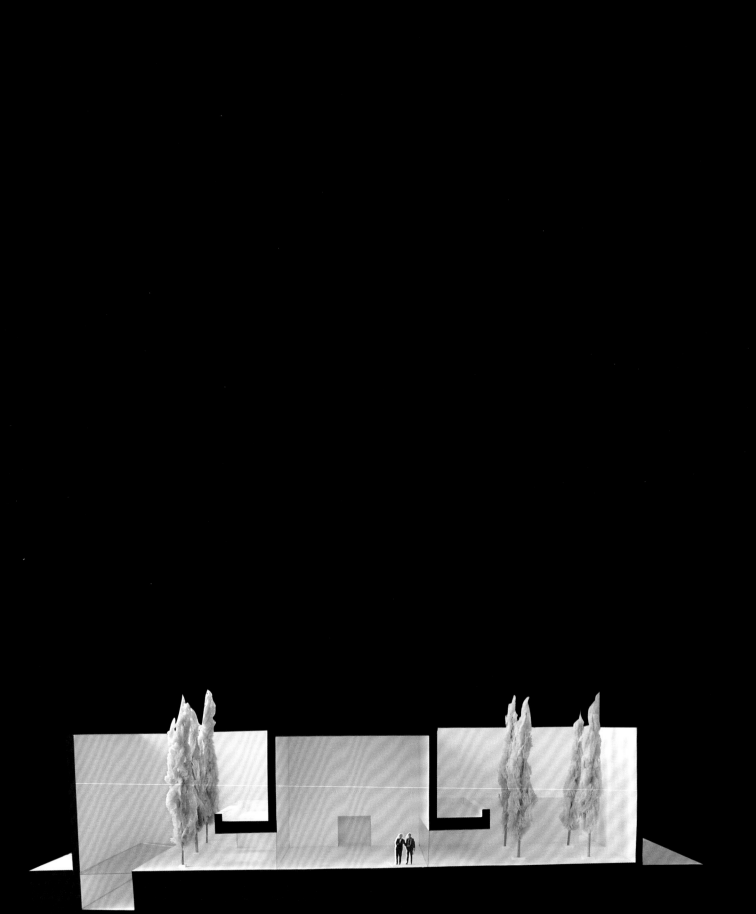

SM Group
Headquarters

SM Group Headquarters

Boadilla del Monte, Madrid, 2003

Like a steel giant lying down. Like a train, like a boat. A building with a metal skin on the edge of the highway.

The headquarters for the SM Group responds well to its site, using state-of-the-art construction technology and demonstrating its ability to age well.

Its location on the very edge of the highway, and parallel to it, leads to a linear outline that effectively responds to its function as well as the possibility for adding future offices. The building's facades have different kinds of openings to capture the necessary light. To the west, a large eye opens to frame the beautiful landscape of Madrid's nearby mountain range. A large concrete podium with service elements was built first, upon which a well-ordered metal structure was raised with a stainless steel skin: a light, metallic tectonic box, sitting on a heavy, stone stereotomic box.

Previous spread. Exterior view.
Right. View from the parking corner.

Above. External view with the platform and skylights.
Right. Main entrance hall view.

Like a steel giant lying down. Like a train, like a boat.
A building with a metal skin on the edge of the highway.

—

Left. View of the offices.
Top. View of the staircase.
Above. View of the staircase and the skylight.

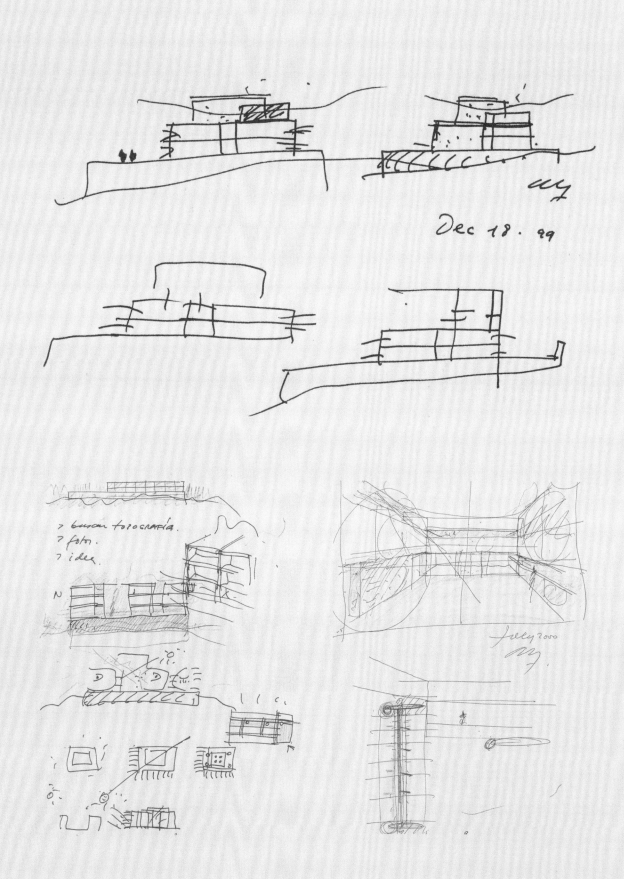

Dec 18. 99

> buscar TOPOGRAFÍA.
> foto.
> idea.

N

July 2000

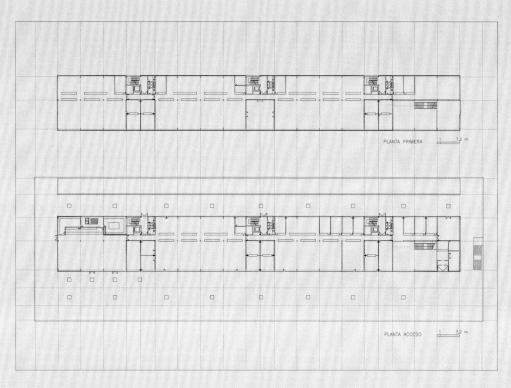

PLANTA PRIMERA 1 ___ 7.2 m

PLANTA ACCESO 1 ___ 7.2 m

ground floor and access plan

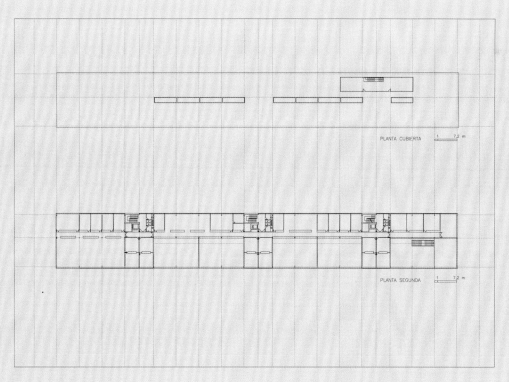

PLANTA CUBIERTA 1 ___ 7.2 m

PLANTA SEGUNDA 1 ___ 7.2 m

roof and second floor plan

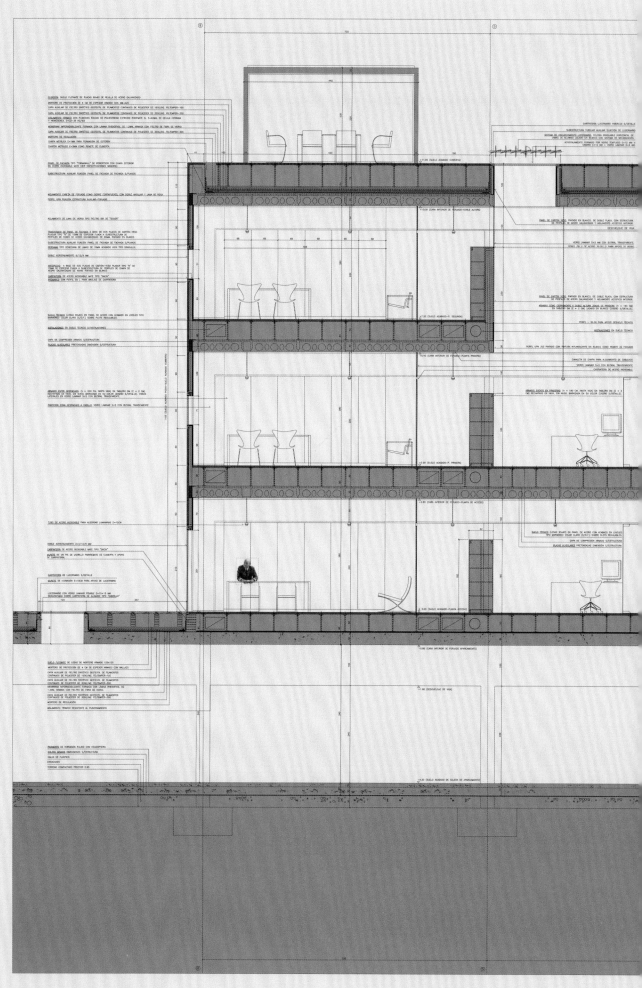

constructive section

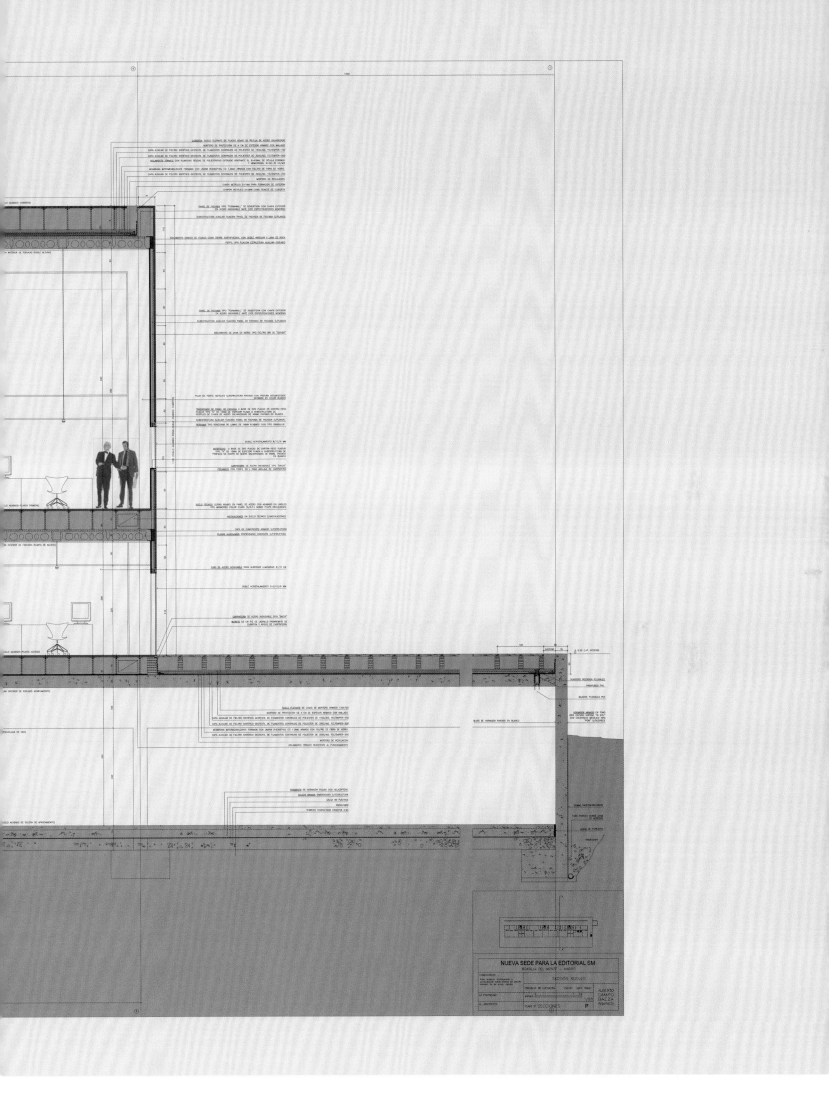

447

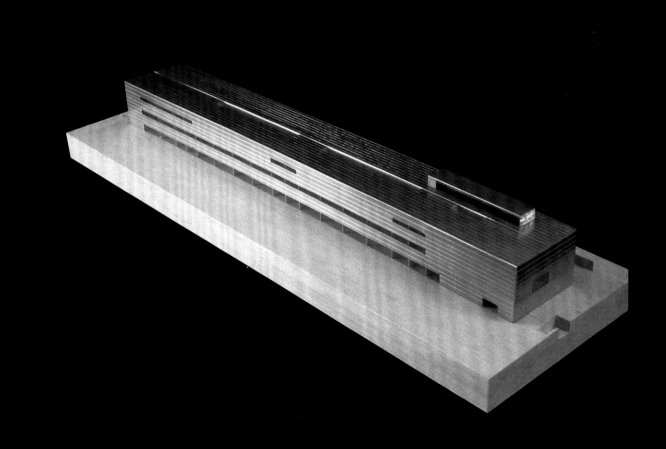

Delegation of Public Health Offices

Delegation of Public Health Offices

Almería, 2002

*In collaboration with Modesto Sánchez Morales,
Francisco Salvador, and José María García*

On an elongated site measuring 40 x 8.5 m with a
maximum height of 7 floors, the offices were built
as a single volume. A straight rectangular parallelepiped was built entirely in stone. The thick walls
contain closets and storage. The windows are
double. Inside, glazed. Shutters made of stone,
the project's most unique aspect, regulate the light
that enters the rooms. When all of the shutters are
closed, the parallelepiped appears as a solid stone
box. The project reaches the extreme of making
the roof terrace in stone as well, creating an interesting belvedere over the city and the sea. In this
way, the idea of a stone box is materialized.

Previous spread. Exterior view.
Right. View with different positions of the stone shutters.

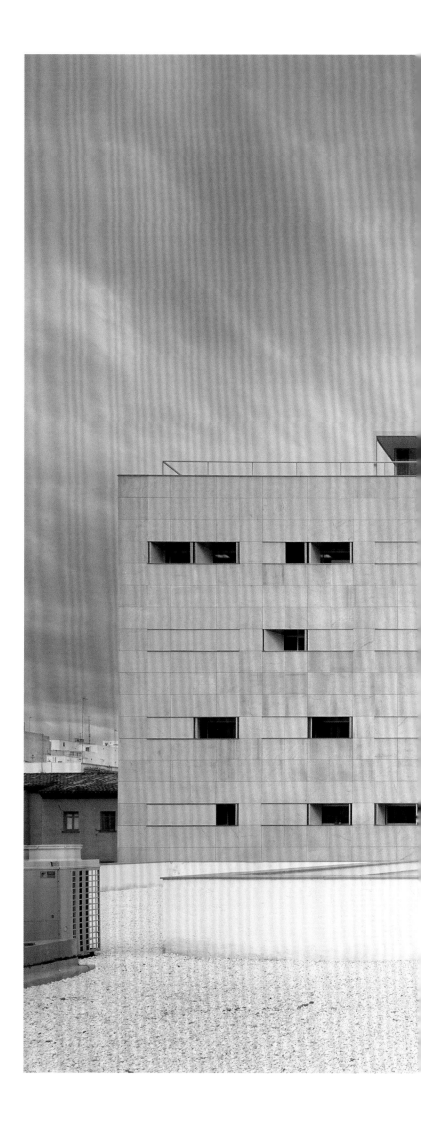

Above. South facade with opened and closed shutters.
Right. East facade.

Top left. View of the staircase.
Left. Interior view of the hall. Glass ceiling.
Right. Staircase to the roof.

Above. View from the top level with the glass box.
Opposite and following spread. View from the glass box.

The project reaches the extreme of making the roof
terrace in stone as well, creating an interesting belvedere
over the city and the sea.

—

Almeria.
una caja de piedra excavada.
que abre sus ojos. boquetes a la luz
a las vistas.

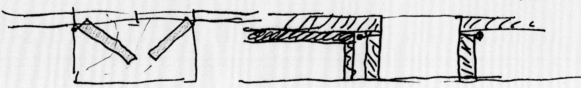

— debo preguntar
a Alain Cottet.
Ricardo Tonani

($\stackrel{a}{\textcircled{a}}$
si a 2 nombres. (: una soeur. –
(: son passport. –
si 2 – I modalité –
2 – II modalité –
2 – III modalité. –
[5 bary de 100 grs) .

en Macael. + inox.

7 × 40 × 7 plantas

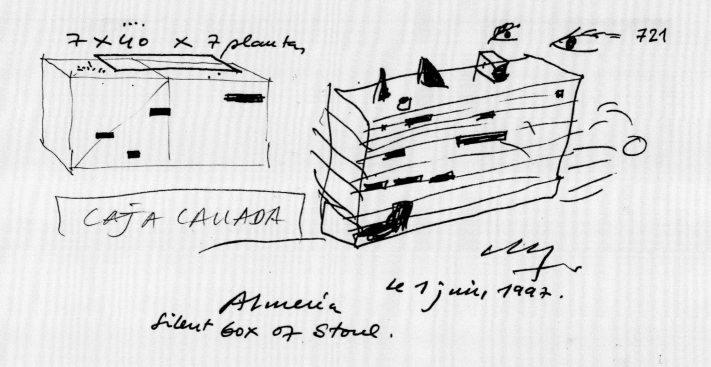

721

CAJA CALLADA

le 1 juin, 1997.

Almería
Silent box of stone.

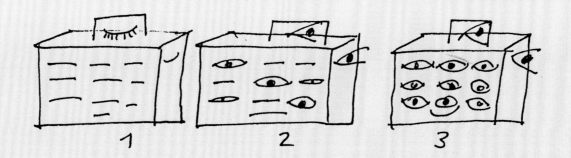

1   2   3

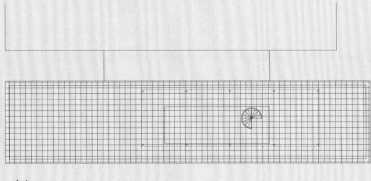

roof plan

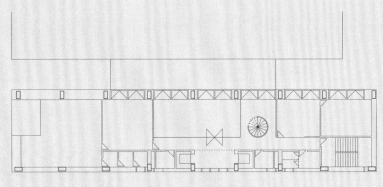

sixth floor plan

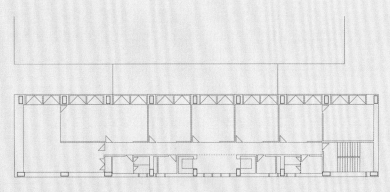

second and fifth floor plan

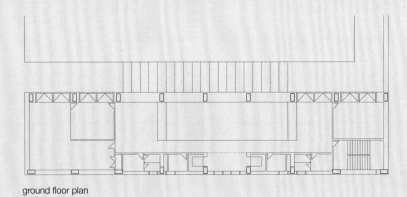

ground floor plan

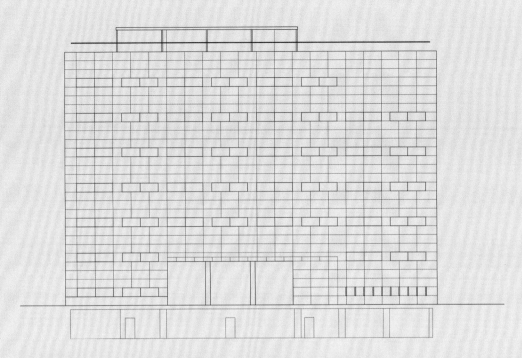

south facade

east facade

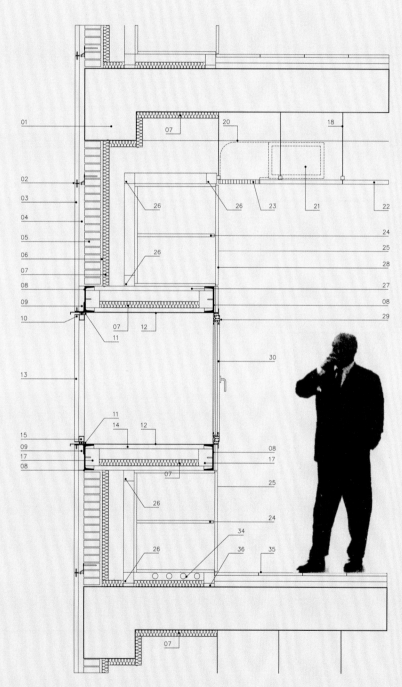

01_Reinforced concrete tie beam
02_Stainless steel anchor
03_Cream-colored Lumaquela sandstone
04_4 cm thick lime mortar
05_12 cm thick brickwork wall
06_Waterproofing mortar render
07_45 mm thick polystyrene rigid insulation
08_A 42-b UPN-180 steel profile
09_70.5 mm steel angle
10_Stone shutter frame of 40.40.4 tubular steel with 30.4 plate for pivoting cylinder of rolling bearing system
11_Pivoting cylinder of rolling bearing system
12_3 mm thick steel plate with flashing white painted to finish lintel window
13_Lumaquela sandstone shutters
14_30 mm thick phenolic board
15_Stone shutter steel frame with pivoting cylinder of rolling bearing system
16_UPN-180 steel profile
17_100 x 120 mm tea pine frame screwed to UPN profile
18_Steel threaded rods
19_Thermal bridge breaking under slab with 45 mm thick polystyrene rigid insulation
20_Hanging beam
21_25 x 40 cm air-conditioning duct
22_White painted false ceiling with hidden fixing system
23_Air-conditioning return diffuser in white aluminum
24_1 cm thick DM edged board shelf with beech veneer finish
25_Filing cabinet of 1 cm thick DM edged boards with beech veneer finish
26_75 x 75 mm tea pine frame for cabinet
27_30 mm thick phenolic board screwed to pine frame
28_DM board with beech veneer finish
29_'Technal' tilt and turn frame in white anodized aluminum
30_6/12/6 mm double insulated glazing
31_100 x 120 mm tea pine frame
32_45 mm thick polystyrene rigid insulation
33_Thermal bridge breaking on slab with 45 mm thick polystyrene rigid insulation
34_Voice and data systems
35_60 x 60 cm Limestone paving slabs
36_25 x 75 mm stand for supporting and levelling.

TYPE OF STONE: LUMAQUELA SANDSTONE

constructive detail

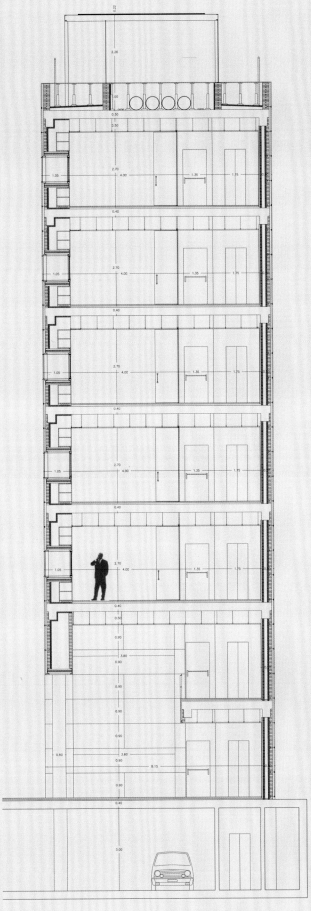

constructive section

Work:
Delegation of Public Health Offices

Location:
Ctra. Ronda, 101, Almería, Spain

Client:
Junta de Andalucía

Project:
1999

Built:
2002

Area:
5,450 m^2

Collaborator:
Gonzalo Torcal

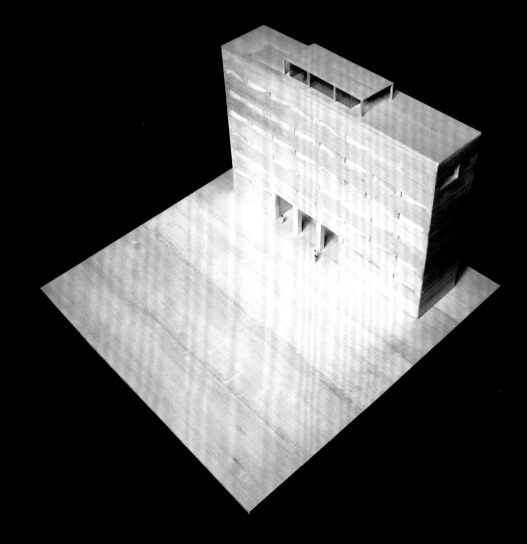

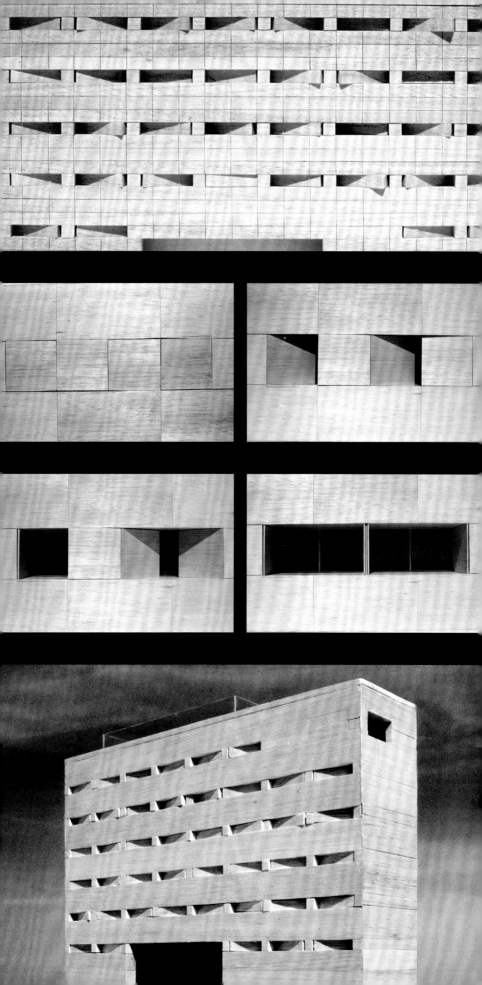

Caja Granada
Savings Bank

Caja Granada Savings Bank
Granada, 2001

IMPLUVIUM OF LIGHT

A large cube is built on top of a podium flanked by two courtyards.

The parking areas, archives, and data processing center are accommodated in this podium.

Offices are arranged inside the cube on seven floors around the central interior courtyard. The cube is built on a 3 x 3 x 3 m grid of reinforced concrete that, in the roof, serves as a light-gathering mechanism, the central theme of this building. The two facades to the south operate as a "brise-soleil" and, filtering this powerful light, illuminate the areas of open offices. The two facades to the north, serving the individual offices, receive the homogeneous and continuous light of this orientation and are closed to the exterior by means of a stone and glass cladding.

The central interior courtyard, a true "impluvium of light," gathers the solid sunlight through the skylights and reflects it against the alabaster surfaces of the walls that enclose the corridors to the north, increasing the illumination of the open offices opposite. The roof rests on four huge columns of exposed concrete. Functionally, the building is compact, flexible, and simple.

In summary, it is a concrete and stone box that traps sunlight within to serve the functions carried out within this "impluvium of light."

Previous spread. South corner.
Right. Exterior view. South facade. Main access.

Atrium

Left and previous spread. Atrium.
Above. Interior roof.
Below. Construction.
Following spread. Interior roof. Exhibition area.

In summary, it is a concrete and stone box that traps sunlight within to serve the functions carried out within this "impluvium of light."

—

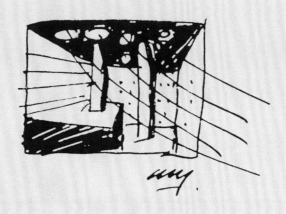

HORMIGÓN

HORMIGÓN ARMADO

may 31.91

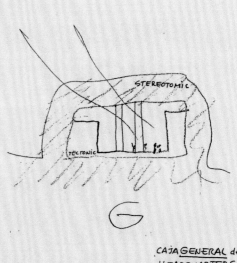

STEREOTOMIC

TECTONIC

G

CAJA GENERAL de GRANADA
HEADQUARTERS
BANK
in
GRANADA – SPAIN
1992
Competition august 92
Winner
1st PRIZE

Granada

483

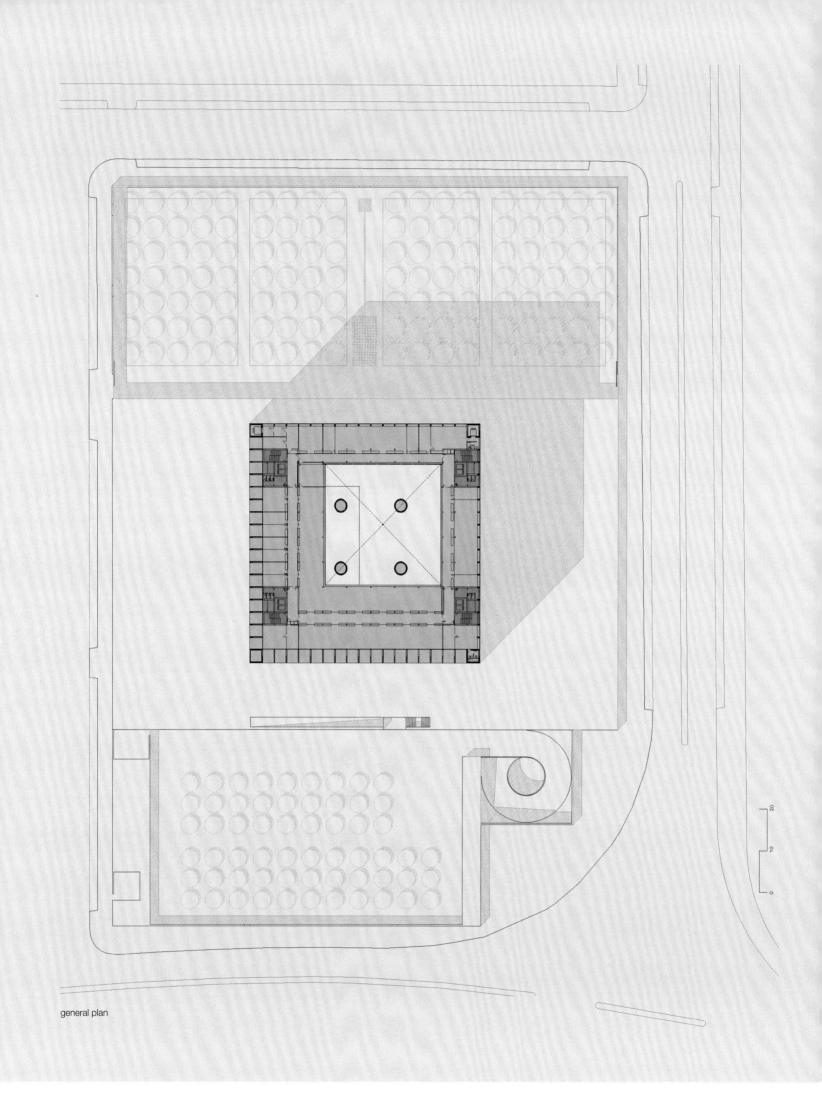

general plan

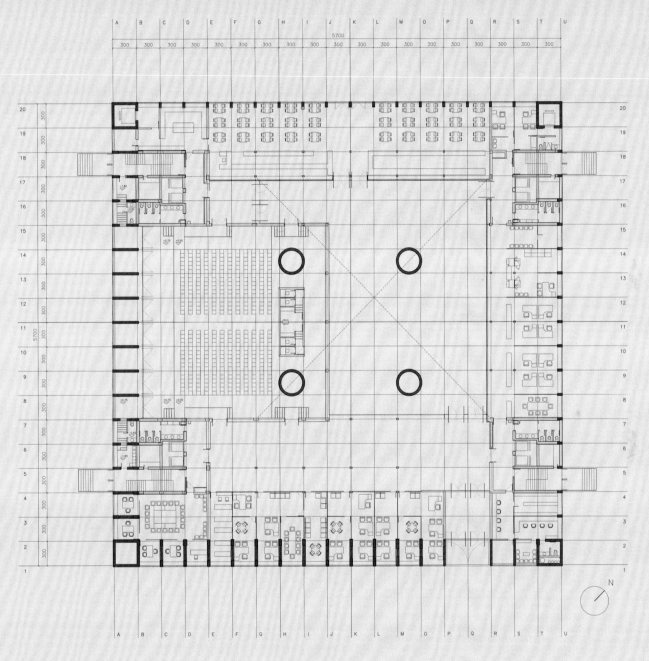

access plan

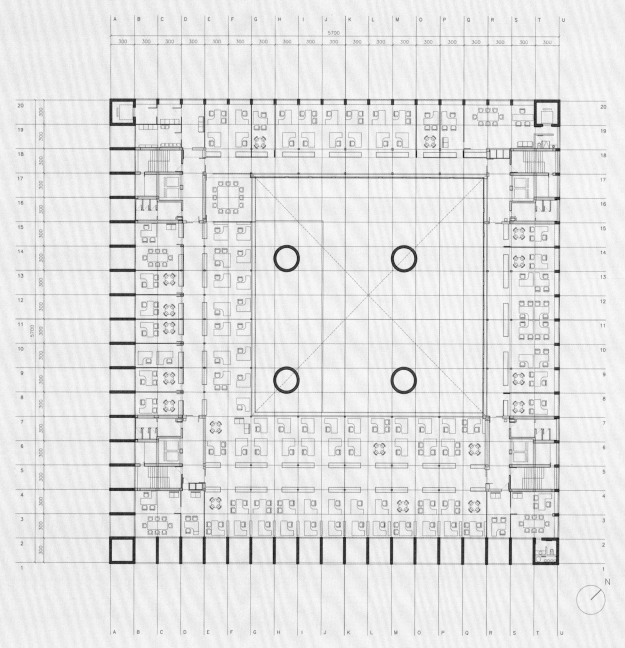

typical plan

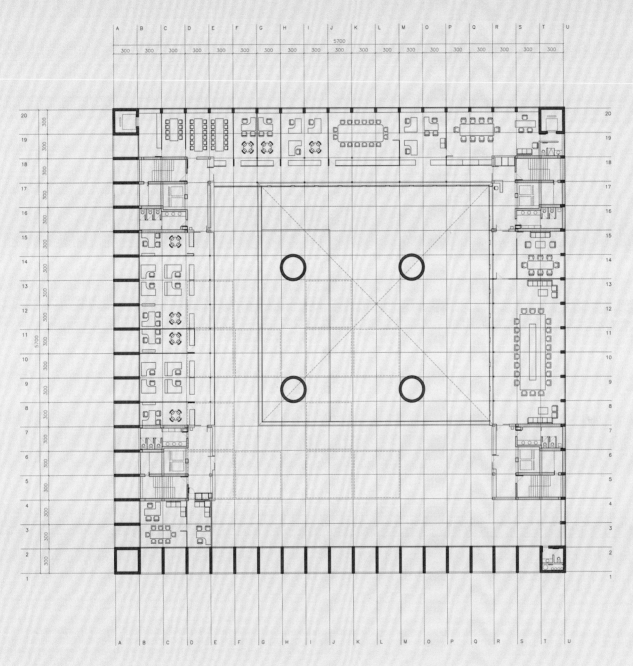

A B C D E F G H I J K L M O P Q R S T U
5700
300 300 300 300 300 300 300 300 300 300 300 300 300 300 300 300 300 300

sixth floor plan

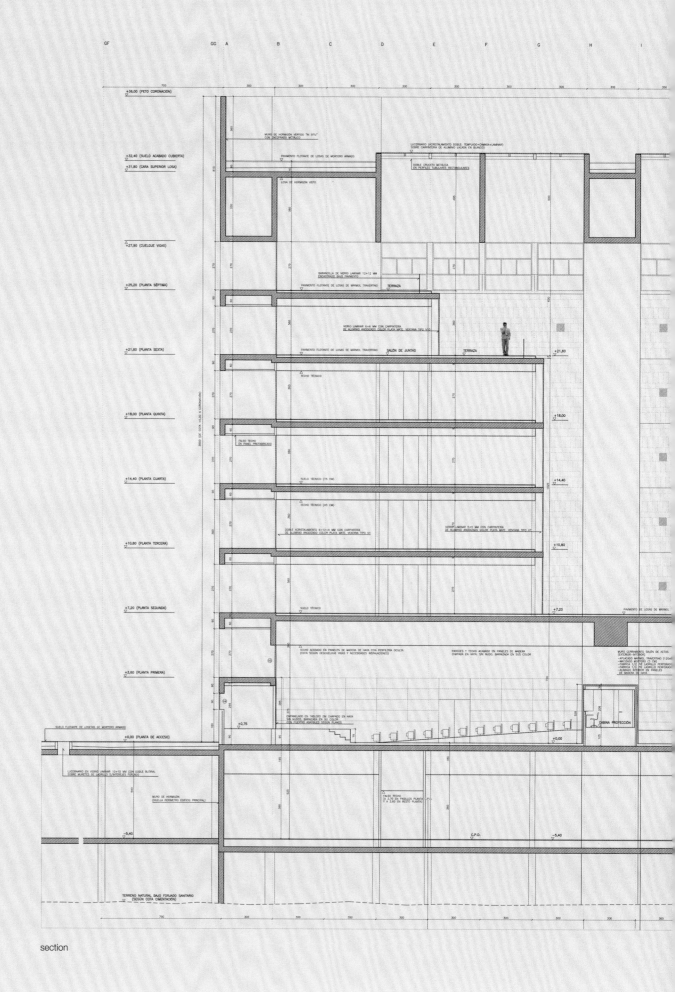

section

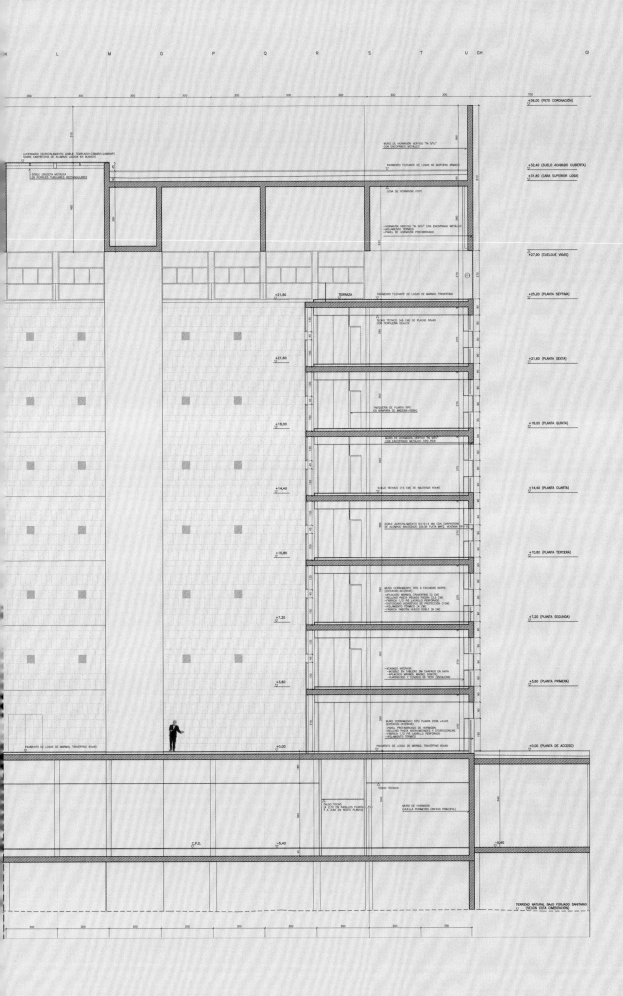

+36,00 (PETO CORONACIÓN)

MURO DE HORMIGÓN VERTIDO "IN SITU"
CON ENCOFRADO METÁLICO

LUCERNARIO (ACRISTALAMIENTO DOBLE TEMPLADO+CÁMARA+LAMINAR)
SOBRE CARPINTERÍA DE ALUMINIO LACADA EN BLANCO

PAVIMENTO FLOTANTE DE LOSAS DE MORTERO ARMADO   +32,40 (SUELO ACABADO CUBIERTA)

+31,80 (CARA SUPERIOR LOSA)

DOBLE CRUCETA METÁLICA
DE PERFILES TUBULARES RECTANGULARES

LOSA DE HORMIGÓN VISTO

HORMIGÓN VERTIDO "IN SITU" CON ENCOFRADO METÁLICO
-AISLAMIENTO TÉRMICO
-PANEL DE HORMIGÓN PREFABRICADO

+27,90 (CUELGUE VIGAS)

+21,80   TERRAZA   PAVIMENTO FLOTANTE DE LOSAS DE MÁRMOL TRAVERTINO   +25,20 (PLANTA SÉPTIMA)

TECHO TÉCNICO (45 CM) DE PLACAS 60x60
CON PERFILERÍA OCULTA

+21,60   +21,60 (PLANTA SEXTA)

TABIQUERÍA DE PLANTA TIPO
EN MAMPARA DE MADERA+VIDRIO

+18,00   +18,00 (PLANTA QUINTA)

MURO DE HORMIGÓN VERTIDO "IN SITU"
CON ENCOFRADO METÁLICO TIPO PERI

SUELO TÉCNICO (15 CM) DE BALDOSAS 60x60   +14,40 (PLANTA CUARTA)
+14,40

DOBLE ACRISTALAMIENTO (6+12+4 MM) CON CARPINTERÍA
DE ALUMINIO ANODIZADO (COLOR PLATA MATE, VENTANA TIPO V)

+10,80   +10,80 (PLANTA TERCERA)

MURO CERRAMIENTO TIPO A FACHADAS NORTE:
(EXTERIOR-INTERIOR)
-APLACADO MÁRMOL TRAVERTINO (3 CM)
-RELLENO PASTA PEGADO PIEDRA (1,5 CM)
-FÁBRICA 1/2 PIE LADRILLO PERFORADO (TOM)
-AISLAMIENTO TÉRMICO (4 CM)
-FÁBRICA TABICÓN HUECO DOBLE (9 CM)

+7,20   +7,20 (PLANTA SEGUNDA)

-ACABADO INTERIOR
-MUEBLE EN TABLERO DM CHAPADO EN HAYA
-APLACADO MÁRMOL MACAEL (ASEOS)
-GUARNECIDO Y TENDIDO DE YESO (ESCALERAS)

+3,60   +3,60 (PLANTA PRIMERA)

MURO CERRAMIENTO TIPO PLANTA COTA +0,00
(EXTERIOR-INTERIOR)
-PANEL PREFABRICADO DE HORMIGÓN
-RELLENO PASTA ANTIHUMEDADES Y EFLORESCENCIAS
-FÁBRICA 1/2 PIE LADRILLO PERFORADO
-AISLAMIENTO TÉRMICO

PAVIMENTO DE LOSAS DE MÁRMOL TRAVERTINO 60x60   +0,00 (PLANTA DE ACCESO)
PAVIMENTO DE LOSAS DE MÁRMOL TRAVERTINO 60x60   +0,00

TECHO TÉCNICO

FALSO TECHO   MURO DE HORMIGÓN
(A 2,70 EN PASILLOS PLANTA   (HUELLA PERÍMETRO EDIFICIO PRINCIPAL)
Y A 3,80 EN RESTO PLANTA)

C.P.D.   -5,40   -5,40

TERRENO NATURAL BAJO FORJADO SANITARIO
(SEGÚN COTA CIMENTACIÓN)

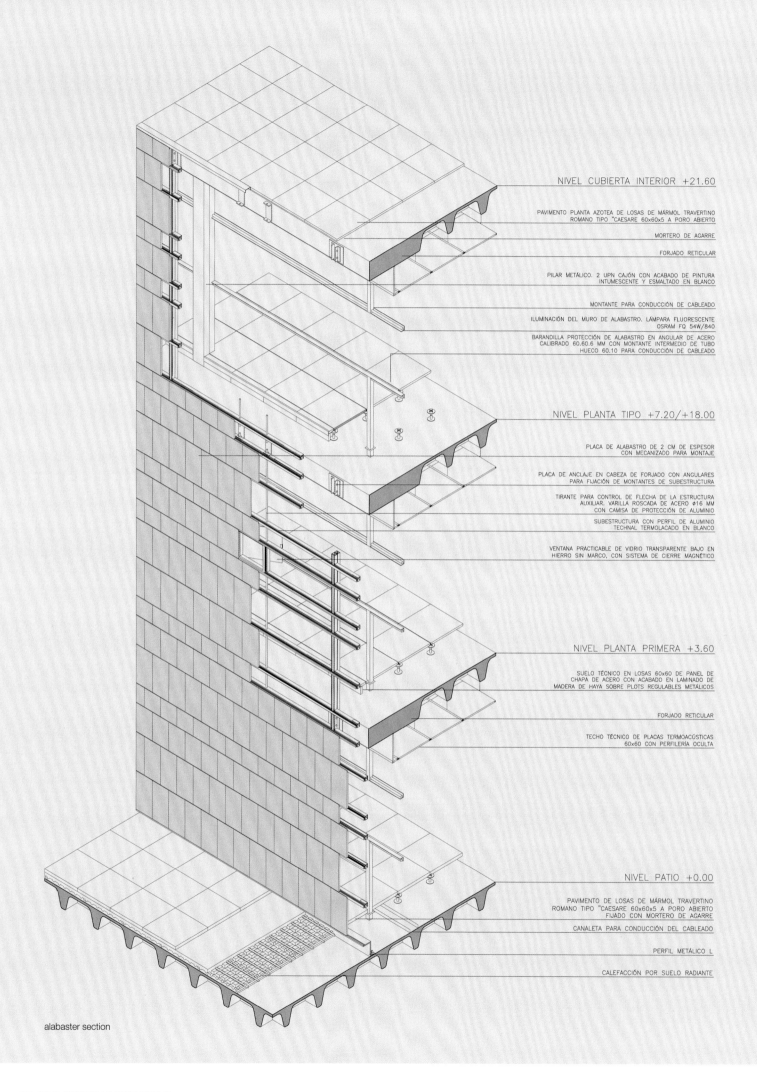

NIVEL CUBIERTA INTERIOR +21.60

PAVIMENTO PLANTA AZOTEA DE LOSAS DE MÁRMOL TRAVERTINO
ROMANO TIPO "CAESARE 60x60x5 A PORO ABIERTO

MORTERO DE AGARRE

FORJADO RETICULAR

PILAR METÁLICO. 2 UPN CAJÓN CON ACABADO DE PINTURA
INTUMESCENTE Y ESMALTADO EN BLANCO

MONTANTE PARA CONDUCCIÓN DE CABLEADO

ILUMINACIÓN DEL MURO DE ALABASTRO. LÁMPARA FLUORESCENTE
OSRAM FQ 54W/840

BARANDILLA PROTECCIÓN DE ALABASTRO EN ANGULAR DE ACERO
CALIBRADO 60.60.6 MM CON MONTANTE INTERMEDIO DE TUBO
HUECO 60.10 PARA CONDUCCIÓN DE CABLEADO

NIVEL PLANTA TIPO +7.20/+18.00

PLACA DE ALABASTRO DE 2 CM DE ESPESOR
CON MECANIZADO PARA MONTAJE

PLACA DE ANCLAJE EN CABEZA DE FORJADO CON ANGULARES
PARA FIJACIÓN DE MONTANTES DE SUBESTRUCTURA

TIRANTE PARA CONTROL DE FLECHA DE LA ESTRUCTURA
AUXILIAR. VARILLA ROSCADA DE ACERO Ø16 MM
CON CAMISA DE PROTECCIÓN DE ALUMINIO

SUBESTRUCTURA CON PERFIL DE ALUMINIO
TECHNAL TERMOLACADO EN BLANCO

VENTANA PRACTICABLE DE VIDRIO TRANSPARENTE BAJO EN
HIERRO SIN MARCO, CON SISTEMA DE CIERRE MAGNÉTICO

NIVEL PLANTA PRIMERA +3.60

SUELO TÉCNICO EN LOSAS 60x60 DE PANEL DE
CHAPA DE ACERO CON ACABADO EN LAMINADO DE
MADERA DE HAYA SOBRE PLOTS REGULABLES METÁLICOS

FORJADO RETICULAR

TECHO TÉCNICO DE PLACAS TERMOACÚSTICAS
60x60 CON PERFILERÍA OCULTA

NIVEL PATIO +0.00

PAVIMENTO DE LOSAS DE MÁRMOL TRAVERTINO
ROMANO TIPO "CAESARE 60x60x5 A PORO ABIERTO
FIJADO CON MORTERO DE AGARRE

CANALETA PARA CONDUCCIÓN DEL CABLEADO

PERFIL METÁLICO L

CALEFACCIÓN POR SUELO RADIANTE

alabaster section

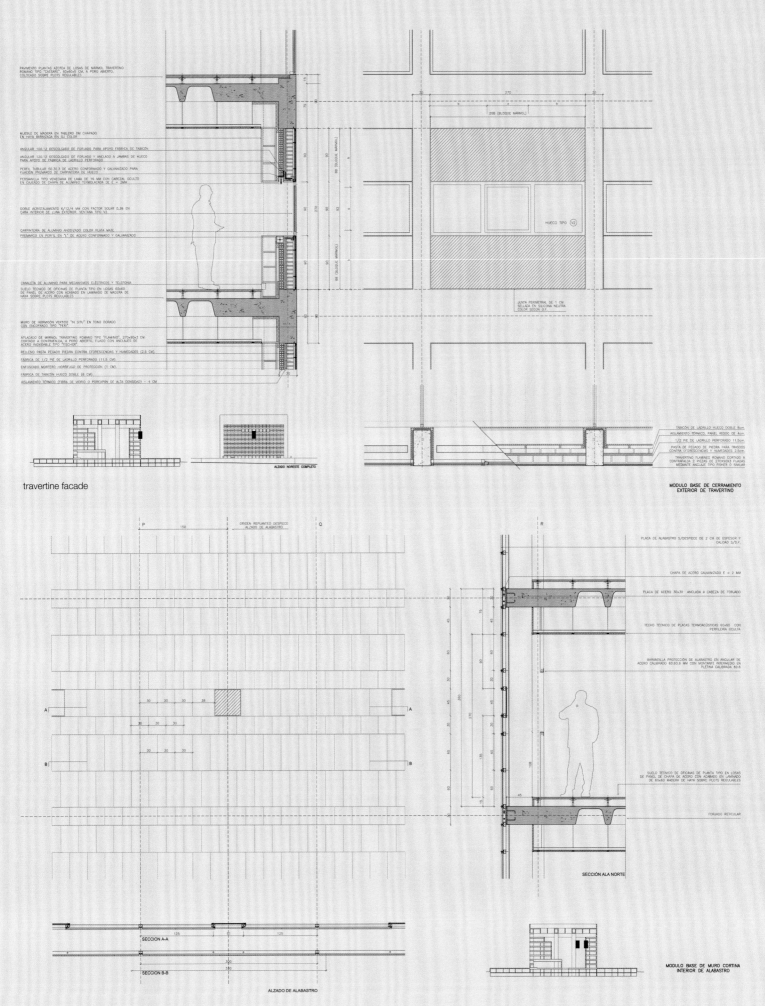

travertine facade

ALZADO NORESTE COMPLETO

MODULO BASE DE CERRAMIENTO
EXTERIOR DE TRAVERTINO

SECCION A-A

SECCION B-B

ALZADO DE ALABASTRO

alabaster facade detail

SECCIÓN ALA NORTE

MODULO BASE DE MURO CORTINA
INTERIOR DE ALABASTRO

Work:
Caja Granada Savings Bank

Location:
Avenida Fernando de los Ríos 6, Granada, Spain

Client:
Caja Granada

Project:
1998

Built:
2001

Area:
40,000 m²

Collaborators:
Felipe Samarán (codirector of construction),
Ignacio Aguirre, Gonzalo Torcal, Raúl del Valle,
Emilio Delgado, María Concepción Pérez, Tomás
García Píriz, Antón García Abril, Francisco Arévalo,
Pedro Pablo Arroyo, Patricia Esteve, Héctor Ruiz,
Daniel Fraile, José Miguel Castillo

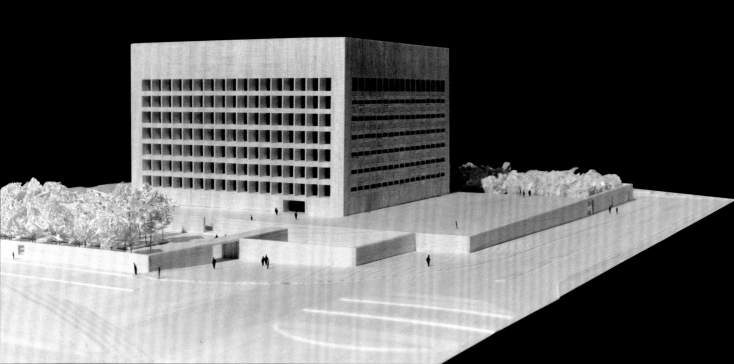

Asencio House

Asencio House

Light, the intense light of Cádiz, is the primary material with which this house is built. A house that is a diagonal space pierced by diagonal light.

The floor plan is a square divided in two halves, or better yet, into four equal parts. The front half houses the communal living and dining spaces along with the library. The back part, in addition to the vertical circulation, houses the more private spaces: the bedrooms and bathrooms. The program is thus arranged in a functional manner.

The section is a diagonal concatenation of double height spaces.

The construction is simple, and finished in white, like the Andalucían houses in the region. The house seems always to have been there. It is only once inside that one discovers the secret play of light and shade, of space and time. It is as simple as it is precise.

Previous spread and right. Exterior view. West facade.

Top. Interior view. Living room and dining room.
Above. Interior view. Living room and library.
Right. Interior view. Library.

Light, the intense light of Cádiz, is the primary material
with which this house is built. A house that is a diagonal
space pierced by diagonal light.
—

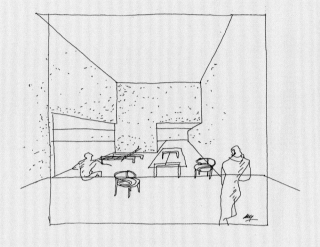

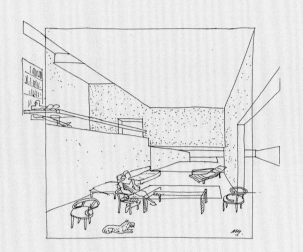

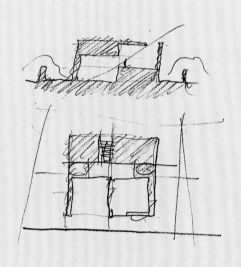

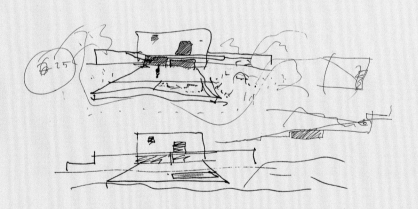

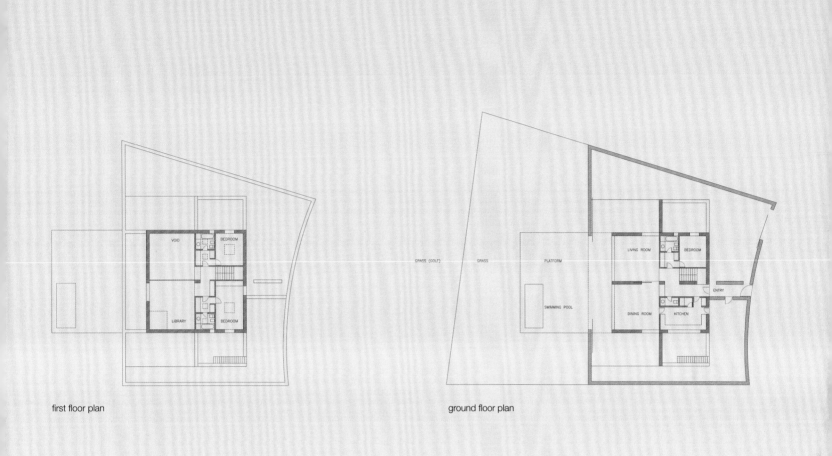

first floor plan

ground floor plan

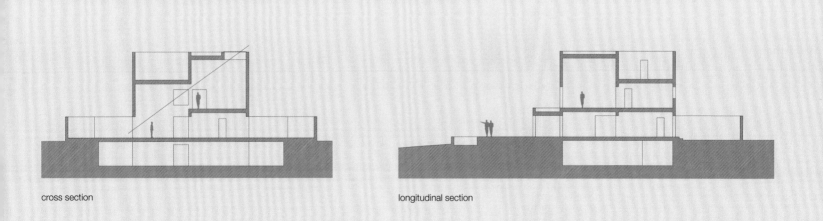

cross section

longitudinal section

503

section detail

Work:
Asencio House

Location:
Urb. Nivo Sancti Petri,
Chiclana de la Frontera, Cádiz, Spain

Client:
Javier Asencio Marchante
María Josefa Pascual Sánchez Gijón

Project:
1999

Built:
2000

Area:
370 m²

Collaborators:
Ignacio Aguirre, Miguel Vela

De Blas House

De Blas House

Sevilla la Nueva, Madrid, 2000

This house is a response to its location: on the top of a hill, southwest of Madrid, with splendid views of the mountains to the north.

A platform was created to settle upon: a concrete box the podium on which a transparent glass box was placed, delicately covered with a light and simple structure of white-painted steel.

The concrete box, rooted to the earth, houses the program with a clear schematic distribution: a service strip to the back and the served areas to the front. Inside, square windows open, framing the landscape as a distant view.

The glass box on top of the platform is a lookout point, to which one rises from within the house. From this vantage point, the landscape is under-lined so that it appears closer.

The glass box, without carpentry under the metal structure, extends almost to the edge of the north-ern facade and is set back on the southern facade to provide shade. Below, a "cave" is a space for refuge. Above, the cabin, a display case, is a space for contemplating nature. The double symmetry in the composition of the columns lends the house a still and serene character.

Previous spread: Exterior view. Podium and glass box.
Right: Exterior view. South facade.

Above. Podium.
Right. Exterior view. North facade.

The house is intended to be a literal translation of the idea of a tectonic box supported on a stereotomic box. It is a distillation of the most essential in architecture. Once again, more with less.

—

Below. Living room.
Right. Glass box.
Following spread. Northeast corner.

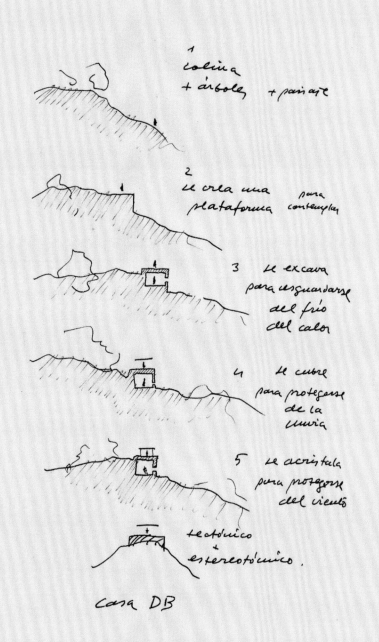

1 colina
+ árboles + paisaje

2 se crea una   para
plataforma   contemplar

3 se excava
para resguardarse
del frío
del calor

4 se cubre
para protegerse
de la
lluvia

5 se acristala
para protegerse
del viento

tectónico
+
estereotómico.

casa DB

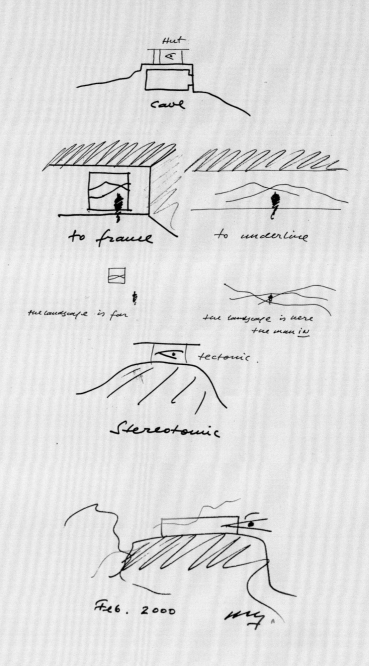

Hut

cave

to frame

to underline

the landscape is far

the landscape is here
the man in

tectonic.

Stereotomic

Feb. 2000

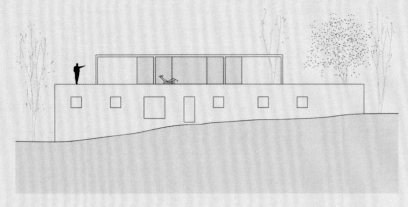

facade

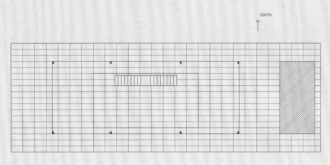

podium plan

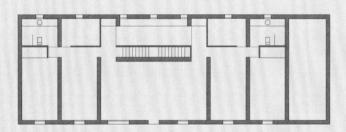

ground floor plan

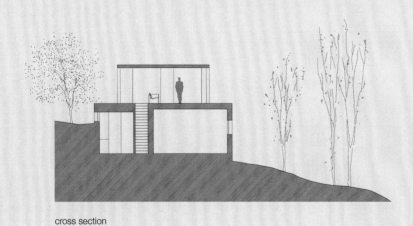

cross section

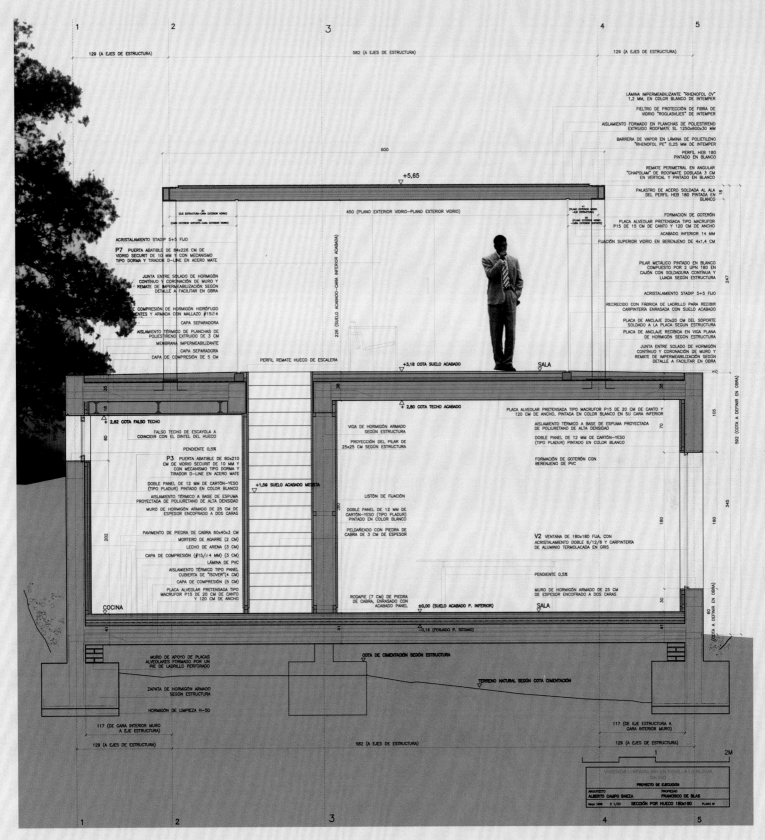

constructive section

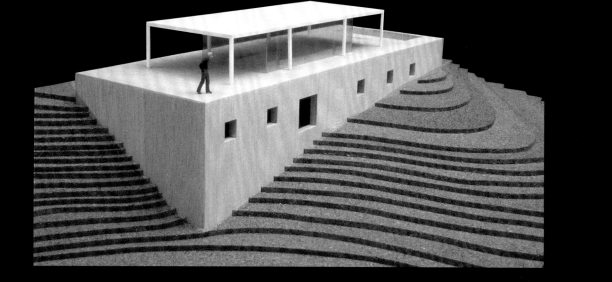

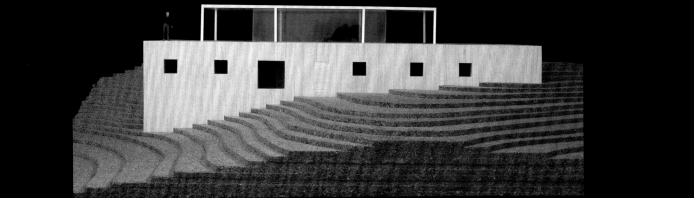

Center for Technological Innovation

Center for Technological Innovation
Inca, Majorca, 1998

SECRET GARDEN

The project was to build high-tech offices on a triangular-shaped site within an industrial area.

In order to do so, we created a garden. A tall "marés" stone wall was raised following the triangular lines of the site, creating an enclosed area.

The entire site was excavated for a basement level and a horizontal plane was set over it, a slab covered in travertine. The inner face of the garden walls was also clad in the same stone.

A podium bounded by a wall was thus created: a travertine box open to the sky. Over this box, a 6 x 6 m orthogonal grid was drawn. Separated from the walls, a parallel offset to the sides of the triangle was roofed over white cylindrical metal pillars, cantilevering 2 m to either side of the line of columns. This space is glazed, without carpentry, creating a continuous space through the horizontal plane of the travertine floor.

Previous spread. North corner. Transparency.
Right. East corner.
Following spread. Patio.

Above left. Entry.
Above right. Lobby.
Below left. Aerial view.
Below right. Patio from roof.

Previous spread. Patio view from the east corner.
Above West corner.
Right. East corner.
Following spread. Exterior stand.

Once again, architecture is created with a stereotomic
base in stone, a box like an upside-down podium
over which a light tectonic element rests. The whole
executed with enormous precision and the utmost
economy of means.

—

Left. Interior view.
Right above. Patio.
Right below. West glass corner.
Following spread. Patio general view at night.

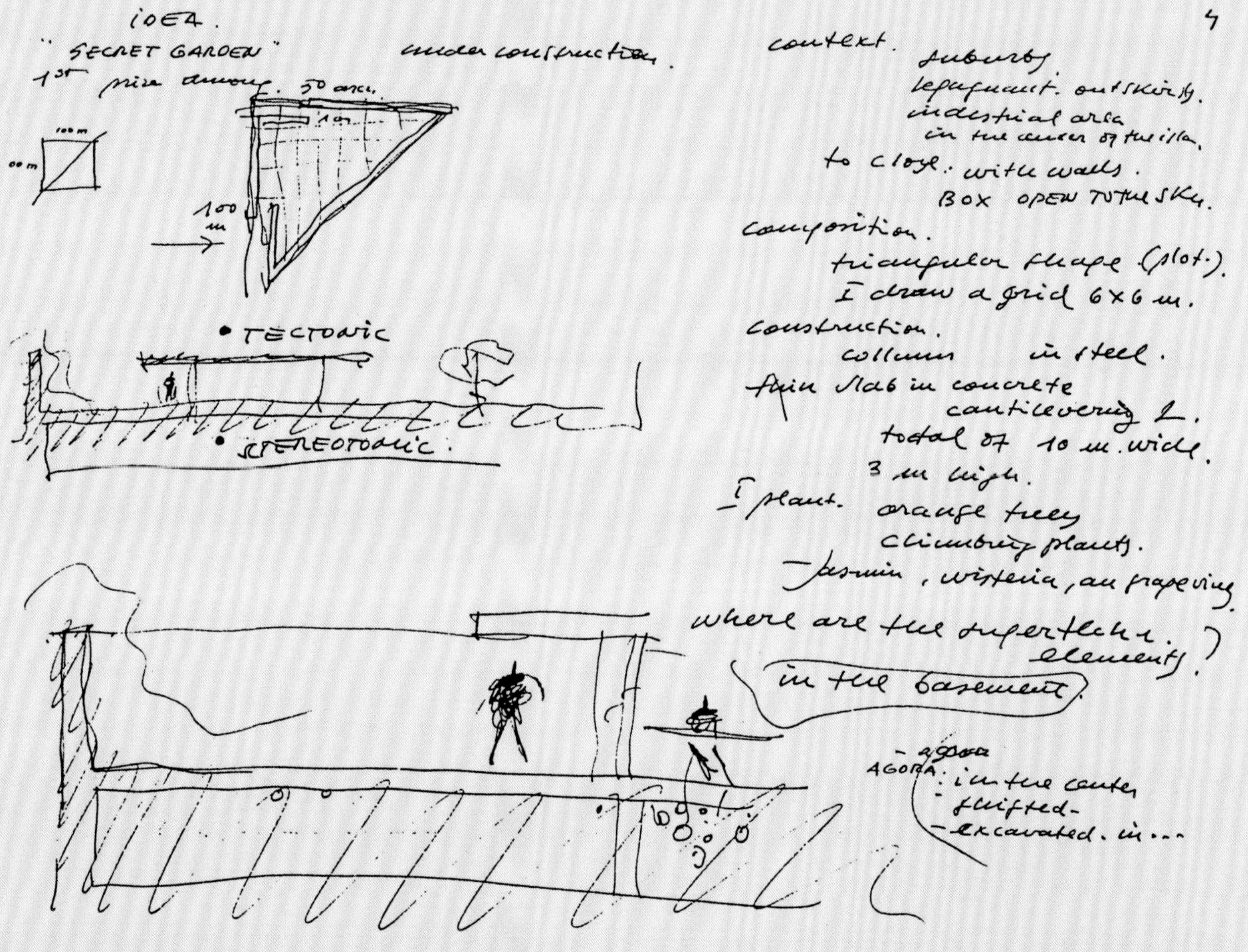

IDEA.
"SECRET GARDEN"   under construction.
1st prize among. 50 arc.

context. suburbs,
lepafuant. outskirts.
industrial area
in the center of the city.
to close: with walls.
          BOX OPEN TO THE SKY.
composition.
          triangular shape (plot.).
          I draw a grid 6×6 m.
construction.
          column   in steel.
fhin slab in concrete
                    cantilevering 2.
          total of 10 m. wide.
          3 m high.
I plant. orange trees
          climbing plants.
          Jasmin, wisteria, au grapevine.
where are the superflui.
                    elements.
          in the basement

• TECTONIC

• STEREOTONIC

AGORA: in the center
          - shifted -
          - excavated. in ...

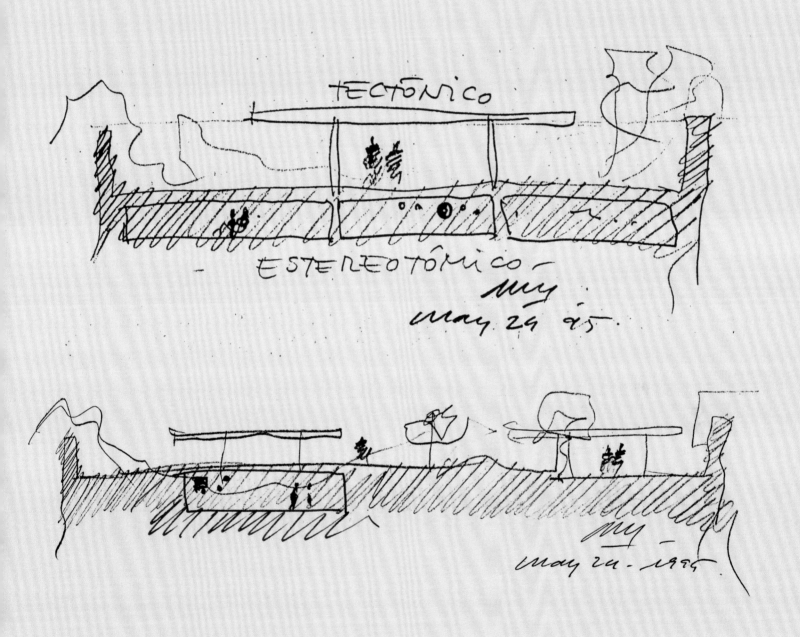

TECTÓNICO

ESTEREOTÓMICO

May. 29 - '95.

May. 24 - 1995.

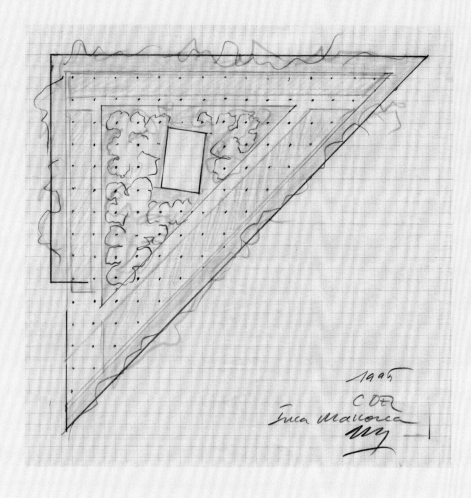

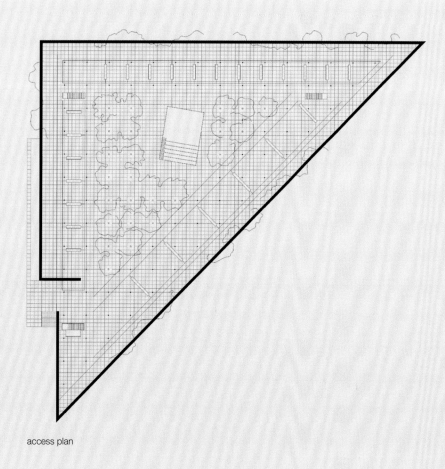

access plan

IDEA.

"SECRET GARDEN"   under construction.

1st prize among. 50 arc.

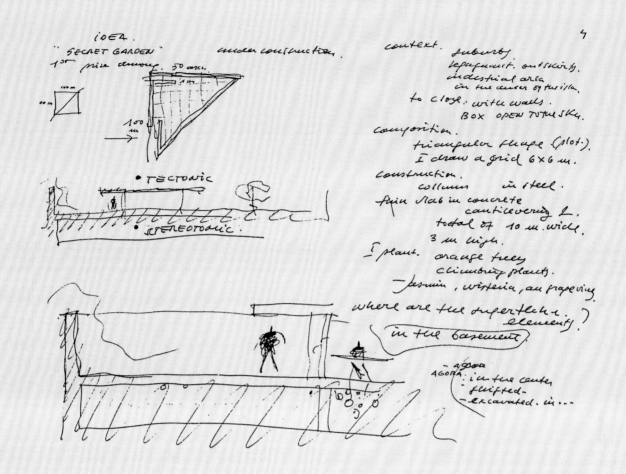

• TECTONIC

• STEREOTOMIC.

context. suburbs.
repugnant. outskirts.
industrial area
in the center of the city.
to close. with walls.
BOX OPEN TO THE SKY.

composition.
triangular shape (plot.)
I draw a grid 6×6 m.

construction.
columns in steel.
thin slab in concrete
cantilevering 1.
total of 10 m. wide.
3 m high.

I plant. orange trees
climbing plants.
— jasmin, wisteria, an grapevine.

where are the superfluous.
elements ?)
in the basement

— agora
AGORA: in the center
— shifted —
— excavated. in...

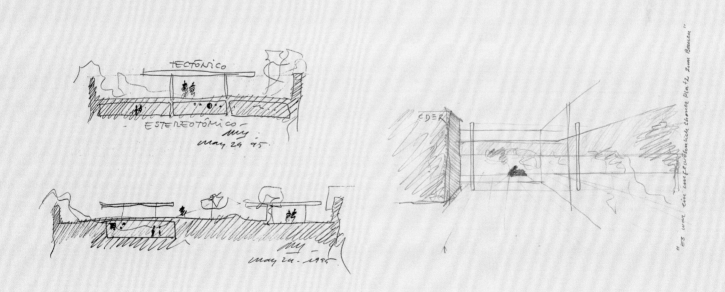

TECTÓNICO

ESTEREOTÓMICO —
my.
May 29 '95.

may 24. 1995

CEDER

"ES war ein unfreundlicher düster Platz zum Bauen"

543

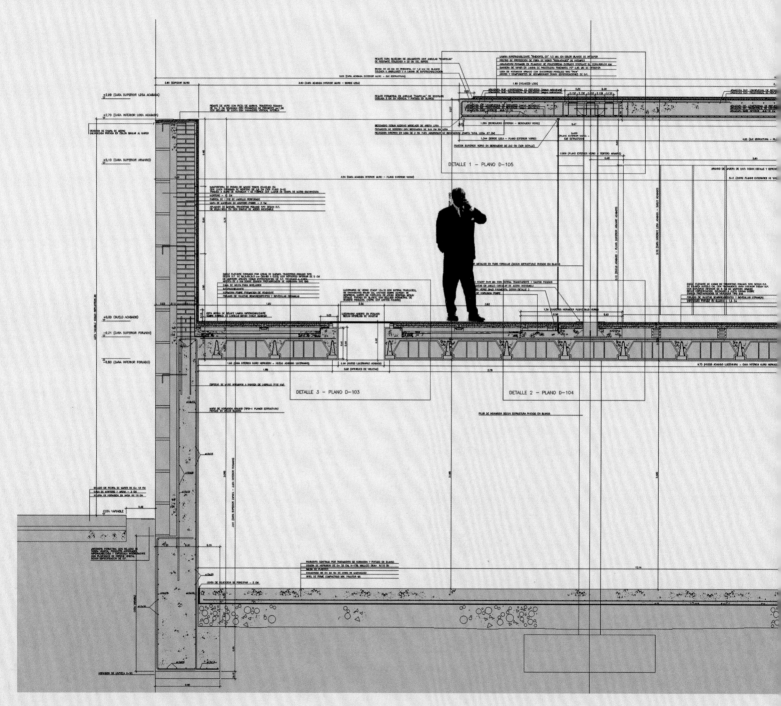

constructive section

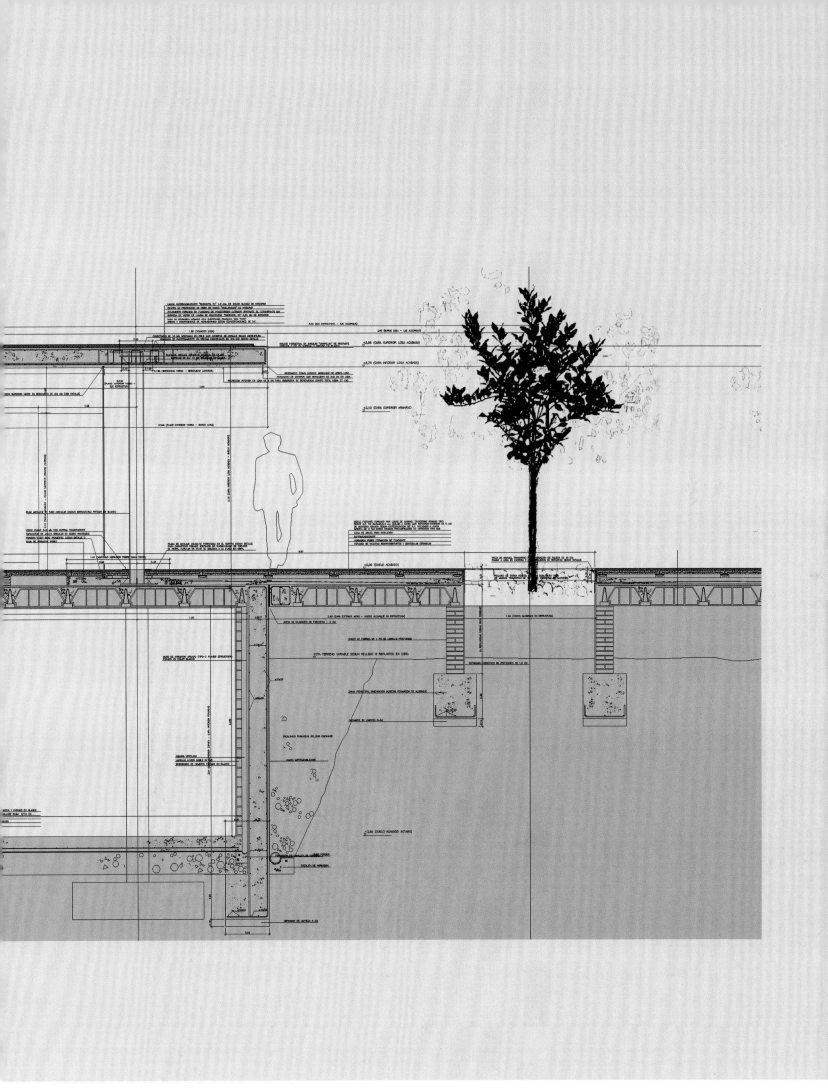

Work:
Center for Technological Innovation

Location:
Gremi Selleters, 25, Polígono Can Matzari,
Inca, Majorca, Spain

Client:
Gobierno Balear

Project:
1995

Built:
1998

Area:
5,000 m²

Collaborators:
Antonio Pérez Villegas, Ignacio Aguirre,
Antón García Abril

Gaspar
House

Gaspar House

At the client's insistence on absolute independence, it was decided to create an enclosed precinct, a "hortus conclusus" or closed grove. The house, defined by four enclosure walls of 3.5 m, is based on a square measuring 18 x 18 m, which is subdivided into three equal parts. Only the central portion is roofed. The square is then divided transversely by two 2 m high walls into three parts, with the proportions A, 2A, A, the service pieces being located on the sides. The roof of the central space is taller, 4.5 m high. At the points where the low walls intersect with the taller ones, four openings of 2 x 2 m are made and simply glazed. It is through these four openings that the horizontal plane of stone paving expands, effectively obtaining a continuity of interior and exterior.

The white color of all the parameters contributes to the clarity and continuity of the architecture. The double symmetry of the composition is emphasized by the symmetrical placement of four lemon trees, which produce contemplative reflections.

Previous spread. Patio and swimming pool.
Right. Exterior view. West facade. Access.

Left. Patios. Transparency.
Above. Patio and swimming pool.

The light in this house is horizontal and continuous, mirrored by the east-west orientation of the courtyard walls. Simply, a horizontal, continuous space is tensed by a horizontal light.

—

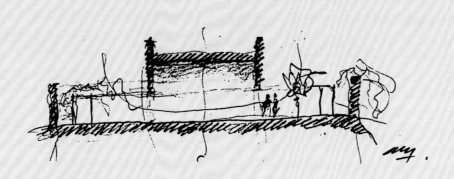

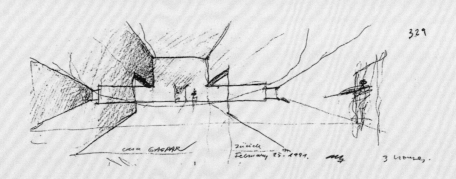

329

casa GASPAR   Zürich
February 23. 1991.   3 houses.

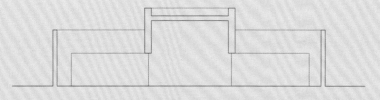

longitudinal section

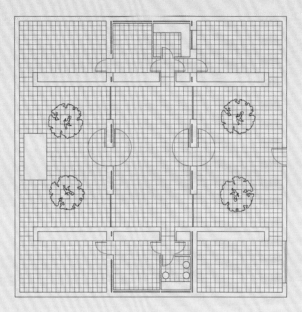

plan

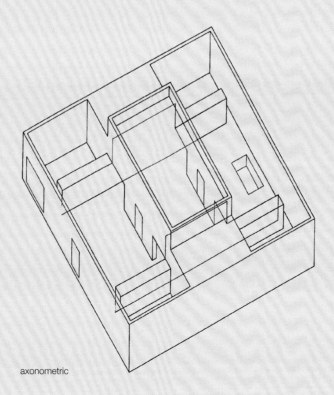

axonometric

Work:
Gaspar House

Location:
Vejer de la Frontera, Cádiz, Spain

Client:
Gaspar Guerrero Castro

Project:
1988

Built:
1992

Area:
120 m²

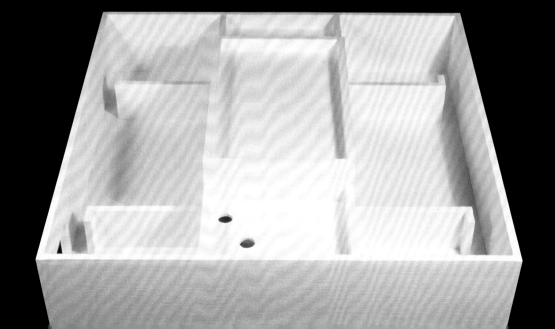

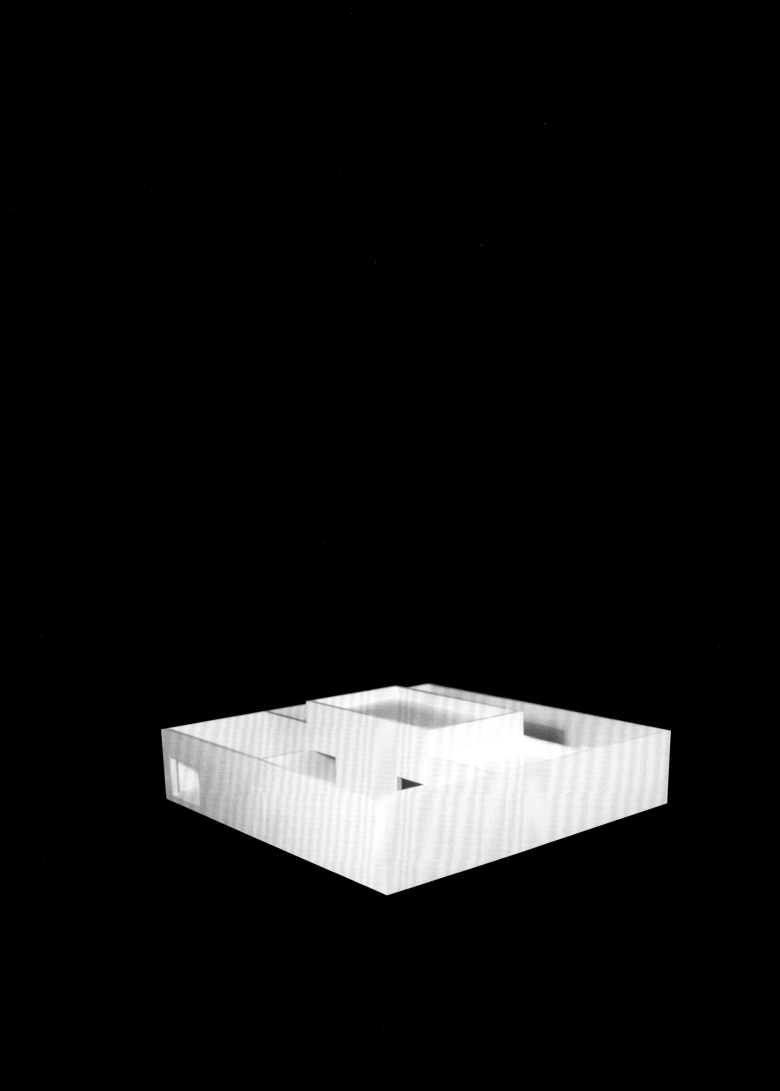

Drago Public School

Drago Public School
Cádiz, 1992

This building, with its great white facade overlooking the sea, is conceived as a continuation of the long and extensive white walls of the old "maritime" cemetery of Cádiz.

A finished volume is worked with in order to mend the urban fabric within the limits marked by the streets.

The irregular trapezoidal site is regularized through the efficient mechanism of a square courtyard around which the circulation winds. Its square form is accentuated by four palms arranged on its stone paving.

The more public spaces are located in the part of the building that looks to the sea, and are more intensely controlled. A deep, double order opening expresses to the city the public nature of the building and groups together the library and cafeteria spaces. The shadowed depth is tensed by the solid sunlight captured by the high circular skylight.

The space that hierarchically presides over the building is the main triple height hall where all of the circulation patterns converge. Its verticality is tensed by diagonal light from the high skylights, and made continuous by the eye opening to the sea, supported by an intermediate plane that makes that view possible. A vertical space tensed by a diagonal light.

Previous spread. Exterior view. West facade overlooking the sea.
Right. Northwest corner.

Top. West facade detail. Balcony.
Above. Panoramic view from balcony.
Right. Exterior view. West facade detail.

This spread. **Main hall.**

This building, with its great white facade overlooking the sea, is conceived as a continuation of the long and extensive white walls of the old "maritime" cemetery of Cádiz.

—

Left. North facade.
Above. West facade overlooking the sea.
Below. Seafront view.
Following spread. View from the sea.

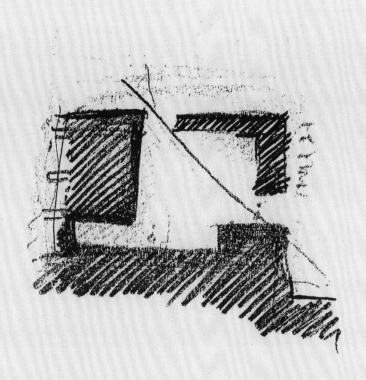

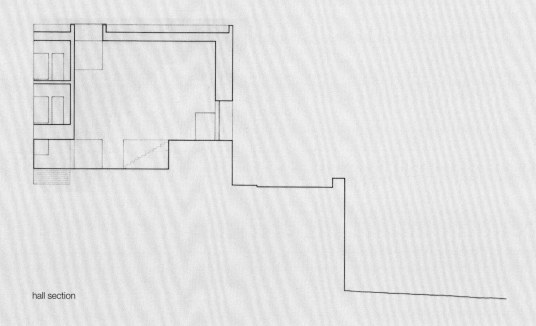

hall section

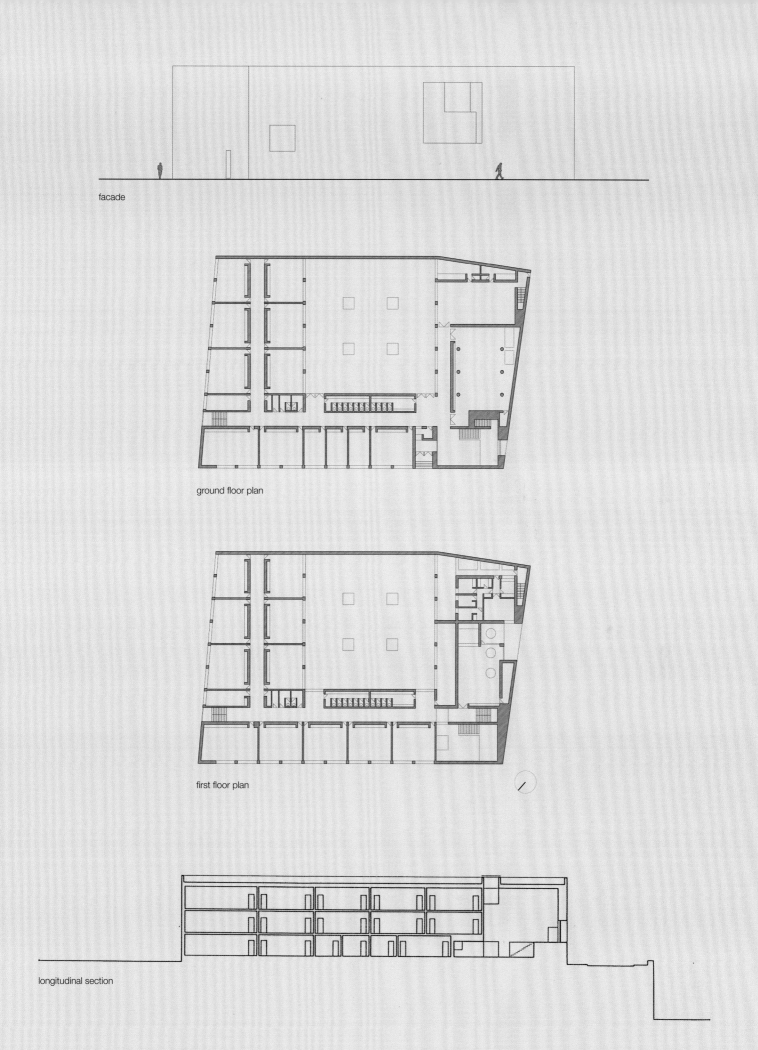

facade

ground floor plan

first floor plan

longitudinal section

Work:
Drago Public School

Location:
Cádiz, Spain

Client:
Ayuntamiento Cádiz

Project:
1988

Built:
1992

Area:
120 m²

Collaborator:
Alejandro Gómez

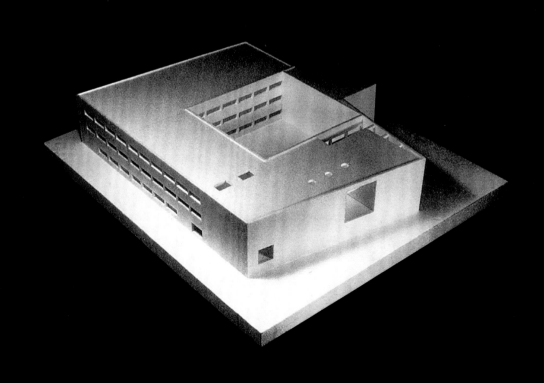

Turégano House

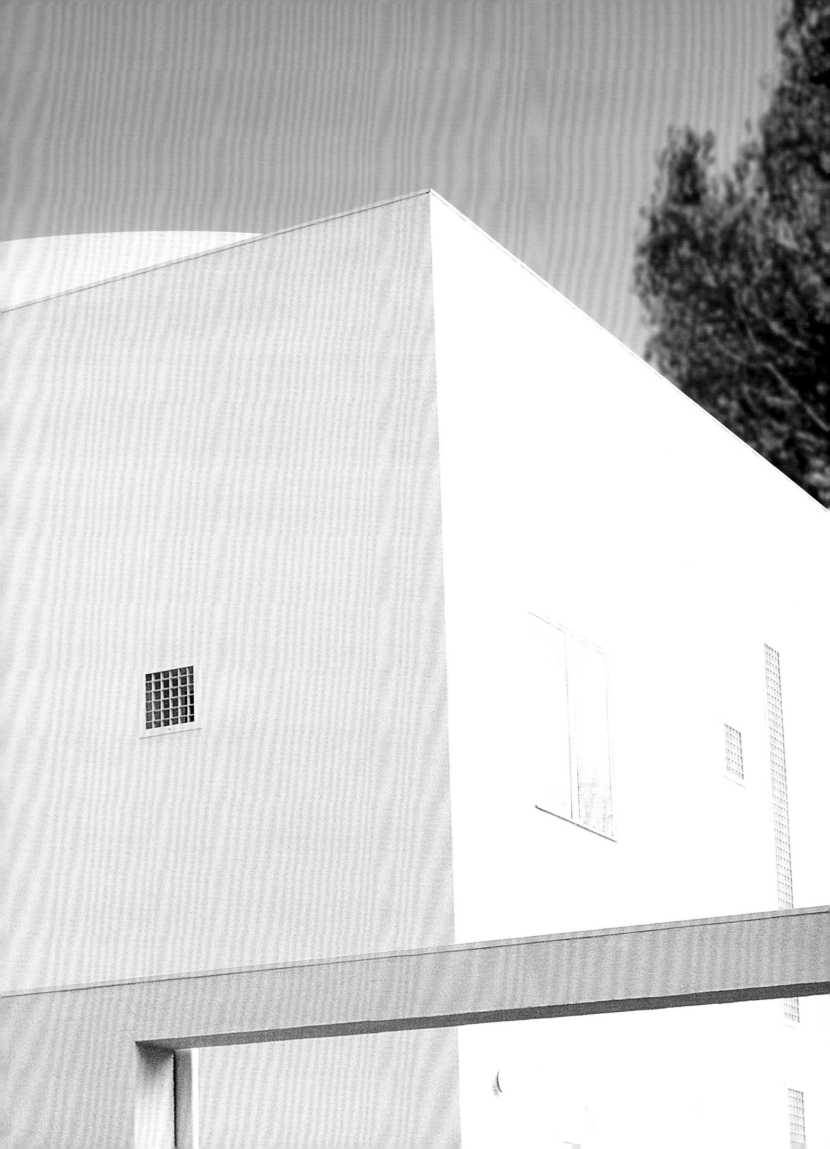

Turégano House

Pozuelo, Madrid, 1988

In collaboration with Pedro L. Valle López

This house is the result of a competition the owners called for among their architect friends.

The topography, midway down a hillside, the rigorous compliance with building codes, and the maximum economy of means were compositionally resolved in a white and cubic "cabin" that measures 10 x 10 x 10 m.

The white cube is divided in two: the northern half, with the service areas, and the southern half, with the served spaces. The first includes a central strip with bathrooms, water closets, and stairs. The bedrooms and the kitchen face directly north. The living room and dining room, located in the served half, are of double height, with the study in the highest point. The study peers over the dining room, which in turn looks upon the living room, thus producing a diagonal space of triple height. The cubic nature of this white hut is accentuated by the window glazings flush with the facade, and by the color white with which all is resolved.

Light, the central theme of this house, is gathered, captured, by windows and slots as it makes its journey from east to southwest, becoming, in its movement, the spatial protagonist of this project. Simply, it is a diagonal space pierced by a diagonal light.

Previous spread. **North facade. Main access.**
Right. **Exterior view. Southeast corner.**

Above. Window detail. West facade.
Right. South facade.

Light, the central theme of this house, is gathered, captured, by windows and slots as it makes its journey from east to southwest, becoming, in its movement, the spatial protagonist of this project. Simply, it is a diagonal space pierced by a diagonal light.

——

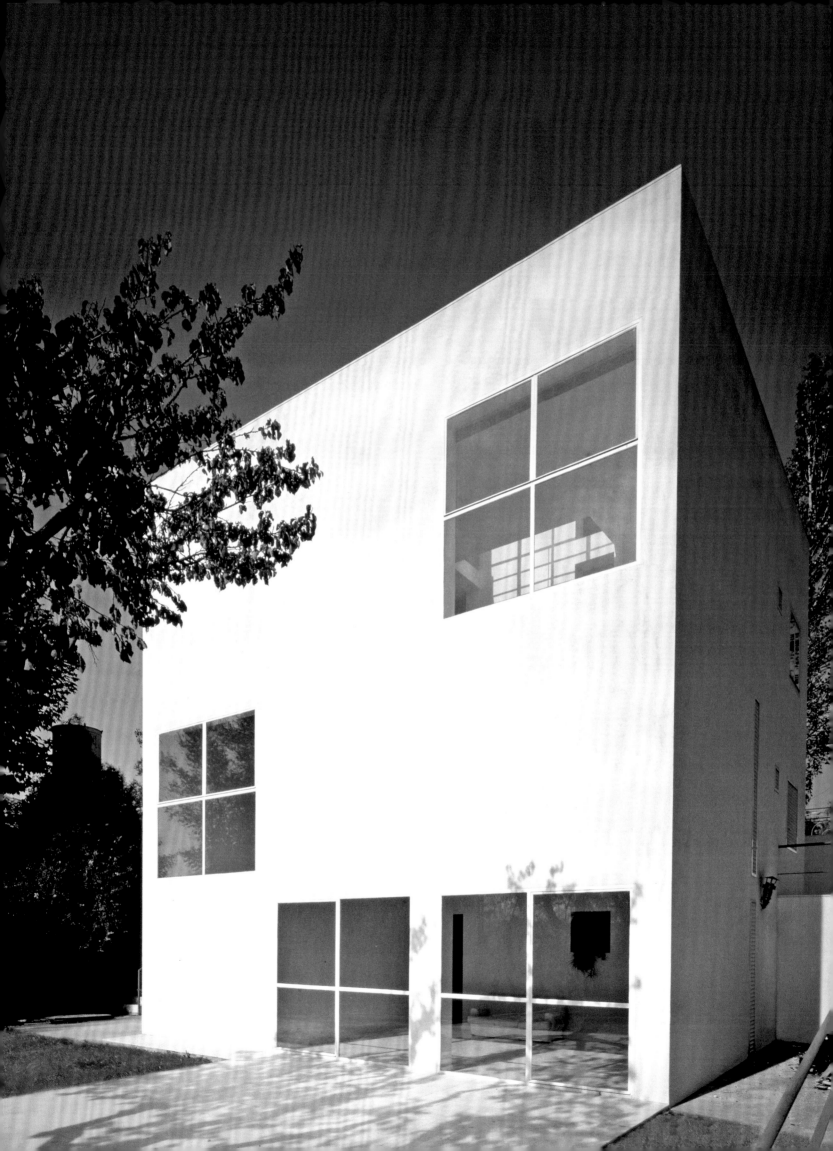

Left. Living room. Diagonal space.
Above. Dining room. Double height.

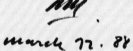

march 12. 88

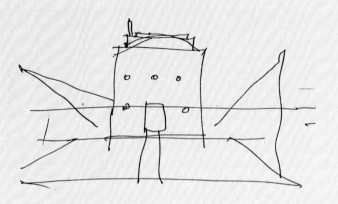

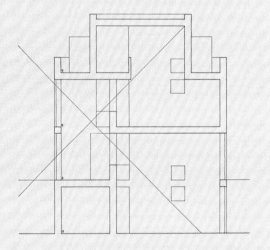

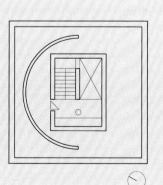

plans

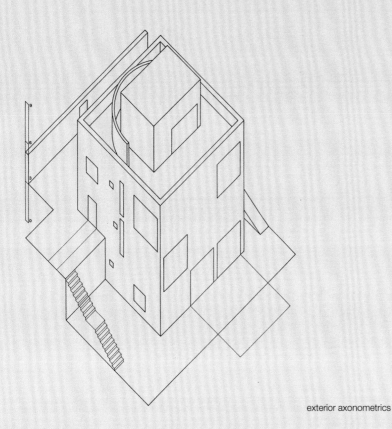
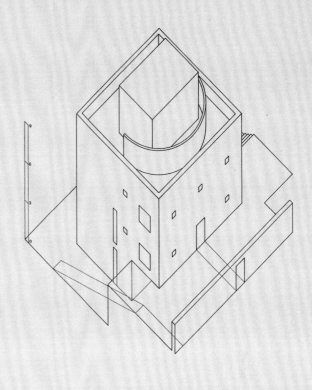

exterior axonometrics

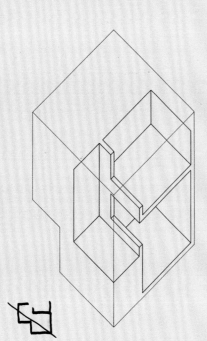
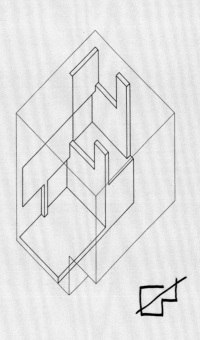

interior axonometrics

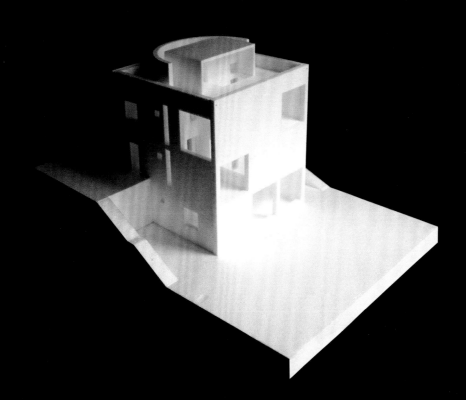

dear Alberto!

How marvellous / Prize
and for that wonderful
project "congratulations"
and all the best for
your working time with
it — I am deeply impressed
with the daring columns —
the exciting space — the light —
what a good committee
of assessors.
Your orange trees are still
in the gardeners care they
will be planted in decem-
ber they will give us a lot
of joy but never attain a
height of "33 meters" my columns
in Kuwait are only 26 meters
good luck and the
warmest greetings from
he and me + my daughter lin
who was here when we received
your letter.
    yours John Utzon

alberto!
how marvellous —
the colours are back
in architecture and in
such a grand manner.
congratulations.
I can't wait to see them
finished
Thank you for the fine
picture
    yours John.

what a beautiful reinforce-
ment.

World / Spain / Madrid

USA ● (13)

SPAIN ● (DETAILED MAP)

MEXICO ● (05, 06)

ITALY (03, 15)

FRANCE

● ZAMORA (09)　　　　　　　● ZARAGOZA (14)

● MADRID
(DETAILED MAP)

PORTUGAL

TOLEDO (12) ●

BALEARIC
ISLANDS
　　　　　　　● MAJORCA (22)

GRANADA (11, 19) ●

CÁDIZ (08, 10, 16, 20, 23, 24) ●

● ALMERÍA (18)

AFRICA

CANARY ISLANDS

Salinas de Janubio
LANZAROTE (25, 34) ●

● TENERIFE (47, 50, 57)

POZUELO (04, 25)

MADRID (01, 04, 07, 17, 21, 25)

BOADILLA DEL MONTE (17)

SEVILLE LA NUEVA (21)

LIGHT IS MORE
On Alberto Campo Baeza

Interview
by Manuel Blanco

I have followed the lines of Alberto Campo Baeza's work over the years in a long series of exhibitions that began with the show titled *Light Is More*, a dictum I created in an attempt to sum up his work and that was obviously born of a fusion of Mies's "less is more" and Campo Baeza's self-defining "more with light," vindicating his use of light. The title thus paid tribute to Campo Baeza and to the master whose Crown Hall, IIT, housed the exhibition. After Chicago, the Urban Center in New York became a celebration of architecture with Kenneth Frampton, Richard Meier, Beatriz Colomina, Mark Wigley, Steven Holl, and Massimo Vignelli there to receive us. Vignelli had long supported Campo Baeza's work and was behind the commission for Olnick Spanu, the magnificent house that we presented there as a new piece.

In 2004, the exhibition grew and I transformed it into an installation in which Campo Baeza's light contended with Palladio's in *Campo Baeza alla luce di Palladio*, at the Basilica in Vicenza, where Alberto Campo Baeza was chosen master of the year by ABACO under the recommendation of Francesco Dal Co. In 2005, we went to Istanbul for the concluding ceremony of the UIA conference at the Byzantine Basilica of Saint Irene, where we presented an anthological exhibition of his work. More than 3,000 architects gathered for the opening, among them Tadao Ando, who would later select Campo Baeza to exhibit his work at the prestigious Gallery MA of Tokyo, over whose scientific committee Ando presided. Among the long list of figures who saw this show in Tokyo along with Tadao Ando were Toyo Ito, Kengo Kuma, Yoshio Taniguchi, and Kazuyo Sejima, making the exhibition an encounter between Spanish architecture, represented by Campo Baeza and a group of young architects working with him there, and a wide representation of Japanese architects. In *Campo Baeza. The Creation Tree*, I offered an installation at the MA Gallery, constructing a landscape out of Campo Baeza's work. It featured a large tree made out of his drawings, branch by branch, with each one of his seminal design projects over the background of Guerrero House, a white wall as an image of his work, a pond of photographs at its feet, and the already legendary Day Care Center for Benneton in the distance. The red moon or the rising sun that presided over the landscape framed Campo Baeza, speaking to us about light, surrounded by his maquettes and by a long analysis I provided of all the themes that appear in his work.

Campo Baeza is probably one of the best-known architects of his generation. His clear, precise work, which is both utterly free of excess and lacks nothing, is always recognized, identified, and remembered. His handling of light and the passage of time confer a very special quality to his spaces, allowing time to slide through them, marked by the light that caresses them, lingering there and becoming eternal. His work grows more intense over time and this is most likely the result not only of an ever increasing distillation of his architecture, but also of his careful choice of projects and the deliberately small number of commissions he accepts compared with other studios of equal renown. Following the thousands of drawings he has made, one may appreciate the personal quality of his work, which relies on a magnificent and small group of collaborators who complement his vision. Some of the most interesting young Spanish architects have worked in his studio or under his guidance at the university. His teaching, research, and creative work complement one another, forming a single endeavor. I've had the privilege of enjoying a great number of conversations about architecture with Alberto Campo Baeza "off the record." The publisher has asked us to provide "for the record" the conversation transcribed below:

WHAT IS ARCHITECTURE FOR ALBERTO CAMPO BAEZA?

In general, I still find it difficult to say what architecture is. I could tell you that for me, as a person, architecture is an enormously important part of my life. I'd also qualify that: it is not the only thing in my life, but it is still a passion. Those of us who are dedicated to creative work are privileged. Human beings with the capacity for artistic creation are truly privileged, in the most profound sense of what one means by artistic creation.

Stefan Zweig expresses it well in the text you and I have discussed more than once, "The Secret of Artistic Creation." It's already there in the title. And while he says many very interesting things, the most central almost answers what you've asked me, and that is, the ability we human beings have to create something that afterward transcends us.

We create something that later goes beyond us. We disappear, but our works remain. This happens with any creative endeavor, but in our creative work as architects, much more so.

Obviously, I'm not telling you "what architecture is." I'm telling you what it is for me: the possibility of creating something wonderful that can remain.

That something, what is it? Well, it's building, building ideas. For me, it's creating spaces that are going to serve to make people happy, spaces in which I try to apply everything I know, using the instruments that architecture has been working with throughout history.

When I speak of instruments, I'm referring to scale, proportion, and measure, to control of construction, control of structure, control of light, and of all of the elements that constitute the architectural space. And all of this, obviously, at the service of man.

So, we may ask ourselves again, what is architecture? And we would speak of Vitruvius and of *utilitas*, *firmitas*, and *venustas*. One could say that the hardest thing to achieve is *venustas*, because beauty is what we would all like to attain. Because clearly construction, good construction, is something an architect has to do well. And it's also obvious that the function must be served. So, beauty is the hardest thing.

Plato tells us that beauty is the splendor of truth. Plato of course presents the matter as a philosophical proposition, which from the point of view of architecture could be translated as: architecture, when true, produces a true beauty that is capable of transcending us, that can go beyond us. It is not the vain beauty of a moment, nor is it a passing fashion.

What is architecture? It is a creation that is going to serve humankind by means of beauty. People say, "Architecture has to serve, it has to be useful and well constructed." Yes, of course it does, but I already take that for granted. I can't understand a wonderful idea for a building that turns out to be impossible to build; that's not architecture. It might be a dream, but if that dream cannot be made reality, cannot be constructed and well constructed and be useful, truly useful, then it is not architecture.

Clearly architecture tends to be born of necessity. We are not called "to make architecture." No. A need appears and from that need, an architect must be able to combine the ingredients to provide a solution to that need. But that's not all. He has to give the best solution to that need, to give an answer, providing not only the best possible construction, solving the problems of construction, but also, he must reach that something else, something more, which is the *quid* of the question, the central idea.

I've always alluded to the idea of the idea, pardon the redundancy. I mean, the necessity that there be an idea. But this too is not that original; it's just as necessary in creating a poem. One must know what it is one wishes to say, the idea of a poem. In a poem, there is something one wishes to say, which later will be translated into the properly arranged words. That is, there must be a previous idea, which is what I mean when I speak of synthesis or distillation. Which, in the case of architecture, is the distillation of a greater quantity of ingredients than there is in other creative endeavors.

Compared to painting, music, poetry, and philosophy, architecture is the most complex, because so many other factors intervene. Someone might well say, "You lose freedom because you have to construct with heavy materials." So many factors are entailed in architecture and there are fewer factors in a poem. Is the poet freer than the architect? I'd say so.

I have no trouble comparing poetry or music with architecture, because I enjoy poetry and music enormously.

WHAT IS THIS PROCESS OF CREATION IN ALBERTO CAMPO BAEZA, THIS DREAM OF ARCHITECTURE? YOU KNOW I'VE SEEN YOUR DRAWINGS, I'VE SEEN ALL THE SKETCHBOOKS AND NOTEBOOKS IN WHICH THIS PROCESS HAS EVOLVED AND DEVELOPED, BUT HOW IS IT BORN?

It isn't easy. If I had to find some way to define that point of departure, I'd say it is a dream. And what's this dream like? I would say that it is strict, precise, and exact. And very, very difficult.

And I return to poetry, which I've often used as an example and will do so once again because I believe it fits what we're talking about very well. Poetry is not a matter of setting out to combine words without further thought. A friend of mine wrote a poem called "Poemar" [poetry-making] in which all of this is expressed very clearly:

"Making poems is no more than trapping the words that fly through the air. Strip them and wash them and dry them and brush them. And arrange them with a certain mischievousness. Make them agree and bring them together or marry them forever. And then, when you unite them, a miracle occurs, they make sound, they stop time, they touch your heart and mine, and we burst into tears."

["*Hacer poemas no es más que atrapar las palabras que vuelan por el aire. Desnudarlas y lavarlas y secarlas y peinarlas. Y ordenarlas con cierta picardía. Acordarlas y juntarlas o casarlas para siempre. Y entonces, al unirlas, se produce el asombroso milagro de que suenan, de que detienen el tiempo, de que el tiempo se para, de que tocan tu corazón y el mío y rompemos a llorar.*"]

Well, making architecture is something like that. It requires enormous precision. Remember the quote by María Zambrano, who says, when referring to poetry: "Poetry is word in agreement with number." Well, architecture is the same. Of course it's difficult for us and I still find it difficult. For example, the matter of light, which is central for me, but not because it is central for me, but because it is central in architecture. I would like to have more knowledge. I invented a tale in a well-known text about light, in which I said that Bernini had made some tablets of light, which he loses and which later end up falling into Le Corbusier's hands. What I wanted to say in this story is that I would like to have an exact control over light, knowing that light is a material and that it is the most luxurious material and that it must be treated as stone is, with the same materiality as stone, and that it has to be controlled just as stone has to be.

In the building we're making in Zamora, we've spent months on the stone and dedicated an enormous amount of hours to defining the size, thickness, and placement of each stone in this beautiful wall that will appear in front of the cathedral. I want to put very big stones there. They have to be the largest stones possible. And I'm asking for the greatest thickness that can be achieved for the greatest size of the wallboard that current technology allows for stone. Knowing it's a stone that covers a wall that has a previous structure. Obviously, I can reach greater dimensions than those used with traditional stone throughout history. We're in the third millennium, and I want to work with stone, in front of the cathedral of Zamora, with the spirit and the technology of our time.

People find all of these things strange, and they're not at all strange. It's like putting words in a poem and suddenly a word acquires a new meaning. I'm currently finishing a text in which I compare architecture with music and I begin quoting Fray Luis de León and his "…*la música estremada por vuestra sabia mano gobernada…*" ("…Music tempered by your wisely governed hand") from his wonderful ode to Salinas. I quote the word "*estremada*" that in current spelling is written with an "x," in its original spelling with an "s." Even these small details are not the details of a neurotic. I worry about the architects who under the motto "God is in the details," which is what Mies van der Rohe used to say, spend all day like neurotics over each millimeter that they design, stuck on the banister or the baseboard. Obviously what is important is the general idea, and it's worth the trouble to take care of these details in as far as they contribute to making this general idea work.

ALLOW ME TO RETURN TO MY QUESTION: IN HIS BOOK ABOUT FALLINGWATER, EDGAR KAUFMANN JR. RECOUNTS HOW HIS FATHER CALLED HIM ON THE PHONE, SAYING "…I'M ARRIVING TOMORROW MORNING." NOTHING HAD BEEN DRAWN WHEN THE MEMBERS OF FRANK LLOYD WRIGHT'S STUDIO GO TO SLEEP, AND WRIGHT DRAWS THE HOUSE AT FIVE OR SIX IN THE MORNING. WHEN THE MEMBERS OF HIS STUDIO GET UP, THEY DRAFT IT AND MAKE THE FINAL DRAWINGS.

WRIGHT DRAWS THIS HOUSE THAT NIGHT. IT'S NOT THAT WRIGHT CREATES THE HOUSE THAT NIGHT. A BUILDING OF THAT COMPLEXITY WAS ALREADY CREATED, IT ALREADY EXISTED IN WRIGHT'S HEAD AND WRIGHT PUTS IT ON PAPER THAT NIGHT.

IN THE CASE OF ALVAR AALTO, THERE IS A SEED THAT FLOWERS, FROM THE FIRST SKETCH HE DRAWS TO THE LAST FLOOR PLAN, BUT ONE CAN RECOGNIZE THE FINAL PROJECT IN THE FIRST SKETCH. WE KNOW LOUIS KAHN'S PROGRESSION AND HOW HE MOVES FROM FORM TO DESIGN: UNDERSTANDING STRUCTURE AS FORM, WHAT HE WANTS THE WORK TO BE, WE CAN FOLLOW IN THE LINES SKETCHED HOW HE REACHES HIS FINAL DESIGN. OR THE

PROCESSES, ALMOST LIKE AUTOMATIC WRITING, IN FRANK GEHRY'S FIRST SKETCHES AND IN HIS FIRST MAQUETTES THAT APPEAR IN EACH ONE OF HIS PROJECTS.

HOW DOES THE FIRST IDEA OF A WORK BY ALBERTO CAMPO BAEZA COME TO BE? HOW IS THIS IDEA DEVELOPED OVER THE PROCESS OF CREATION? I'VE SEEN THE INITIAL DRAWINGS, I'VE SEEN THE 75,000 DRAWINGS IN YOUR FILES, BUT HOW DOES THAT FIRST IDEA APPEAR AND FLOWER? AND THESE IDEAS, DO THEY APPEAR ON PAPER, DO THEY APPEAR IN YOUR HEAD, DO THEY ARISE AS AN IDEA, A CONCEPT? WHAT IS THEIR GESTATION?

The answer to that question isn't easy, but if I must choose one of the options you've presented, I'd say, in my head. Clearly, in my head.

A drawing might serve as a reference and can help at certain times to suggest or develop, but the idea very clearly comes from my head. And for that same reason, I would say that I need time, a lot of time. I believe the elaboration of architecture or its composition requires a long time.

I don't mean that it took Virgil eleven years to write the *Aeneid*, but rather that even for that first moment, which is what you're asking about, time is needed. As much time as for the first moment of human life. In human life, means are given in order to have a child, and sometimes it works and sometimes it doesn't. What is the culminating moment? Nobody knows. I think architecture is very difficult for me and takes me a lot of time. And furthermore architecture is not like Mozart's music. I've written it somewhere, there are no Mozarts in architecture.

It doesn't depend on size, precisely because so many factors are involved, even for a small thing. One must also have a clear idea about what one wants for very large buildings.

Yesterday we were reviewing the projects for this book and once again the maquettes for the Copenhagen Philharmonic appeared. The building's like a large beached rock, a beached rock that obviously I make parallelepipedic, straight, rectangular, divided into four large steps on which afterward a large transparent glass box is placed that faces the water. Within the large rock are the auditoriums, the more closed-in areas that need to respond to the acoustics. And in the upper glass box, the public spaces looking at the city and at the water. Well, this idea for a large project was born after a long process and clearly will have to be translated later into specific measurements and a concrete program.

About your question and this moment of the birth of an idea: I'm certain it's in my head. You can be on a trip thinking more than drawing, thinking, and it appears. Or certain ideas appear first and are followed by another stronger or clearer idea. It's a complex process.

It's not fortuitous; it is something that has been very worked out in my case. It's not something that suddenly appears like an angelic inspiration, no. It is something for which I need an enormous amount of time.

I don't think I'm so original in this; throughout the history of architecture, you see architects who interest you and whose production is relatively limited.

I distrust contemporary architects who produce more projects than a good creative mind can generate in depth.

Of course, many architects can make a great number of works. The capacity to produce quantity is easy these days, with the means we have, with large firms and immense production companies. I'm not afraid of it. But to produce with depth and quality, knowing that one is building for history, that's another thing. I think true creators, poets and musicians, painters and philosophers, create for history. We are making history, we are building history.

I remember a curious story from one of my visits to Zamora. They told me that a very nice and very effective classmate of mine wanted to join us for lunch. He ate with us and was very pleasant, and he told me, "Alberto, I've built 2,000 works." I showed my amazement and he added, "but not only in Zamora, in Madrid too and all over the world." The meal was enjoyable, but when we returned to Madrid, I asked myself, "Good God, how many have I built?" I pulled together all my books and other publications on my work and began counting. And I had only thirty-seven constructed works. At first, I said, "What a disaster!" But then, as it happens, I'm very calm and can only be grateful for all I have and I don't want more. I'm doing what I believe I should and can and am enjoying myself and try to remain rigorous in my judgment. By chance, on my bedside table that night was a book by Bill Bryson, Shakespeare's latest biographer. And also by chance, on the page where I'd stopped reading, he spoke of how Shakespeare had written only thirty-seven plays. So that eased my mind and I slept happily that night. The genesis of architecture needs time. Time and maturity. Time to age.

Another aspect I'd like to stress is that what one proposes are theoretical issues. Michael Bockemühl, the art critic, speaking of Rembrandt, my favorite painter along with Goya and Velázquez, said that what Rembrandt did was "translate concepts, make them visually possible by means of his painting."

I think that is what one is trying to do. When I make a building with a platform facing a landscape, I am proposing theoretical issues that can relate this new space to the landscape. And when I propose what a corner means in the building we were talking about before in Zamora, I am certain that, independently of the size of the stone that we use, I care much more about the theoretical issue of the cornerstone.

At what point does a square building have its maximum tension? Where the walls join, in the angle. That first stone is the foundation stone, which is the stone on which my building rests, but I would also say that it is the stone where all architecture rests, the so-called cornerstone of which the Holy Scriptures speak. So, I'm going to try to make this first stone the largest and the thickest. It will be the biggest stone that the producers with their modern machines are able to bring to light. Then, the following stones will have to be smaller so that this so-called cornerstone looks even bigger. And obviously the basement will require larger stones than the upper stories; that's pure logic.

These very theoretical issues that arise when we speak of the cornerstone or the corner, or of what the corner means in architecture, are what interest me. The corner in Mies van der Rohe or Palladio or Bernini: these architectural solutions are theoretical issues that can be translated materially.

When we professors speak of how architecture rests on the ground, its contact with the soil, with the earth, how it emerges from the earth, how it rests on the earth, and how it connects to the sky, we are speaking of issues that may seem very theoretical but are very real, material. It's that encounter between the theoretical issues and reality that interests me.

Just as Bernini, when sculpting *The Rape of Persephone by Neptune*, couldn't care less how much beard Neptune has, or whether he wears a crown, or whether Persephone is pretty or not. What he cares about is showing the softness of the hard marble by means of his sculpture: the possibility of making something hard soft, of showing how the very hard and smooth marble gives way under the fingers that press into Persephone's thigh. Bernini is making a purely theoretical proposition there, in addition to the fact that the sculpture is beautiful, or the movement of the cloth and the movement of the body are lovely, which are obviously present in the work as well. There are many factors and I would say, in this sense, too, that sculpture is very close to architecture.

WE ARE TALKING ABOUT THE CONSTRUCTED IDEA.

Yes, clearly. And its relationship to painting, sculpture, and music is very clear as well.

The other day I read something lovely in Alex Ross's book *The Rest Is Noise*. It's a marvelous book and recounts a very interesting fact. How in 1905 Richard Strauss premiered *Salomé*, based on a text by Oscar Wilde and with very provocative music, in Graz. Mahler, Alban Berg, a disciple of Mahler's, Schoenberg, and Puccini, who came all the way from Italy, all go to Graz to attend the premiere. All of them were there. At that time Strauss was proposing a new music that those of us who like music love. A music that sounds familiar to us now but at that time was scandalous.

I'm saying all of this to point out what I'd like to do with architecture: to make the most vanguard architecture, the most representative of our moment that simultaneously is able to last over time.

I am a man of the third millennium, not just a man of the twenty-first century, and I would like this to be reflected in my work. To make this architecture of the third millennium is it really necessary to twist, break, scream, shout, and do everything that one finds these days in the magazines? I don't think so; this is something different. It's something more profound. In the Zamora project, the site has an irregular shape and we are adhering to the site. So, the stone box that opens to the sky is a box with irregular forms that are controlled but broken because of the layout of the city that we are responding to.

Can architecture resemble some outlandish object? I don't think so. But aren't the forms of most of the buildings that fill our magazines outlandish? Yes, but I think architecture cannot and should not be superficial. It has to belong to the time in which we are living, and at the same time be capable of withstanding time, of lasting. The difficult desire of duration that Paul Eluard spoke of.

WE SEEM TO BE COMING UP TO SOMETHING I WANTED TO ASK YOU. MANY YEARS AGO ALBERTO CAMPO BAEZA SAID, "I AM NOT A MINIMALIST, I DO MORE WITH LESS."

AND I WON'T SAY I WAS SURPRISED BY, BUT I VERY MUCH LIKED THE FACT THAT THE "MORE WITH LESS" THAT YOU WROTE MANY YEARS AGO TO DEFINE YOURSELF, RECENTLY APPEARED AS THE SLOGAN OF A CONGRESS IN PAMPLONA ORGANIZED BY THE ARCHITECTURE AND SOCIETY FOUNDATION THAT ATTRACTED MANY IMPORTANT INTERNATIONAL ARCHITECTS ALONG WITH A LOT OF SPANISH ARCHITECTS.

"MORE WITH LESS" AS A RESPONSE TO THESE TIMES OF CRISIS, BUT THERE IS ANOTHER "MORE WITH LESS" THAT IS ABSOLUTELY IMPLICIT AND EXPLICIT AS THE THEORETICAL STATEMENT OF CAMPO BAEZA'S WORK.

I WOULD LIKE TO DEVELOP THIS THOUGHT, WHAT IS "MORE WITH LESS"?

"More with less" is very clear, and again I'll give an example from poetry. In the end, analogies with other creative endeavors are very useful and explain a lot.

A poet is not a minimalist of literature. Imagine people telling poets, "This guy's a minimalist." No, this guy is a poet. He's a poet who is able to make something that can break your heart with the least amount of words. In poetry a few words put one way say almost nothing and put another say everything, producing the breath of poetry, the soft puff of air.

What you and I have talked about, so often, and it's characteristic of all creative work, is the suspension of time. That aspect that can seem so mysterious, that is the creator's ability to suspend time.

Suspending time sounds almost like pure philosophy, doesn't it? But in fact, it really happens. The other day I walked into the Cathedral of Cádiz and I almost levitated, the light there was so lovely.

On my last visit to New York, as I stared at Velázquez's portrait of Juan de Pareja at the Metropolitan Museum of Art, space and time flew. Or when you read a poem. Right now I'm reading Sophia de Mello, a wonderful Portuguese poet from the last century who centers almost everything in the word. Reading her elevates you and time runs away.

That is what I mean by "more with less." Not minimalism, but rather "more with less." And sometimes words are not enough, but this is it: to squeeze all the juice out of the lemon to its very last drop.

CAN WE SPEAK OF A SEARCH FOR THE ARCHETYPE?

Yes, of course we can speak of the search for the archetype. Lately I've written something about it. I don't think trying to build types is vain or without purpose. It means trying to make a more universal architecture. When the circumstances, the ingredients, are very similar, the answers should, logically, have a lot in common.

Right now I'm struggling with the project I've got on my desk. In this case, the ingredients are wonderful: a beach house on the edge of the sea, on a site with a slight slope toward the water with dunes in front, so I have to establish the plane on which that marvel can be contemplated. I have to lift myself over the dune a little and in the end you ask: Is this house going to belong to the kind of typology, to the archetype, of the podium house with the temple on top, the cave and the cabin with the cabin on top? As much as I struggle against it and run myself in circles trying to escape the "curse," once again, I find myself working on this typology.

It's a matter of establishing the horizontal plane: the exact establishment of the horizontal plane on the exact point so as to be able to face a landscape with its distant—infinite—horizon, which is the sea. It is a matter of being there. The human being facing the universe.

I made a joke at the inauguration of my last piece, Between Cathedrals in Cádiz, which is, once again, a horizontal plane on high facing the sea between the city's two cathedrals. And I told those present, with the mayor and the bishop in front, "And you will note that from here, we see America." And you could see America; of course you could see America, there beyond, on the line of the horizon.

WHAT TYPES CAN ONE FIND IN CAMPO BAEZA'S ARCHITECTURE?

In his text for this book, Jesús Aparicio made a series of synoptic tables with diagrams in which he groups the types very well. There are houses on a horizontal platform when the landscape offers a distant horizon, and there are introverted, closed houses when the landscape nearby is so inadequate as to require the creation of their own landscape.

The last house, the Moliner House in Zaragoza, is a case in point. I enclose myself within the walls the regulations allow, and I create a box that is closed to its unspeakable surroundings and that is open to the sky, creating an interior landscape. Alternatively, in situations with a distant horizon, when I have a wonderful exterior landscape, I try to appropriate it by means of the horizontal plane, underlining it and stressing it. But when the exterior landscape is unacceptable, you close in on yourself and create your own landscape, which is the sky.

One can take the Moliner House and open the most transparent part of the house, the ground floor, to that created landscape. And on the upper floor, once again close inward so as not to see the inadequate surrounding landscape and bring in the northern light through a few large clear windows. And in the lowest part, the basement, place the bedrooms that receive light through excavated courtyards.

So, a very clear outline for a house appears, in which I speak of sleeping, living, and dreaming and may recall Bachelard. To sleep, which is to die a little, in the deepest sense. To live on the transparent floor, in the garden. To dream in the highest, in the translucent space, in the clouds, in the library.

Curiously, last week I received a Japanese magazine that featured the latest house by Kazuyo Sejima, and it's exactly like it, not in shape, but in layout and idea. The lower walls are curved, while mine are lined up straight and parallel. But it's the same idea; the house is buried, it opens on the *piano terra* to these walls that she shapes while above it is transformed into something different. It's responding to a way of inserting a house in a high-density area with other buildings that have no interest whatsoever. It's as simple as that.

WE'RE TALKING ABOUT A SPECIFIC LANGUAGE, ABOUT A LANGUAGE THAT HAS ALREADY BEEN GESTATED AND GENERATED, ABOUT HOW THIS LANGUAGE HAS BEEN BROKEN AND HOW NEW IDEAS AND NEW FAMILIES SUDDENLY APPEAR.

Yes and no. If language is expression, obviously it's recognizable, just as I speak Spanish and Kazuyo Sejima speaks Japanese. She will express herself in Japanese and I in Spanish. There will be times that an idea may coincide and its expression be different, and nonetheless, the idea is very similar, not to say the same.

And should the question go in the other direction, of talking about Campo Baeza's language, I don't have a preconceived language. Obviously I have my tendencies, and I can defend the use of white at certain times because it resolves a series of matters very clearly.

The latest project on my desk right now is in Lanzarote. It's a project on an island where everything is black; the earth is volcanic with bits of picón charcoal. The project is an enormous podium, a horizontal plane that holds and is encrusted into the earth and wants to become earth, merge with the same volcanic soil, and it is in black. Colors and materials depend on the place.

For the Museum of Contemporary Art that has not yet been built in Cádiz, in Vejer, in Montenmedio, which is an infinite white band, I made a few tests and for a time was working with colors within that infinitely long box until I finally gave up. Because it was more out of a will to start using colors, than that the project asked for them. What is natural in Barragán may be difficult for me, and one needn't copy him, though I admire Barragán a lot, nor use the color that he used masterfully.

And in regard to the language of form, I can still have rectangular shapes. But if I use them, it is not because I'm stuck on them, or because "that is the language of Campo Baeza," but rather because they seem to be the most rational solution. When the plot requires a contralto or a countertenor instead of a soprano, we use a countertenor.

WE FIND A SUDDEN LEAP OF SCALE IN YOUR WORK. THERE IS A LEAP IN SCALE IN THE CAJA GRANADA SAVINGS BANK [THE HEADQUARTERS FOR THE GRANADA SAVINGS AND LOAN]. IS THERE A BEFORE AND AFTER THAT WORK?

Clearly there is a before and an after. I'd never made such a large building before, though I'd worked on other designs with Julio Cano Lasso, such as the Universidad Laboral of Almería, that were just as large or larger.

But the question is obvious when you've worked on a small scale, the domestic scale, the scale of private homes and of small schools, the scale on which I'd almost always worked before. One could also mention the library at Orihuela, which is another building of a certain size, or the offices for the Andalucían Regional Government in Almería, which also was on a larger scale.

But in a full sense, the Caja Granada building is the largest I've done. It was a matter of confronting a different scale, a different size, and I believe we faced the challenge gracefully.

Clearly the next big building was Andalucía's Museum of Memory, and I think the answer there was also the right one. I tried to establish a dialogue between the new building and the Caja and to continue constructing the new city.

The first building was a point of reference in the more or less disorderly outskirts, with buildings next to it that are as large as the Caja Granada but that don't look anything like it. In the case of the next building, beside the first, the reading that most interested me was how to relate the new building to the earlier one and to the city, in this case, marked by the river that lies at its edge.

There's a theme that is still lacking in the new building, which is the forecourt, a level that leads us to the edge of the river, where the river becomes a part of the new city. And I call these two buildings a new part of the city and I hope that if the Kengo Kuma building, the opera, is constructed, it will also be in this line. I believe Kengo Kuma has proposed a different form, but one that he also understands by means of the platform that his building sits on. And you, as the curator in charge of the exhibition in Japan, saw how Kengo Kuma was moved when he looked at our model, because the forecourt from which his building will emerge was already reflected in our maquette.

So, my building has to look toward the river, and not toward the street behind. It does so clearly with that large eye that appears along the top of the screen.

I'm trying to answer your question about the change of scale, the before and after. And I would say that there hasn't been such a great change. Obviously, there's a before and an after, but no one can say that this architect only makes houses. Campo Baeza makes architecture.

I've figured out the course I'm teaching on housing this year, and I'm presenting, first, a small house, then collective housing, and finally, a tower. And I've given it the significant title "An architect is a house." By which I mean, no architect worth anything in the history of architecture has not made a house. Palladio is the Villa Rotonda, Mies is Farnsworth House, Le Corbusier is Villa Savoye, and Utzon is Can Lis.

WHEN I WALKED INTO THE CAJA GRANADA SAVINGS BANK FOR THE FIRST TIME, AND REMEMBER IT WAS DURING KENNETH FRAMPTON'S VISIT, THE FIRST TIME KENNETH FRAMPTON SAW IT, HE STOOD LOOKING AROUND THE SPACE IN AMAZEMENT, AND WHAT SURPRISED ME WAS THAT IT HAD THE SAME INTENSITY THAT EACH AND EVERY ONE OF YOUR HOUSES HAS, TRANSFERRED TO A LARGE SPACE. AND THAT THIS LEAP IN SCALE ALLOWED YOU TO MAKE A SPACE EVIDENT, MAKE IT PRACTICALLY HOLY. THAT HEART OF LIGHT THAT I WROTE TO YOU ABOUT AT ONE POINT, IN WHICH TIME STOPPED.

AND HERE I HAVE NO CHOICE BUT TO SPEAK OF LIGHT, THE LIGHT IN CAMPO BAEZA AND THE MEANING HIS UNDERSTANDING OF LIGHT HAS IN HIS WORK.

FOR THE EXHIBITION AT CROWN HALL, I SUMMED UP YOUR WORK, PLAYING WITH THE "MORE WITH LIGHT" THAT YOU WROTE AND PARODYING MIES, IN THE TITLE "LIGHT IS MORE" BECAUSE IN YOUR CASE LIGHT IS MUCH MORE…

I think it's very clear that light is the raw material of architecture, its first material. And it would be very stupid to say that light is Campo Baeza's discovery. Light is always at the center of architecture, starting from the cave. I imagine that when they were moving that large stone to close off that primitive cave, some cracks of light would be the prelude to everything that came next.

Of course light is a wonderful material, and I think that what works in Caja Granada is having achieved that suspension of time, that sense of suspended time; the building works as if it were a sundial, which is what the Pantheon does. If I had to speak about what is behind the Caja Granada, in terms of proportion and dimension and the central idea, I'd speak of the Pantheon. We could speak again of the essential mechanisms of architecture: scale, proportion, and the precision of dimensions.

In a house, the matter of light is treated differently. As I did in the Turégano House, because there are double spaces that interconnect and there is a large window to the southeast, and the light comes in from high, and at a certain moment it crosses the space. A very lovely light occurs there. But in other houses, such as Gaspar House or Guerrero House, size and function are not going to talk about light the way they do in the Caja Granada. Or in the Olnick Spanu House or the Moliner House, there it's working on transparency, on the continuity of the space. That too is a matter of light, obviously, but it's treated in another manner.

When we speak of light, we identify it with sunlight, with solid light that can cut across space, tighten it and produce the emotions that only arise in that kind of space. In my last article, comparing architecture with music, I wrote, "…The air is serene and dressed in loveliness and a light never used before…" That's what I'd heard from Juan Navarro Baldeweg some time ago. He spoke with subtlety about how architectural works are like musical instruments. Because, just as music is air that is later tempered, tuned, or made to vibrate through the strings or be blown from the primitive flute to the most sophisticated instrument, architecture is light.

Getting back to your earlier question about scale, when an architect moves to a large scale, light can be treated as a material in a very special way. And I think that's what I've tried to do in these buildings, what I'm still trying to do. In the building in Lanzarote, it's the same thing. I construct three spaces that through a series of circumstances are the same size. But the light makes these three spaces very different. We'll be working with skylights on three different scales.

In an initial study we worked with different shaped skylights, but in the end we're going to go to something much more precise and work with skylights in different scales. I think it will be a very precise exercise in light.

Light, I insist, and will repeat for the hundredth time, is the most luxurious material we architects work with. Like stone, only that light is given freely and stone costs money. Light is without a doubt the most luxurious material, but as it is given to us free, we value it less.

I think many architects forget they have such a wonderful material to work with. And they use very expensive materials when everything is much simpler. Working with light, obviously, and now I'm returning to the beginning of our conversation, has to be in the genesis of the idea. That is, I have to know whether the light interests me or not and how it interests me in a given project for those functions. You cannot always make spaces, the almost religious or holy spaces as you've called them, like those at the center of the Caja Granada.

You cannot work with that kind of space in an educational center. If the function is to teach, spaces where the focus is wisdom, which is the teacher, are what's needed. And that's that. They must be well organized and well lit, and afterward one can create a space in the lobby where all the circulations converge, as we've done in the Day Care Center for Benetton. The classrooms work transparently with the light from the garden, with continuity, which is the most logical for a classroom with young children. And nonetheless, the hallways converge in a central vertical space where the light from high is worked with and where such lovely things happen, as I've recounted more than once, that the children themselves have written: "I have touched the light." And you can see the children touching the pools of light on the wall. And another child, generously saying, "this house was made by God."

I think the comparison with music helps us understand the parallel between a well-constructed building that light passes through and the well-constructed musical instrument that air passes through. A violin is not the same as a piano. The well-built piano would have to start from an idea that is very different from that of the violin. You cannot make a violin in the shape of a piano. And once you have a clear idea of what you want, you must know how to construct it well. Construct, tune, and play.

THE TENSION OF THE SPACE IS KEY IN YOUR WORK.

Yes, in my work and in all worthwhile architecture, space is tightened, tuned. In the case of the skylights in the Day Care Center for Benetton, we studied models using some cones that gather light with its precise orientation and dimension, just as one would tune a violin. And afterward, obviously, light comes in and people see that it works because the instrument has been well conceived, well constructed, and well tuned.

One could say "but that's so complicated!" I say it's not, because that is the architect's job. The job of the architect is to be useful, but in addition to being useful, or at the same time that the space is useful, it must be beautiful. And we return once again to Vitruvius and to *venustas*, and to truth and beauty.

There is a more generic term that also pertains to the work of creation, that can sum up everything we've been talking about in regard to scale, measurement, proportion, and precision, and that is "order." Order, to establish the order of the space, to arrange the world. That is the role of architecture.

WHAT REMAINS FOR ALBERTO CAMPO BAEZA TO DO?

I could say a lot, but well, in truth, whatever God wants.

What remains for me to do? To continue trying to understand how technology makes it possible for us to conceive new or different spaces. See what I'm defending now? We've moved from light, a very concrete but sublime thing, to order, which could seem more philosophical, and now to technology. It is easy to understand how skyscrapers came to be, once the elevator made them possible. The other day I read a thesis that talked about the gondola, the apparatus used to clean a very tall building. For the new doctoral candidate, that was the key, but in fact, the elevator is the core of the matter. There must be a mechanism that can move us quickly, vertically; this is what changed everything so that skyscrapers could be made, just as sheet glass in large sizes made the continuity of horizontal space possible. Without steel and sheet glass in large dimensions, Mies van der Rohe would not have been able to conceive his continuous spaces. Nor would Le Corbusier have been able to conceive his spaces without concrete.

I think technology allows us to understand what we architects can do. The other creative fields such as painting, poetry, or music have a greater degree of freedom.

THERE IS SOMETHING THAT HAS ALWAYS IMPRESSED ME A LOT AND IT IS THE EXTREME GENEROSITY, NOT ONLY OF YOUR WORK BUT ALSO OF YOUR PERSONAL RELATIONSHIPS. AND IT TAKES ME TO A DIFFERENT PLACE, TO THE SCHOOL, AND TO A GROUP OF PEOPLE WHO HAVE SURROUNDED YOU, STANDING IN YOUR LIGHT OR IN YOUR SHADOW, AND THAT NOW APPEAR EVERYWHERE.

IF YOU WANT, WE WON'T MENTION NAMES, OR IF YOU WISH, WE WILL. BUT FOR ME, IT WAS IMPOSSIBLE TO PUT TOGETHER THE EXHIBITION *A CITY CALLED SPAIN*, IN WHICH I WANTED TO PORTRAY ALL OF THE GENERATIONS WORKING OVER THE PAST TEN YEARS, WITHOUT FINDING A VERY SIGNIFICANT GROUP OF ARCHITECTS TIED TO YOU PERSONALLY. AND I HARDLY FIND THIS IN ANY OTHER

FIGURE IN SPANISH ARCHITECTURE, EXCEPT PERHAPS IN RAFAEL MONEO, BECAUSE GREAT FIGURES IN SPANISH ARCHITECTURE HAVE COME OUT OF MONEO'S STUDIO AND FROM AMONG HIS PEOPLE. WHAT DO YOU ATTRIBUTE THIS TO?

Thank you for those comments; it's generous on your part. I've also often said that I have the immense good fortune of being surrounded by people who are better than I. And it's not just a nice thing to say, it is the truth.

And it is my great good fortune. Federico García Lorca expressed it well in his much-quoted line, "I write for those who love me." Well, then, one is lucky to be enormously loved, but I insist on the importance of being surrounded by people worthier than I. I believe that too is the right choice. In every aspect of life, you would be stupid if you surrounded yourself with people who weren't as good so that you could shine. You make a point of surrounding yourself with the best people so as to be in good company.

Here I'd even dare to give names, due to some very recent instances that I think are significant and that sometimes aren't interpreted properly. This past week, Juan Carlos Sancho Osinaga, a splendid architect who makes top-quality architecture along with his wife, Sol Madridejos, got tenure as a full professor of design at the School of Architecture of Madrid. And last year, Jesús Aparicio Guisado also made tenure as a full professor of design at the School of Architecture of Madrid. I have only praise for Suso Aparicio, a person who deserves it all. Both men were assistants of mine years ago, until naturally and logically they became independent at the school, as professors. So, the years go by, and the teachers who had been my assistants are now full tenured professors. That hasn't happened with any of the other design and project professors.

And I've "hardly done anything" for this to happen; that is, I haven't done anything strange or anything that I shouldn't do or that wouldn't encourage them and give them freedom. It's the same with one's children, you can give them all the protection you want, but it's counterproductive: you have to give them freedom.

Freedom is at the center of my life. In architecture and in teaching and in my personal life.

THIS HYMN TO FREEDOM MAY BRING US TOWARD A CONCLUSION HERE. WE'RE TALKING ABOUT A BODY OF WORK WITH GREAT FREEDOM.

SPEAKING OF FREEDOM BRINGS TO MIND THE THIRTY-SEVEN BUILDINGS, SPEAKING OF FREEDOM BRINGS TO MIND THE INTENSITY, THE CONSISTENT INTENSITY, THAT MEANS NO WORK IS DILUTED OR WATERED DOWN AND INSTEAD HAS ITS FORCE, EACH AND EVERY PROJECT. IT BRINGS TO

MIND SPECIFIC EXAMPLES. THE TOWER FOR TELEFÓNICA THAT WAS NOT BUILT AND THE NEIGHBORHOOD OFFERED IN PLACE OF THE TOWER, ALSO REJECTED; IT BRINGS TO MIND YOUR CHOICE OF WHICH PROJECTS TO TAKE ON.

WHAT HAS THIS FREEDOM MEANT IN CAMPO BAEZA'S WORK AND WHAT PRICE HAS THIS FREEDOM HAD IN CAMPO BAEZA'S WORK?

The question is a clear one, and I'd tell you that my answer is also very simple: that is, it's worth it. Freedom is worth the trouble. The price is very high, but it is worth it, and thank God I am in a situation in which I can only be grateful. But yes, it has had its cost.

You've said so gracefully in mentioning the Telefónica Tower. When instead of the tower, they suggested I make a neighborhood, and so a neighborhood is made. What was done is just fine, but I think the tower would have been better, for Telefónica as well, not only as a major piece, but also as an understanding of the city of Madrid, the place and topography.

Independently of whether or not the tower was appropriate in its conception as a tower with the four nuclei in the corners and the emerging elements, it was truly beautiful. But above all, there was the matter of understanding the city and the territory clearly. To make the highest tower in the city, at the highest point in Madrid, which would have been seen from great distances, would have served as a future reference for what was going to be built. That Telefónica Tower would have been the right choice.

It's useless to speak of the price of this attitude, of not agreeing to the other solution, which, economically, would have been terrific for me. Consistency offers satisfaction that money never does.

Which leads me to the last anecdote from my latest project, the one now under construction in Zamora that I've already mentioned several times. At a certain moment, there were complications due to that damn stone, with some quarries trying to force us or force the owner, the Regional Government of Castilla y León, and pressuring us, so that I said: if this inappropriate colored stone is used in an inappropriate size, I'm leaving the job. I'm not interested in finishing the work in that manner. If they try to force that stone on me I'm leaving. And I would have left.

We work intensely, as you say, with great freedom, a freedom that comes from honesty, which I think is the other word that could match freedom. It also gives all the works their intensity. Of course they're intense! Because I have never let down my guard. Obviously some have turned out better than others, but even in those, it's there, the intensity with which it was made, beating like a heart.

All of this is very clear and is worth the trouble. We spoke before of Shakespeare and his thirty-seven plays and my thirty-seven

constructed projects, and I think it's absolutely worth the trouble. Economically? Money is the great temptation for an architect, because architecture is capable of producing a quantity of money that breaks anything. But I also believe one needn't be a hero to escape that temptation.

ONE THING WE HAVEN'T SPOKEN ABOUT IS THE SIZE OF YOUR STUDIO, THE NUMBER OF COLLABORATORS.

RIGHT NOW, I AM VERY CURIOUS TO SEE HOW THE LARGE FIRMS ARE GOING TO SURVIVE THESE SO-CALLED TIMES OF CRISIS. HOW MANY ARE IN YOUR STUDIO? FIVE OR SIX PEOPLE?

Three, there are three of us, not six. But I'll repeat, I think life establishes naturally certain rhythms that are good to follow. There are buildings, projects, commissions that enter the studio and then are watered down. Two terrific commissions in Madrid that by the time we put the contract on the table escaped, they'd been watered down. There are people who confuse the enthusiasm one has for architecture and try to take advantage of the situation. The three people in my studio are enormously worthy, so we can control what we have with absolute precision.

At my studio, I don't know whether this will be printed or not, but we don't work on Saturdays and Sundays. The office is closed. We start at nine in the morning, we close from two to five, and then work from five until nine.

With this schedule and with truly efficient people, we can make a Caja Granada, we've made the MA, we've brought forward all of the things that would seem to have come from a larger studio. As in everything in life, I think that if you organize and plan well, it's possible to do very well.

IS THIS A FORMULA FOR THE NEW TIMES AHEAD?

It's a formula for the new times and for the old ones. I think the big mistake some architects whom I love and admire make is that of falling into the trap of getting more people, so that they need more work.

Sometimes having more people does not provide better solutions. Sometimes the load is heavy on my collaborators and handling the construction is intense, but then, it's also done within a well-controlled order.

DOES THAT MEAN THAT EACH WORK IS DECIDED ENTIRELY BY ALBERTO CAMPO BAEZA?

I would say so, and I don't mind saying so. It doesn't take one bit of merit away from my collaborators.

Obviously, they're not going to consult me if the seventh brick in the fourth row on the third corridor has a chipped corner. I would do that when I was young, when I was a newly graduated architect and worked with Julio Cano Lasso. I knew those things at that time, I was proud to know what was going on in each millimeter of the construction. I'm speaking about the work's overall plan, having broad strokes, which are clearly those I most value. I think that a work is its strong design, though I also value every stroke. In Velázquez, one sees the work as a whole and the work up close and the work in close detail, and it stands up to these three readings. I think my buildings do as well.

WHAT DO YOU MOST VALUE IN YOUR WORK?

Among the things one tries to do in architecture, and before I'd discovered many of my intentions, I would say the ability to withstand time. That may sound extreme, but I think if the works are truly worthwhile, they withstand time.

The ability to be recognizable. A recognizable architecture that can remain in one's memory.

To speak of time, of the ability to withstand time and to remain in people's memory, would require a much longer discourse.

I like it that people can remember Gaspar House. It really excites me when people still say when they see me, "That's the architect who made the Gaspar House." Gaspar House was built twenty-some years ago and it is very small, but it's radical, clear, seminal. Or the De Blas House or the Caja Granada.

They are works that withstand time and remain in people's memory, and that is important.

I've spoken to you before about making people happy. I think people live happily in my buildings, both in the houses and in the others—Cajas, etc.

I've told the story thousands of times about the first day the employees walked into the Caja Granada to work, and how one of the people going there to work was moved as he entered the large space. Because obviously that space, which you call holy, is very powerful. Every time I go back to the Caja I say hello to that person.

I think the works' ability to serve in this respect and to make the people there comfortable and happy is a good objective.

In the end, that's my intention: to build ideas capable of being materialized so that people live happily in them.

MANUEL BLANCO IS AN ARCHITECT AND HOLDS A PH.D. HE IS A PROFESSOR OF ARCHITECTURAL ANALYSIS AT THE DEPARTMENT OF ARCHITECTURAL COMPOSITION OF THE ESCUELA TÉCNICA SUPERIOR DE ARQUITECTURA AT ETSAM, THE MADRID SCHOOL OF ARCHITECTURE, WHERE HE HAS ALSO TAUGHT THE DOCTORAL SEMINAR ON ARCHITECTURAL ARCHIVES AND DOCUMENTATION SINCE 1987. FIRST DIRECTOR OF SPAIN'S NATIONAL MUSEUM OF ARCHITECTURE AND URBANISM IN 2007, HE WAS ALSO CURATOR FOR THE SPANISH PAVILION AT THE 10TH VENICE BIENNALE FOR ARCHITECTURE IN 2006 WHERE HE PRESENTED *ESPAÑA [F.] NOSOTRAS, LAS CIUDADES*, A DEPICTION OF OUR SOCIETY THROUGH THE PEOPLE INVOLVED IN THE CITY AS A VIDEO INSTALLATION IN WHICH A HUNDRED WOMEN SPOKE SIMULTANEOUSLY ABOUT THEIR WORK. BLANCO WORKED ON THE EXHIBITION *PETER EISENMAN: THE CITY*, WHICH WAS RECENTLY INAUGURATED. IT WAS CONCEIVED AS THE CENTER OF INTERPRETATION OF THE CITY OF CULTURE OF GALICIA, A PROJECT FROM PETER EISENMAN, AND IS THE FIRST SPACE OF THE COMPLEX TO BE OPENED TO THE PUBLIC. HE IS ALSO PRESENTING, IN ATHENS, *UNA CIUDAD LLAMADA ESPAÑA*, AN INSTALLATION CREATING A MAP OF SPAIN USING SPANISH CONTEMPORARY ARCHITECTURE FROM THE PAST DECADE. HE IS AN INDIVIDUAL MEMBER OF THE INTERNATIONAL CONFEDERATION OF ARCHITECTURAL MUSEUMS (ICAM). HE IS ALSO A FOUNDING MEMBER OF THE INTERNATIONAL COUNCIL OF ARCHIVES, SECTION ON ARCHITECTURAL RECORDS (ICA-SAR) AND WAS A MEMBER OF THE STEERING COMMITTEE FROM 2005 TO 2009. HE ORGANIZED AND WAS DIRECTOR OF THE INTERNATIONAL CONGRESS ON ARCHITECTURAL ARCHIVES (CAA) IN 2004. HIS PUBLICATIONS AND KEYNOTE SPEAKER INTERVENTIONS IN NUMEROUS CONFERENCES HAVE FOCUSED ON NEW TRENDS AND APPROACHES IN ARCHITECTURAL ARCHIVES AND THE NEED TO CREATE A REAL WORLDWIDE NET INCLUDING ALL KINDS OF INSTITUTIONS THAT PRESERVE, EXHIBIT, OR RESEARCH ARCHITECTURAL RECORDS.

IDEAS
REMA
FORM
DISAS

Afterword
by David Chipperfield

Beautiful Isolation
The Work of Alberto Campo Baeza

We have the opportunity to review the work of Alberto Campo Baeza at a moment of change. The effect of the global financial crisis has caused a severe reconsideration of development and seems to announce the end of an extraordinary period for Spanish architecture, a period that has seen contemporary Spanish architecture recognized internationally for its quality and its invention. The 1992 Olympic Games held in Barcelona seemed to announce Spain's development as a modern European state and the end of the difficult and isolated years of the Franco regime. Architecture and design became the representation not only of a commitment to building a new modern state with up-to-date infrastructure but also a general optimism about modernism.

Those of us living outside of Spain came to admire the "new Spanish architecture" and its architects. Over these years few other countries could compete with the production quality or atmosphere of Spanish architecture. The commitment of the different regions and cultures to build new public infrastructure, museums, railway stations, schools, and public spaces was supported by a well-educated and talented architectural community that has produced some of the most interesting projects of the past twenty years.

This period includes many generations of architects and seemed to give an opportunity not only to established architects but to younger architects, not only to projects in Barcelona and Madrid but all over Spain. While drawing on the modernist heritage of the great Spanish architects, José Manuel de la Sota, Francisco Javier Sáenz de Oiza, Josep Antoni Coderch, etc., a new openness and desire to experiment became possible.

The work of Alberto Campo Baeza sits within this period and yet like his work also manages to sit beyond this time. An architect defined by his "Spanishness" yet completely international. An architect who has achieved great fame but who maintains a modest office. An architect who has designed some of the most beautiful houses but seems totally comfortable working with large-scale projects and within complex urban contexts.

There are many strategies that architects can adopt in their working method. One approach may be described as the tendency toward "isolation." That is to identify particular qualities and empathize these qualities to an extreme, to avoid a conventional reconciliation of physical qualities in favor of exaggeration and contrast. This method of composition isolates certain components or elements of design and rather than being in the service of composition they become the composition. These qualities are identified with such clarity that they become the subject.

In the work of Alberto Campo Baeza we can witness this approach manipulated with great skill and to extraordinary effect. The identification and isolation of abstract and physical qualities underpin every project. In this manner the explicit qualities of light, view, enclosure, and weight become not only the language of the projects but their very substance.

The seduction that one experiences in the buildings of Alberto Campo Baeza is the consequence of their explicitness. There is no confusion about the architect's intention; each building announces its promise through its clear resolution. Fundamental to their success is the appropriateness of the projects' intent, to intensify the experience of being within the building, and in turn to the context within which the building sits.

Like his architectural mentors Mies van der Rohe and Tadao Ando, Campo Baeza has managed to develop an architecture with its own language, which is both personal and impersonal. An architectural language that is autonomous and not contextual yet manages to establish a powerful relationship with its setting. Indeed it seems that the elemental nature of the architecture allows the architect to engage the place as part of its composition, both in a tangible and ineffable manner.

The quality of Campo Baeza's architecture and his approach was apparent in his first projects but became explicit with a series of projects completed at the end of the 1980s and beginning of the

1990s. These were the Turégano House (1988), the Drago Public School (1992), Asencio House (1990), and Gaspar House (1992).

The photography of the courtyard of the Gaspar House became the "pinup" image of the early 1990s. This one image condenses in a unique moment the possibilities of such a simple and isolated architecture. Who could resist sitting in this beautiful space with its profound stone floor, a single tree growing out of a deep cut into the floor, with nature framed by the perfect lines of the enclosing abstract walls?

Here we could see once again the optimism of modernism, with all of its rewards, abstract space, a shocking interplay of inside object that seems to set itself apart from context but, through its play of enclosing and opening, seems to create a relation with its setting; secondly an interior composition of spaces, enjoying intentional sectional overlapping (internal views) and larger scale openings to the outside (external views); and finally an abstraction of an architectural language organized by these concepts of the view, light and interlocking.

The De Blas House (1998) departed from the simple volumes of the previous projects and instead developed a strategy of contrast. This allows the ideas of isolation to be played in a more extreme way, as the contrasting conditions (openness, closedness, wall, frame, light, dark) can be characterized and enforce

It is a tribute to the architect that the larger projects—Caja Granada, SM Group Headquarters, Day Care Center for Benetton, and Andalucía's Museum of Memory—are not only controlled like the smaller projects but they form a consistent body of work surprising in its legibility and its extreme discipline.

and outside space separated by a single frameless sheet of glass and a poetic contrast between architecture and nature. A stark white architecture that seemed to both isolate itself and yet be part of the place.

The image talks of something else that is the experience of the viewer. We are not looking at an architecture that is designed only to be looked at; we are in an architecture that is designed to be in. The issue of scale is not only the consideration of proportion but of the positioning of the occupant and mediating the relationship of the individual and their environment.

In these four projects Campo Baeza developed the strategies that founded the basis for investigation in his evolving body of work. I would identify these as: firstly the autonomous building each other. The temple-like form on its massive base creates an identifiable typology. The exquisite elegance of the proposal (Mies meets Ando) creates a house that seems both monumental and domestic. Campo Baeza succeeds again at creating a place that is irresistible. The house is not only a house but a place. The contrasting conditions of autonomy and grounding seem to be simply achieved with this temple strategy. The house floats like a boat above the landscape yet is gracefully dug into the site. The qualities of rootedness and openness, ground and horizon are isolated and concentrated and became the very subject of the project. We can witness this concept developed in the Olnick Spanu House in the more luxurious setting of New York State.

Campo Baeza's most significant work to date is the Caja Granada Savings Bank (2001), an uncompromising cubic building of ten stories, built in concrete. The organization of the building arranges a perimeter zone of offices around a central atrium. Confronted with a project of this size, the architect manages to maintain his strategy of isolation, creating an internal interior space of nearly religious atmosphere. Four giant columns and careful modeling of the interior space create a building that is both monumental and humane. The explicit physical and compositional quality ensures a building defined not by its complex program but by architecture. In this way, the building achieves the same clear authority as the smaller projects. This authority, given by the simple organization of the architectural elements and the reduction of the surface detailing, gives an intensity to the building that is difficult to achieve in such a large project. Campo Baeza has convincingly translated his strategy to a large-scale work. By intensifying the elemental composition of the building the monumental becomes humane and the humane becomes monumental.

It is a tribute to the architect that the larger projects—Caja Granada, SM Group Headquarters, Day Care Center for Benetton, and Andalucía's Museum of Memory—are not only controlled like the smaller projects but they form a consistent body of work surprising in its legibility and its extreme discipline.

The contribution that any architect makes is measured by the legacy of their built work. However we cannot dismiss the more general contribution made to our architectural culture by an architect's commitment to teach, debate, and write. Within these terms one must acknowledge Campo Baeza's approach and success in performing these activities. Campo Baeza has operated in a precise manner of architectural practice, a manner that gives a dynamic relationship between professional and intellectual activities. Refusing to develop a large practice, he has managed to concentrate his energies on a few projects at any one time and to maintain an ongoing commitment to teaching and writing about architecture. This exemplary example (one much better understood in Spain than in other countries) in some ways explains the vivid qualities of his architecture, and maintains the role of the architect not only as a professional but as a cultural figure.

DAVID CHIPPERFIELD WAS BORN IN LONDON IN 1953. HE STUDIED AT KINGSTON SCHOOL OF ART AND THE ARCHITECTURAL ASSOCIATION IN LONDON. AFTER GRADUATING, HE WORKED AT THE PRACTICES OF DOUGLAS STEPHEN, RICHARD ROGERS, AND NORMAN FOSTER. DAVID CHIPPERFIELD ARCHITECTS WAS ESTABLISHED IN 1984 AND THE PRACTICE CURRENTLY HAS OVER 180 STAFF AT ITS MAIN OFFICES IN LONDON, BERLIN, MILAN, AND SHANGHAI. THE PRACTICE HAS WON MORE THAN FIFTY NATIONAL AND INTERNATIONAL COMPETITIONS AND MANY INTERNATIONAL AWARDS AND CITATIONS FOR DESIGN EXCELLENCE, INCLUDING RIBA, RFAC, AND AIA AWARDS AND THE RIBA STIRLING PRIZE IN 2007. IN 2009, DAVID CHIPPERFIELD WAS AWARDED THE ORDER OF MERIT OF THE FEDERAL REPUBLIC OF GERMANY AND NAMED KNIGHT BACHELOR FOR SERVICES TO ARCHITECTURE IN THE UK, AND NEW YEAR HONORS 2010. HE HAS TAUGHT AND LECTURED EXTENSIVELY.

Epilogue
by Kenneth Frampton

The Temenos and the Belvedere in the Recent Work of Campo Baeza

Undeterred by the vagaries of fashion, Alberto Campo Baeza has kept his faith for over half a century with the Platonic purity of his unique architectural vision, amplified of late by shifting his work to the time-honored paradigms of the temenos and the belvedere. In this regard, it may be claimed from an experiential standpoint that the temenos is primarily tactile, while the belvedere is quintessentially visual, and that where the one is experienced through the dynamic movement of the body across the static mass of a stereotomic platform, the other stems from a distant panorama seen from an elevated vantage point. Other existential conditions qualify our experiences of these archetypal forms; on the one hand, the life-sustaining shelter of the house and on the other, the eternal silence of a tomb. The former appears most recently in Campo Baeza's work in an elegant neo-Palladian house with a nine-square plan built on a hill overlooking the Sierra de Guadarrama near Madrid, while the latter surfaces in Campo Baeza's proposal for an eight-cubic-meter concrete tomb, set on a concrete podium with a solid concrete door, projected for the Capoluogo Cemetery in Venice in 2017. This 2 x 2 x 2 m volume, illuminated by corner windows, will be reiterated in an equally commemorative work, the Robert Olnick Pavilion conceived as a gallery to be added to the Magazzino Italian Art museum in Cold Spring, New York.

The house as temenos first appears in Campo Baeza's architecture in his House for the Infinite, projected for a beach near Cádiz, in 2014. Designed for a bluff overlooking the ocean, this house-cum-podium is entered from above via a single stair descending on axis to serve the main volumes of living and dining spaces, located left and right on the floor below. Each of these spaces have floor to ceiling plate glass walls facing the sea. The bedrooms of this house, located one floor further down, are closer to the beach and hence are discretely lit by much smaller square windows.

Campo Baeza will turn to a more monumental version of the same theme for a beachfront site in Mexico, where one descends into a vast empty shell of space open to the constantly changing vicissitudes of an oceanic climate and thus completely accessible to birds and other forms of wildlife. This is an architecture of cyclopean dimensions where the temenos/roof is supported by beams 1 m in depth resting on square columns that are 1 m wide. Adjoining each support is a 1 m square skylight open to the air from which descend shafts of Piranesian light, the angle of which is constantly changing according to the sun. This crepuscular space, which has the aura of an industrial ruin, is ostensibly designed as a multifunctional space while the site plan suggests that a house proper may be eventually included within the overall scheme but set off at an angle to one side.

It is hard to imagine something more removed from this than the refined five-story Cala House projected for the outskirts of Madrid in 2015 as a cubistic rationalization of the Loosian Raumplan, the main difference being that where Adolf Loos favored incremental breaks between floor levels, Campo Baeza projects "rotating" double height studio volumes in which a mezzanine overlooking a two-story volume is itself a double height space.

An exceptional realized work of recent date is the Rotonda House, completed in 2021 and built on a hilltop on the outskirts of Madrid to the west of the city.

In this instance, a 12 x 12 m plan is divided up into a "classical" nine square grid, giving the whole house a Palladian character. The sole exception to this is the belvedere terrace at the top of the house, where the nine square grid is translated into a thin steel framework supporting an equally light shade roof housing a dayroom in the center and looking out from a generous terrace over a spectacular landscape. It should be noted that in the architect's imagination this is the terrace on which, of a summer's evening, Mies and Palladio will meet for an aperitif. Inspired by such transhistorical arcadian fantasies, Campo Baeza continues to cultivate and refine his unique vision of a disciplined lyrical architecture of pure form.

KENNETH FRAMPTON IS AN ARCHITECT, HISTORIAN, AND ARCHITECTURE CRITIC, AND AUTHOR OF NUMEROUS BOOKS AND ESSAYS ON THE HISTORY AND THEORY OF ARCHITECTURE. FRAMPTON STUDIED ARCHITECTURE AT THE GUILDFORD SCHOOL OF ART AND THE ARCHITECTURAL ASSOCIATION SCHOOL OF ARCHITECTURE IN LONDON, AND WAS THE RECIPIENT OF THE GOLDEN LION FOR LIFETIME ACHIEVEMENT OF THE 16TH INTERNATIONAL ARCHITECTURE EXHIBITION OF THE VENICE BIENNALE.

IONAL

Biography
Distinctions
Collaborators
Photographic Credits

ENCES

Biography

Alberto Campo Baeza was born in Valladolid, Spain, where his grandfather was an architect, but from the age of two, he lived in Cádiz where he saw the light.

He is an emeritus head professor of design ETSAM, the Madrid School of Architecture, where he has been a tenured professor for more than thirty-five years. He has taught at the ETH in Zurich and the EPFL in Lausanne as well as the University of Pennsylvania in Philadelphia, Kansas State University, Catholic University of America (CUA) in Washington DC, and L'Ecole d'Architecture in Tournai, Belgium. More recently, he has been named Clarkson Chair in Architecture by the University of Buffalo, and Walton Critic Speaker at the School of Architecture and Planning of CUA. In 2018–2019 he was visiting professor in the School of Architecture of Barcelona, ETSAB. From 2017 to 2020 he was emeritus head professor of design. In 2021 he served as visiting professor at the New York Institute of Technology.

He has given lectures all over the world and has received significant recognition such as the Torroja Award for his Caja Granada and the Award of the UPM University for his Excellence in Teaching. In 2013 he was awarded the Heinrich Tessenow Gold Medal, the Arnold W. Brunner Memorial Prize of the American Academy of Arts and Letters, the International Architecture in Stone Award in Verona, and the RIBA International Fellowship 2014 from the Royal Institute of British Architects. Also, in 2014 he was elected full member of the Royal Academy of Fine Arts of San Fernando in Spain. In 2015, he was awarded the BigMat Grand Prize in Berlin and the International Prize of Spanish Architecture (PAEI).

In 2015, he won the 1st Prize Ex Aequo to build the new Louvre. In 2017, he was awarded the Attolini Lack Medal of the Anahuac University of Mexico, and in 2018, the Honoris Causa Doctorate of the San Pablo CEU University and the Piranesi Prix de Rome. In 2019 he was named Honorary Fellow of the American Institute of Architects in New York and won the Gold Medal of Spanish Architecture of the Spanish Higher Council of Architects Association. And in 2020 he received the Honoris Causa Doctorate from the Lusíada University of Lisbon and from the National University of Rosario, Argentina.

His works have been widely recognized. From the houses Turégano and De Blas, both in Madrid, to Gaspar House, Asencio House or Guerrero House in Cádiz, Rufo House in Toledo and Moliner House in Zaragoza. And the Olnick Spanu House in Garrison, New York, the House of the Infinite in Cádiz, and the Cala House in Madrid. Or the BIT Center in Inca-Mallorca, the public space Between Cathedrals in Cádiz, the Caja de Granada Savings Bank and the MA, the Museum of Memory of Andalucía, both in Granada. And a nursery for Benetton in Venice, or the Offices in Zamora for the Regional Government of Castilla y León. In 2017 the Sports Pavilion for the University Francisco de Vitoria in Madrid was finished, and, at present he is working on the extension of the Lycée Français in Madrid. In 2020 he won the competition for the new bridge over the Piave River in Belluno, Venice.

More than thirty editions of the books with his texts "La Idea Construida" [The Built Idea], "Pensar con las manos" [Thinking with Your Hands], and *Principia Architectonica* have been published in several languages. In 2014 he published *Poetica Architectonica*, in 2015 *The Built Idea* was translated into English and Chinese and in 2016 his latest texts were published under the title *Varia Architectonica*. Recently, all his work has been gathered in a book *Complete Works* by Thames & Hudson. In 2017, he published *Teaching to Teach*, in 2019 *Palimpsesto Architectonico*, and, in 2020, he published *Rewriting and Trece trucos de Arquiectura*.

He has exhibited his work in the Crown Hall by Mies at Chicago's IIT and at the Palladio Basilica in Vicenza, in the Urban Center In New York, at the Saint Irene Church in Istanbul, and the Tempietto of San Pietro in Montorio, Rome. In 2009 the prestigious MA Gallery of Toto in Tokyo made an anthological exhibition of his work that in 2011 traveled to the MAXXI Museum in Rome. In 2013 his work was exhibited in the American Academy of Arts and Letters, New York, and in the Pibamarmi Foundation in Vicenza, in 2014 at the School of Architecture of Valencia, in 2015 in Cádiz at the College of Architects, and at the Spanish Embassy of Iran in Teheran. More recently, his work was exhibited in 2016 at the Oris House of Architecture in Zagreb, in 2017 at the University of Buffalo School of Architecture, in 2018 at the Museum of the University of Alicante, in 2019 at the Fundaçao EPD in Lisbon, and in 2020 at the Oris House in Zagreb.

In 2021 he won the National Prize for Architecture.

Distinctions

Competitions

1971 First Prize, Festival Palace
SANTANDER.

1973 First Prize, Castle Parador
CUENCA
With Julio Cano, M. M. Escanciano,
A. Mas, and J. M. Sanz.

1977 First Prize, Town Hall
Fene - LA CORUÑA.

1978 First Prize, Cathedral Plaza
ALMERÍA.

1979 First Prize
MEC. National Schools Competition.

1982 First Prize, University Gymnasium
MADRID.

1992 First Prize, Caja Granada
Headquarters
GRANADA.

1994 Third Prize, Social Housing
IBIZA.

1995 Third Prize, Social Housing
Leganés - MADRID.
First Prize, Center for Technological
Innovation
Inca - MAJORCA.

1998 First Prize, Public Health Offices
ALMERÍA.

1999 Second Prize, Telefónica Offices
MADRID.

2004 First Prize, Junta de Castilla y León
Offices
ZAMORA.

2015 Ex Aequo First Prize
Conservation and Storage Facility
Louvre Museum
LIEVIN.

2016 Honorable Mention
Lima Museum of Art Extension
LIMA, PERU.

2018 First Prize
Lycée Français Extension Buildings
MADRID.

2020 First Prize
Bridge over the Piave river
In collaboration with Fhecor
Ingenieros
BELLUNO, ITALY.

Awards

1986 Honor Award – City Hall of Madrid
San Fermín Public School
MADRID.
Honor Award – Official College of Architects
San Fermín Public School
MADRID.

1987 Honor Award of the Jury – BA Biennial
"10 Arquitectos Españoles" Exhibition
BUENOS AIRES.
Gold Medal International Critic – BA Biennial
"10 Arquitectos Españoles" Exhibition
BUENOS AIRES.

1989 Special Award – Sofia Biennial
San Fermín Public School
Turégano House
SOFIA.
Honor Award – City Hall of Madrid
Jesús del Pozo Boutique
MADRID.

1993 PAD Award Stone
Public Library in Orihuela
ALICANTE.
Commendation – Eric Lyons Award
Gaspar House
LONDON.

1994 Special Award – Sofia World Triennial
Drago Public School
Gaspar House
SOFIA.

1996 Special Award – Union of Architects
of the Republic of Kazakhstan
Drago Public School
KAZAKHSTAN.

1999 Selected Project – FAD Prizes
Center for Technological Innovation
BARCELONA.
Selected Project – MOPU
V Bienal of Spanish Architecture
Center for Technological Innovation
MADRID.

2000 Golden Lion – Venice Biennale
Spanish Pavilion
VENICE.

2001 Gold Medal – Miami Biennale
De Blas House
MIAMI.

2002 COAM Award
De Blas House
MADRID.
VETECO Award
Caja Granada Headquarters
MADRID.
COA Baleares Award
Center for Technological Innovation
MAJORCA.
García de Paredes Award
Official College of Architects
Caja Granada Headquarters
GRANADA.

2003 DuPont Benedictus Award
De Blas House
WASHINGTON, DC.

Fernando Wilhelmi Award
Real Academia de Bellas Artes
Caja Granada Headquarters
GRANADA.

2004 Torroja Award
Ministerio de Fomento
Caja Granada Headquarters
MADRID.
Arco Award – COA Almería
Public Health Offices
ALMERÍA.

2005 Architecture in Stone International Award
Public Health Offices
VERONA.
COAM Award
SM Group Headquarters
MADRID.
Macael Award – Asociación de la Piedra
ALMERÍA.

2008 Macael Award – Asociación de la Piedra
Andalucía's Museum of Memory
ALMERÍA.

2009 International Critic Award – BA Biennial
Daycare Center for Benetton
Silver Medal – BA Biennial
Andalucía's Museum of Memory
BUENOS AIRES.

2010 Nomination
Arnold W. Brunner Memorial Award
American Academy of Arts and Letters
NEW YORK.
Nomination – Saloni Award
Andalucía's Museum of Memory
BARCELONA.
FAD Awards – Finalist
Between Cathedrals
BARCELONA.
Opinion Award – FAD
Between Cathedrals
BARCELONA.

2011 Nomination – Mies van der Rohe Award
Andalucía's Museum of Memory
EUROPEAN UNION.
Finalist Building of the Year
Plataforma Arquitectura
Andalucía's Museum of Memory
SANTIAGO.
Observatorio D'Achtall Award
Casa Sefarad-Israel
MADRID.
La Voz Award, Art Category
Diario La Voz
CÁDIZ.

2012 Nomination – AIT Award
Rufo House
Offices in Zamora
FRANKFURT.

Special Mention – Sánchez Esteve Award
Official College of Architects
Between Cathedrals
CÁDIZ.
Colegiado de Honor
Official College of Architects
CÁDIZ.
UPM Award
Excellence in Teaching Award
Universidad Politécnica de Madrid
MADRID.

2013 Heinrich Tessenow Gold Medal
Heinrich Tessenow Society
GERMANY.
International Award Architecture in Stone
XIII Edition
Offices in Zamora
VERONA.
Arnold W. Brunner Memorial Prize
American Academy of Arts and Letters
USA.
Mies van der Rohe Award. Selected Work
European Union Prize for
Contemporary Architecture
Offices in Zamora
EUROPEAN UNION.

2014 Academician
International Academy of Architecture
SOFIA.
Academician
Section of Architecture
Medal 38th
Royal Academy of Fine Arts of San Fernando
SPAIN.
RIBA International Fellowship
Royal Institute of British Architects
LONDON.
Asencio House
Cultural Heritage
Andalusian Institute of the Historical Heritage
Consejería de Educación, Cultura y Deporte
JUNTA DE ANDALUCÍA.
Architect of the Year AD Award
Architectural Digest
SPAIN.
Mention
2013 Spanish Architecture Award
Offices in Zamora
CSCAE
SPAIN.
Premio de Arquitectura Enor
Finalist
Offices in Zamora
SPAIN.
The International Architecture Award
Offices in Zamora
Chicago Athenaeum
Museum of Architecture and Design
CHICAGO.

2015 International Spanish Architecture Award
International Competition; Conservation and
Storage Facility for the Louvre Museum
Consejo Superior de los Colegios de
Arquitectos de España
MADRID.

BigMat International Architecture Award.
Grand Prize
Consejo Consultivo de Castilla y León
BERLIN.
BigMat International Architecture Award.
Selected Project
House of the Infinite
BERLIN.
Becado de Honor
Colegio Mayor Hernando Colón
Universidad de Sevilla
SEVILLE.
AR House Awards. Finalist
House of the Infinite
The Architectural Review
LONDON.
ACI Award
Innovation Category
House of the Infinite
Asociación de Consultoras Inmobiliarias
MADRID.

2016 XII BEAU Award. Finalist
Spanish Biennial of Architecture and
Urbanism
House of the Infinite
Ministerio de Fomento
SPAIN.
Archilovers Best Project 2015
House of the Infinite
Edilportale
The Architecture&Design Network
ITALY.
Accesit
IX Premios de Arquitectura y Urbanismo
de Castilla y León
Offices in Zamora
Colegios Oficiales de Arquitectos de
Castilla y León
VALLADOLID.
Premios Diseño e Innovación Fuera de Serie
Categoría de vivienda
Accesit
Raumplan House
Unidad Editorial
BARCELONA.
Diploma Compás de Oro
Delegación de alumnos
ETSAM MADRID.

2017 Attolini Lack Medal
Anahuac University
MEXICO.
Architizer A+ Awards
Residential-Private House (XL>5000 sq ft)
Popular Choice
Domus Aurea
NEW YORK.
Diploma II Compás de Oro
Best Professor Competition
Delegación de alumnos
ETSAM MADRID.
Best Professor of Design 2017
Delegación de alumnos
ETSAM MADRID.
VII Premio de Arquitectura Ascensores Enor
House of the Infinite. Selected work
Cala House. Selected work

UFV Sports Center. Finalist
Grupo Enor
VIGO.
FAD Awards
Selected
UFV Sports Pavilion and Classrooms
BARCELONA.
COAM Prize
Sports Pavilion and Classrooms Building
Universidad Francisco de Vitoria
Official College of Architects
MADRID.

2018 Doctor Honoris Causa
Universidad San Pablo CEU
MADRID.
Piranesi Prix de Rome Career Achievement
Award
Accademia Adrianea di Architettura e
Archeologia Onlus
ROME.
Docomomo Ibérico Catalogue
Category A
PPO Pamplona, Fominaya House, García
del Valle House
Technical University in Almería
Category B
PPO Vitoria
DOCOMOMO.
XVII Ascer Awards. Tile of Spain
Honorary Mention
UFV Pavilion
Asociación Española de Fabricantes de
Azulejos y Pavimentos Cerámicos
SPAIN.

2019 Gold Medal
CSCAE. Higher Council of Architects
Associations
SPAIN.
Honorary Fellow AIA
American Institute of Architects
USA.
XII Sika Awards
Selected work
UFV Pavilion
SPAIN.

2020 National Architecture Prize
Ministry of Development
SPAIN.
Doctor Honoris Causa
Lusíada University
LISBON.

2021 Finalist. XV Bienal Española de
Arquitectura y Urbanismo
Books and publications
Barcelona 60's (various authors)
SPAIN.
Doctor Honoris Causa
National University of Rosario
ARGENTINA.

Collaborators

OFFICE TODAY

Luis Ignacio Aguirre López
Alejandro Cervilla García
Miguel García Quismondo
María Pérez de Camino
Tommaso Campiotti
Elena Jiménez
David Vera
Alfonso Guajardo-Fajardo Cruz

SINCE 1971

Gaja Bieniasz
Miguel Ciria Hernández
Gonzalo Algaba Fresneda
Kika Alonso
Antonio Álvarez Cienfuegos
Jesús Aparicio Guisado
Carmen Aparicio Guisado
Jesús Aparicio Alfaro
Francisco Arévalo Toro
Julia Ayuso Sánchez
Pedro Pablo Arroyo
Miguel Barandalla
Manuel Barata
Román Beitia
Antonio Bernacchi
Francisco Blanco Velasco
Dermot Boyd
Adam Bresnick
Miguel Cabrillo
Javier Calvo Mayayo
Ingrid Campo Ruiz
José Miguel Castillo Martínez
Tomás Carranza
Antonio Corona
David Delgado Baudet
Emilio Delgado Martos
Enrique Delgado Cámara
Rafael Díaz
Antonio Dominguez
Jesús Donaire García de la Mora
Paulo H. Durao Sousa
Alexandre Stélios Kauffmann
Alfredo Estébanez
Patricia Esteve
Juan Carlos Fernández
Pablo Fernández Lorenzo
Joaquín Fernández Madrid
José Antonio Flores Soto
Daniel Fraile
Javier Galante
José María García
Antón García Abril
Tomás García Piriz
Fernando Gil
Alejandro Gómez García
Marga González-Calvo de Miguel

Alfonso González Gaisán
Javier González Montero
Enrique González Villa
Agustín Gor Gómez
Daniel Huertas Nadal
Juan Manuel Izquierdo
Jesús Jiménez
Martin Kropac
Shalanka Kurera
Mónica Lamela
Fernando Laredo
Patricia Liñares
Begoña López Rodríguez
Pedro Luis López Ruipérez
Sol Madridejos
Eustaquio Martínez
Raúl Martínez Martínez
Mauro Matarredona
Pablo Millán Millán
Takayuki Miyoshi
Javier Montero
Daniel Montes
Alberto Morell Sixto
Alfredo Muñoz Herrero
Sara Oneto Delgado
Bernardo de Pablo
Petter Palander
David Pascual
Jesús Peñalba
Arsenio Pérez Amaral
Antonio Pérez Villegas
Francisco Ramos
Jesper Ravn
Pablo Redondo Díez
Luis Rodríguez Casanova
Fernando Romero
Juan Luis Roquette
Héctor Ruiz Velázquez
Francisco Salvador
Felipe Samarán Saló
Miguel Ángel Sánchez
Juan Manuel Sánchez La Chica
Modesto Sánchez Morales
Sergio Sánchez Muñoz
Juan Carlos Sancho Osinaga
Rafael Serrano
Andrés Toledo
Gonzalo Torcal Fernández-Corugedo
Ana Toscano
Luis Úrculo Cámara
Javier Utrilla
Pedro Luis Valle
Raúl del Valle González
Francisco Vallejo
Miguel Vela López
Alejandro Vicens
Emmanuel Vodoz
Ángel Ximénez
Juan Yruela

COLLABORATORS IN ENGINEERING/ STRUCTURE

Andrés Rubio Morán
María Concepción Pérez Gutiérrez
Jorge Conde
Eduardo Diez
Jesús Gómez de Barreda
Rafael Abenza
José Domingo Fabre
Juan Antonio Dominguez
Rafael Úrculo Aramburu (*)

(*) Installations

TECHNICAL ARCHITECTS

Rafael Anduiza
José Miguel Agulló
Miguel Bellas
Gerardo Berrocal
Juan José Bueno Crespo
Julio Cañizares
Emilio Casal
Manuel Cebada Orrequia
Diego Corrales
Agustín Cuenca
Juan Domingo Torres
José María Fernández
Juan José de las Heras Montero
Germán Hermida
Miguel Leonsegui
Francisco Melchor
Miguel Mesas
José Miguel Moya
Luis Olmedo García
Julio Pérez Amigo
Fernando Rodríguez
Alfonso Urquí

PHOTOGRAPHERS

Pedro Albornoz
Fernando Alda
Francisco Arévalo Toro
Javier Callejas
Luis Casals
Nicolás Casla
Colette Jauze
Paisajes Españoles
Miguel de Guzmán
Roland Halbe
Duccio Malagamba
Alberto Piovano
Francisco Rojo
Alberto Schommer
Hisao Suzuki

Photographic Credits

Javier Callejas:
Cover and back cover. Pages 4–5, 6–7, 8–9, 10–11, 36–37, 38–39, 40, 41, 43, 44, 45, 46–47, 72–73, 74–75, 76, 77, 92–93, 94–95, 96, 97, 98–99, 100, 101, 102–103, 104, 105, 106–107, 108, 109, 110–111, 112–113, 148–149, 150–151, 152, 154–155, 156–157, 158, 159, 160–161, 162, 163, 170–171, 172–173, 174–175, 176–177, 178–179, 180, 181, 182–183, 184–185, 187, 188–189, 200–201, 202–203, 204–205, 206, 207, 208, 209, 210–211, 212–213, 214–215, 216, 217, 218, 219, 220–221, 234–235, 236–237, 238–239, 240, 241, 242, 243, 244–245, 246, 247, 248, 249, 250–251, 254, 255, 256–257, 258–259, 260–261, 274–275, 276–277, 278–279, 280–281, 282–283, 284, 285, 286, 287, 288–289, 298–299, 300–301, 302–303, 304–305, 306–307, 308, 309, 310–311, 312, 313, 314–315, 316 up, 317, 330–331, 332–333, 334–335, 336, 337, 338, 339, 340–341, 342, 343, 344–345, 346–347, 354–355, 356–up, 357, 358–359, 360–361, 362, 363, 364–365, 372–373, 374–375, 376–377, 378, 379, 380–381, 382, 383, 384–385, 386–387, 617, 628–629

Hisao Suzuki:
Pages 356 down, 394–395, 396–397, 404 up, 436–437, 438–439, 440, 441, 442, 443, 458, 459, 460–461, 472–473, 474, 475, 476–477, 494–495, 496–497, 498, 499, 500–501, 508–509, 510–511, 513, 514, 515, 516–517, 524–525, 526–527, 528 up, 529 up, 530–531, 532, 533, 537, 538–539, 548–549, 552, 553, 556–557, 562–563, 564–565, 566, 567, 568, 569, 570, 571, 572–573, 580–581, 582, 583, 584, 585

Roland Halbe:
Pages 424–425, 427 down, 428, 450–451, 452–453, 454, 455, 456, 457, 480–481

Fernando Alda:
Pages 418–419, 420–421, 422–423, 426–427, 429, 470–471, 479 up

César Béjar:
Pages 128–129, 130–131, 132, 133, 134, 135, 136–137

Estudio Campo Baeza:
Pages 252, 253, 352–353, 550–551, 578–579, 619

Marco Zanta:
Pages 398, 399, 400, 401, 402, 403, 405

Francisco Ortigosa:
Pages 58–59, 60–61, 62, 63, 64, 65, 70–71

Raúl del Valle:
Pages 526–527, 536, 554, 555

Pedro Albornoz:
Pages 529 down, 534–535

Duccio Malagamba:
Page 478

Miguel Quismondo:
Page 352–353

José Miguel Agulló:
Page 332 down

Stampa:
Page 404 down

Alberto Piovano:
Page 479

Gregori Civera:
Page 512

Nic Lehoux:
Page 314 down

Mazmen Fotografía:
Page 528 down

First published in the United States of America in 2023 by
Rizzoli International Publications, Inc.
300 Park Avenue South
New York, NY 10010
www.rizzoliusa.com

Designed by Oscar Riera Ojeda and Lucía B. Bauzá

Publisher: Charles Miers
Editor: Ron Broadhurst
Managing Editor: Lynn Scrabis
Production Manager: Barbara Sadick

Printed in China

2023 2024 2025 2026 2027 / 10 9 8 7 6 5 4 3 2 1

ISBN: 978-0-8478-7278-7
Library of Congress Control Number: 2022936065

Visit us online:
Facebook.com/RizzoliNewYork
Twitter: @Rizzoli_Books
Instagram.com/RizzoliBooks
Pinterest.com/RizzoliBooks
Youtube.com/user/RizzoliNY
Issuu.com/Rizzoli